THE FLY AT FIFTY

THE CREATION AND LEGACY OF A CLASSIC SCIENCE FICTION FILM

BY DIANE KACHMAR & DAVID GOUDSWARD

The Fly at Fifty: The Creation and Legacy of a Classic Science Fiction Film

Published in the USA by:
BearManor Media
P O Box 71426
Albany, Georgia 31708
www.bearmanormedia.com

ISBN 1-59393-315-0

Printed in the United States of America.
Book design by Brian Pearce.

TABLE OF CONTENTS

DEDICATION

This book is dedicated to Vincent Price
Friend, actor, art collector and critic, author, gourmet
and most excellent raconteur.
His great sense of humor and joy of life are missed by us all.

ACKNOWLEDGEMENTS

Diane: I would like to thank the Florida Atlantic University Dean of Libraries, Dr. William Miller for all his encouragement in the pursuit of my professional writing career and recognize the support and resources that my library colleagues, Janice Donahue, Elaine Kelly, Rita Pellen, Maria Berenbaum, Darlene Parrish and the entire Interlibrary Loan department have provided for me.

I also wish to thank my husband John, who always has such great ideas for all my books and whose late night internet searches always find interesting information to add to my manuscripts. I could not do this without him.

David: I would like to thank my wife Heather, who, as with most of my little projects, now knows more about this movie than she ever really wanted to — such is the risk of marrying an author who thinks out loud with alarming frequency and significant volume.

I would also like thank my brother Scott, who graciously continued work on our joint project on horror films of Florida while I researched this book. While I watched a classic like *The Fly*, he sat through *Blood Freak*. I definitely got the better end of that deal.

Except where noted, the photographs in this book were provided to the public for promotional purposes at the time of the movies' release, by the film companies listed in this book. We regret any inadvertent omissions, and will correct them in a future edition.

FOREWORD

BY AL DAVID HEDISON

October is a time for goblins, ghosts and any other assorted monsters that go bump in the night. For almost fifty years now, ever since I made the film *The Fly* in 1958, I have always known it is October when my phone rings and there is someone on the other end of the line who wants to interview me about *The Fly* and Vincent Price.

The first time my phone rang, in 1959, it was *Photoplay* magazine. They wanted me to don a voodoo mask and terrorize a Halloween party thrown by Ray Stricklyn and Jill St. John. I did my bit for studio publicity and the article was duly published — in December. I'm still trying to figure out how *that* story ended up in the Christmas issue.

Little did I know then that the three of us would end up hip deep in monsters in 1960, when we were all cast in the film *The Lost World*. I shared billing with rhinoceros iguanas, monitor lizards, a gecko and even a Caribbean caiman. It is true when they tell you as an actor, *never* work with children or animals. One of the lizards decided to have our special effects cameraman, L. B. Abbott, for lunch one day while he was filming them. Luckily, *I* didn't have a call that day.

I managed to escape monsters for a few years after that. First I did a Korean War film in Kyoto and Okinawa, Japan in 1961, then I filmed the biblical epic *The Greatest Story Ever Told* in Page, Arizona in 1963. Both were monster-free, unless you count the occasional bed checks of my desert dormitory room for scorpions and Gila monsters.

I thought I was safe back in California on Fox Studios Stage 10 in the heart of the city of Los Angeles, when I began filming the *Voyage to the Bottom of the Sea* TV series for Irwin Allen. This lasted for about 6 episodes. Then I received a script that called for a plankton monster to eat me. Being a series regular, I managed to escape this fate. The plankton ate our Guest Star instead, something that would continue to happen with alarming regularity. I spent the next four years being pursued by all manner of undersea and alien denizens, but I always outwitted them somehow. Often I triumphed by dint of superior fire power, i.e. my trusty laser pistol.

I was very lucky when a diving bell atmosphere turned me into a werewolf; that same laser pistol wasn't used on me. Again I lived to tell the tale. I kept my fangs from that episode as a souvenir. I used them as part of a Halloween costume afterwards, but I didn't win first prize. Fangs were not in vogue that year. I should have worn love beads.

In 1973, I got mixed up with voodoo and tarot and a whole bunch of snakes while helping out a friend and then later in the year the Egyptian Goddess Bast almost clawed me to death. I again used my wits and knowledge to escape; she ended up being the one who was massacred by the felines. That was a very haunted year.

Things remained quiet for about a decade after that, except when I would accept an invitation to Fantasy Island. I truthfully cannot recommend the place as a peaceful vacation spot after what happened to me whenever I would go there.

It was another October when my phone rang. I picked it up and heard "help me" in a very familiar falsetto. It was Roger Moore calling to wish me a very Happy Halloween. He had flipped on the TV in the south of France and there was I was getting crushed (once again) in that press.

In 1986, my phone was ringing off the hook. David Cronenberg was remaking *The Fly* with Jeff Goldblum and everyone wanted to know what I thought about that. They must have liked what I said as I found myself invited to the Los Angeles premiere. The remake was a great film, with a very realistic and quite graphic transformation of a man into a fly. However, with all the technological progress we'd made since 1958, they still hadn't figured out how to save the scientist! I nominated Goldblum for an Academy Award that year. That's how good I thought he was in the role of Seth Brundle.

They were still asking me about the Cronenberg remake when Halloween 1987 rolled around. My final assessment was that the film was right on and it was wonderful. I hadn't expected to like it, but the story was beautifully done. I walked out the theater with gooseflesh. It had almost everything I had wanted to do in my 1958 version and couldn't.

For Halloween in 1993, I was part of a costume party on the set of *Another World*. They opted to dress me as a Naval Officer. Only the women were allowed to have claws on that show.

In 2002, they released *The Fly* soundtrack on CD and I was interviewed for the liner notes and did a personal appearance at a record store in Los Angeles in June. I'm not sure why they didn't wait for Halloween for this release, but there was a good crowd there nonetheless.

For the 45th anniversary in 2003, I went to Memphis, Tennessee for a film festival with Brett Halsey, who played my son in 1959 sequel, *The Return of the Fly*. This was also in June. *The Fly* was shown and I talked about my part in it with the audience after the screening. We had great fun doing this event, even though it wasn't Halloween, nor was it the actual anniversary, which would have been in July.

I am prepared for my phone to ring in 2008. It has already started ringing. In the spring of 2007, I was in London, preparing for a trip to Italy at the end of May, when the first call came. I was interviewed for a featurette called *Fly Trap: Capturing a Classic* that became part of the bonus materials on the DVD set *The Fly Collection*, which Fox released on September 11, 2007.

The set includes all three of the early films, as part of a major release for (finally) Halloween. When I returned home to Los Angeles, the phone rang again. I was asked to record an audio commentary track for this same DVD release the following week.

This past June — this has to be the horror equivalent of writing Christmas songs in July — I began working on this book you have in your hand. It doesn't seem like fifty years have passed since I made *The Fly*. I look forward to 2008 and all the new adventures celebrating the fiftieth anniversary of my film will bring.

The phone is ringing. I'd better go answer it.

David Hedison
October 26, 2007

David Hedison at the 2005 WonderFest in Louisville, KY with his alter-ego as a resin kit, built and painted by Neal DeConte.

PHOTO COURTESY OF STEVE IVERSON, 2008 (WWW.CULTTVMAN.BIZ)

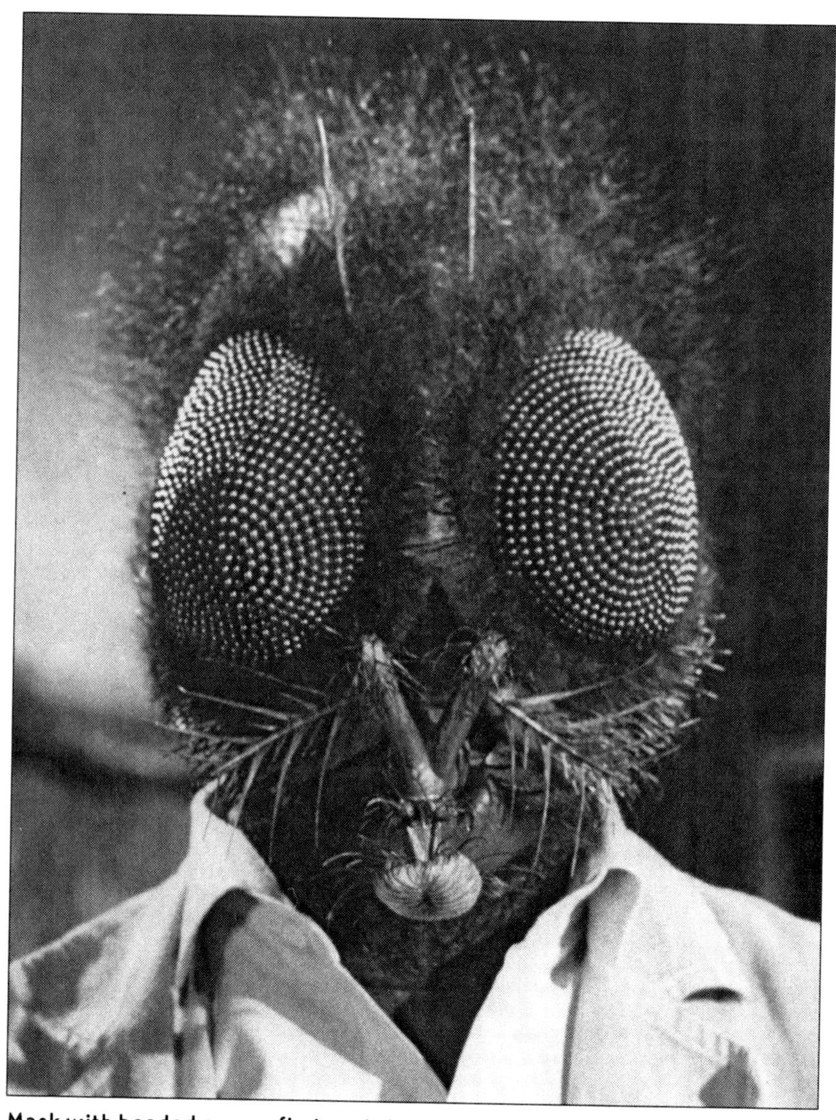

Mask with beaded eyes — first prototype.
PHOTO COURTESY OF BEN NYE, SR. ARCHIVES, 2008

CHAPTER 1

THE MAKING OF A CLASSIC

THE FLY (1958)

20TH CENTURY FOX, CINEMASCOPE, COLOR, 94 MINUTES

Director and Producer .... Kurt Neumann
Screenwriter ...James Clavell, based on the short story by George Langelaan
Cinematographer.. Karl Struss
Editor ....Merrill G. White
Music... Paul Sawtell
Art Directors .... Theobold Holsopple and Lyle R. Wheeler
Set Decorations .... Walter M. Scott and Eli Benneche
Special Photographic effects.............................. L. B. Abbott
Wardrobe Design.. Charles LeMaire
Makeup................................. Ben Nye and Dick Smith
Hairstyles.. Helen Turpin
Costumes..Adele Balkan
Sound .... Eugene Grossman and Harry M. Leonard
Color consultant... Leonard Doss
Assistant Director...................................... Jack Gertsman
Additional Special Effects .... James B. Gordon

CAST

Al (David) Hedison.................................Andre Delambre
Patricia Owens ....Helene Delambre
Vincent Price....................................Francois Delambre
Herbert Marshall .... Inspector Charas
Charles Herbert ....Philippe Delambre
Kathleen Freeman ....Emma, the Cook
Betty Lou Gerson ....Nurse Andersone
Eugene Borden..Dr. Ejoute
Torben Meyer .... Gaston, the Night Watchman
Arthur Dulac .... French Waiter
Franz Roehn ....Police Doctor
Charles Tannen..Doctor
Henry Carter... Orderly
Bess Flowers .... Arts Matron at the Ballet

In June of 1957 *The Fly* short story was published in *Playboy* magazine. It was voted the most popular fiction story of that year and won the Best Fiction Award. The short story was then published in the Annual: *The Years Best Science Fiction.*

Kurt Neumann read the short story and brought to it to Robert Lippert, Sr., an independent producer, for whom Neumann had worked many times. Their best known film collaboration to this date was *Rocketship X-M* in 1950.

Lippert immediately saw the potential in this short story. He quickly bought the movie rights from George Langelaan. He also secured an option for sequels, a financial decision that worked out well for Lippert, given that the studio ended up green lighting two more films from the property.

Loosely affiliated with Fox Studios at this time, Lippert had his own production company, Associated Producers, Inc., that Fox used as a B movie unit. The films were released under the name Regal Pictures. He made a popular, if low budget product and filled a niche that Fox made money on. The studio would provide money and the distribution, but had nothing else to do with the films until they were handed over as a finished product. No say in the casting, anything. Fox didn't even look at the finished pictures. However, Fox maintained the right to approve any project Lippert wanted to make.

Langelaan story in hand, Lippert went to Fox to pitch his latest option for one of his films. Fox also saw the potential of it. They immediately put the film under development. As early as July 1957, Fox was touting the film as the next Regal Pictures spectacular, with production slated for January of 1958.

Lippert put the picture together and hired a crew, but Fox would ultimately make this film. Buddy Adler, the head of production at this time, saw the commercial potential of this property. He needed a box office hit badly. The sci-fi genre was becoming increasing popular with current movie going audiences. Adler's decision to take over this film, made in February 1958, insured the film would be made in color and would have a $450,000 budget, which put it far above the average film made in the genre during this time. This was also significantly more than the standard $90,000 Lippert would have been given by Fox to make this as a Regal film. Less than two weeks after the announcement that Fox was taking over production, Lippert was out of the project.

Nothing was ever said publicly by Fox as to why. It has been suggested, long after the fact, that Lippert was removed from the film because of a non-payment of royalties dispute he had with the Screen Actors Guild over previous Regal film sales to television. This was an increasingly volatile issue and the WGA would ultimately strike on this issue in 1960, after several years of documented abuses.

Fox made Neumann the film's producer in addition to his director duties. Neumann was used to wearing several hats on a film and preferred working that way. He kept most of the crew Lippert had gathered. They had all worked with him on previous Lippert films, creating a production staff already familiar with his style. Fox then gave the production whatever else was needed, including several of their contract players, department heads, and studio space for eighteen days. This film would go on to become the biggest hit of Kurt Neumann's career.

Neumann's direction was straightforward without melodrama and gave the film an understated tone that lends much needed credibility to the fantastic premise. The film benefits from the use of the flashback device and especially by not showing the audience everything all at once. The plot may have involved a machine that still hasn't been invented fifty years later, but Neumann treated the material with dead seriousness and his cast played it for real.

Base Latex mask without the eye pieces.
PHOTO COURTESY OF BEN NYE, SR. ARCHIVES, 2008

They all wanted to make a good film. Neumann was quoted at the time as saying that the day of the shoddy-looking, cheap exploitation feature was over and that the public had become wise and would not tolerate this type of film. This wasn't true. Bad, cheaply made films would remain a staple of drive-in theaters for at least another 40 years, but Neumann's intent was laudable. It was obvious from his words that Kurt wanted this film to be believable, and impart of a sense of plausibility to the story. He backed those words with very solid production values.

Neumann supposedly used Patricia Owens' real fear of insects to make her scream when she pulls the cloth off Andre's head. According to most sources, she had not seen the mask they had made for Hedison up to that point and that was why her reaction was so strong to the reveal.

Owens told a slightly different story. According to her, the first time she saw Hedison wearing the fly mask, she screamed, but it wasn't because she pulled off the cloth. That came later. Owens stated that was the first thing she shot with Hedison in the full makeup was the last scene they had together in the picture, when Andre placed his head under the hydraulic press and signaled her to bring it down. Owens wasn't even sure she was doing the scene right.

She goes on to say that Hedison was a sweet guy and seemed happy when they were making the movie. Patricia does credit this film for helping her get over her insect phobia, so that part of the story is true, despite the later mix-up over which scene it actually was. She said later on whenever she saw a beetle or something crawling, she would tell herself: It's only Al Hedison playing a new role. And the fear would leave her.

There was a little doll used in the spider web as a reference for both Price and Marshall and it has been claimed manipulation of this figure is what kept cracking them up during the filming of this scene. There are tiny figures in the

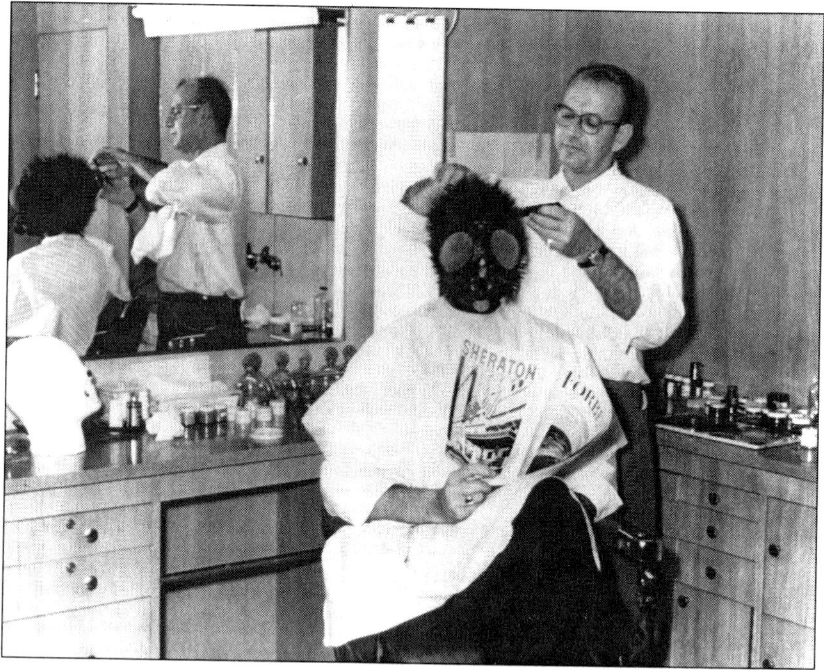

Mask with beaded eyes — final wig being trimmed and fitted.
PHOTO COURTESY OF BEN NYE, SR. ARCHIVES, 2008

web of the cocoon and the spider, but they are barely visible in only a few shots and never move.

Price disagreed. He said there never was any kind of manipulation done for him and Herbert Marshall. They had to pretend to see what was supposed to be there and play the scene as written. They never could get it out. They were supposed to be playing a kind of philosophical scene and then off-screen the script person would pipe up with: "Help me! Help me!" Price said they would scream with laughter every time they heard that falsetto line being drawn out like that and it took about 20 takes to finally get the scene done.

This would become the anecdote Price would always tell about making this film. How he and Bart spent half a day trying to get this scene filmed and how they could not do it without cracking up. In another version of this tale, the one most widely quoted, Price says since they could not look each other in the face, they ended up doing the scene back to back.

In yet another version, Price gets even more specific. He tells about going out into the garden and finding the spider web. In one corner there is the spider puppet and down in the web is the fly with the human head and the fly is saying, help me... help me ... yet he and Marshall had to play a very serious scene in front of this tableau.

They'd start and Marshall would say his line ... and start to giggle. And the little voice would say "help meee... help meee." Price replied with, 'Don't worry, Bart, I've been chasing that damn fly all through the picture!' Then Vincent tried to say his line and started to giggle. Little voice says "help meee ... help meee." Finally Bart said, 'Help you! To hell with you! Help us!'

Vincent Price's daughter Victoria says she was told that neither actor could maintain a straight face, the more they tried to regain their professional composure, the more ludicrous the whole thing seemed until they dissolved into helpless giggles. Each successive take only made it worse, until both men were sitting on the ground with tears of laughter streaming down their faces. No one knows exactly how many takes director Kurt Neumann required to finally get it right.

Price would also describe *The Fly* as science fiction filmed with taste and class and always enjoyed a review he claimed to have read in *The New York Times*, where the reviewer urged everyone: Don't swat it, see it.

Herbert Marshall gave more than the role of the Police Inspector called for. His horrified reaction shot, after crushing the human headed fly and the spider with the rock was extremely well played. You believe he will never forget what he saw and did. Marshall had an artificial leg. Neumann and Karl Struss, the cinematographer, managed to effectively accommodate that fact through the camera set-ups so his slight limp was never that noticeable.

Kurt Neumann died a month after the premiere and a week before the Aug. 29 general release, on August 21, 1958. His death was initially ruled a suicide, attributed to his grief over the unexpected death of his wife six weeks earlier. That ruling would be overturned, but the rumor persistently remains.

James Clavell, who was another person Lippert was employing at this time, crafted a screenplay that was very faithful to the Langelaan short story, except to leave out the man/fly/cat recombination — this deliberate omission was dictated by the studio for taste reasons beyond the budget and makeup limitations of the film.

Studio execs insisted there be a happier ending than the one in the short story, in which Helene commits suicide after writing out her confession of what really happened to make her crush Andre in the steam-hammer. Neumann wanted Clavell, as he would give a staid British tone to the fantastic material; the Director needed a straightforward retelling that kept the core of the short story. *The Fly* was James Clavell's first feature film credit, even though he had been in Hollywood since 1953.

Clavell's serious approach to the screenplay sets his script apart from the standard retribution monster flicks of this period. The other genre films mostly employed a standard "playing god with things we shouldn't mess with" syndrome — a very popular theme of these post-atomic mutation films. Andre's accident is an inadvertent tragedy. It should have worked, could have worked, but since it cannot be undone, all is lost. The process and the result must be destroyed.

In the end Andre was likened to an explorer who sacrificed himself for knowledge in an attempt to make things better for a future generation. Given what happened in the sequels, however, Andre's sacrifice may not have been all that beneficial for the remainder of his relatives that repeatedly tried unsuccessfully to resurrect his research.

The special effects of the actual transportation are very believable. They may be simple lighting, but they are very effective on the screen. This simplicity makes the tragedy seem all the more horrible when it does happen. It was the job of L. B. Abbott to produce the transporter effect by using different shades of blue light and to combine the live action close-up of Hedison screaming with the puppet spider. He made everything and everyone look good in this film.

The Fly is considered one of the better films to come out of the shock school, as many of these post-atomic films are now classified. The entire cast worked very hard to make us believe the story. The director let the tension build by simple suggestion, so the net result is a quiet, uncluttered motion picture that powerfully involved its audience in the tragic story.

One cannot watch the hooded Andre tortuously writing 'Love You' in large, uneven letters on the blackboard and not be moved by the man's plight and horrible decision that he has to make. He has to do away with himself. There is no time for Andre to prepare for his death and absolutely no hope of redemption or reprieve. He is being taken over. And when there is no hope left, some consider the human spirit is already dead. In this sense, all Andre is doing is destroying the remaining shell.

Buddy Adler also had several ideas for this film that did not make it into the theater. His first big idea was to have the white-headed fly get bigger each time we saw it, so the audience would know it had to be killed, before it grew into an uncontrollable monster and went on the inevitable fifties' film rampage that would cause its death. The special effects and make-up department did not have the budget to be able to make this happen and the film was spared this cliché.

The second idea Adler had was to actually show the man/fly/cat mutation described in the short story. Again, there was no additional money available to build a second mask, no matter how dramatic this reveal would have been. A second reveal would have diluted the first, and as the fly head reveal *is* the scene everyone remembers from this film, a second one was not needed.

Adler's third idea, the only one that was actually acted on, was to nix the inclusion of the matchbox burial scene of the now-crushed white headed fly, although there is a publicity still of Vincent Price kneeling by the web with the matchbox in hand. Adler figured correctly that this scene would cause more laughs than tears from the audience. It was deemed too ludicrous, for all its good Christian intentions, to be taken seriously and would have detracted from the stark drama of the film's ending. The reaction of the audience to the speeded up fly voice in the spider web proved how fragile the audience's willing suspension of disbelief was for this film.

The lab set cost $28,000 and included a whole raft of Army surplus material. They cobbled it all together and it looked great. Dr. Frank Creswell was the technical advisor. His job was to insure accuracy of the central lab computer, which was based on a real one at IBM. It had the quick look panel on the front. This panel consisted of 396 lights which would tell whether or not the primary integration system was functioning properly. Creswell made sure this panel only flashed acceptable messages, in case anyone in the audience decided to actually read what the computer was flashing.

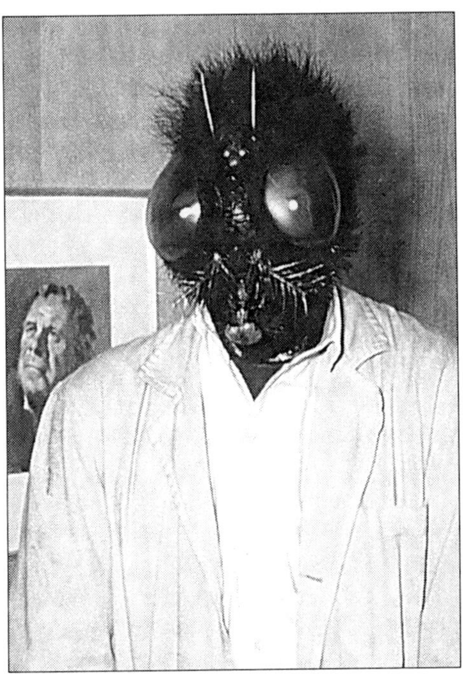

Final mask camera test.
PHOTO COURTESY OF BEN NYE, SR. ARCHIVES, 2008

Filled with flickering computer panels, large control knobs, timers, miles of wiring and ever growing transport booths, the basement lab was modern technology brought to life. One could believe Andre could step into his now telephone booth sized transporter and be de-materialized, only to reappear in the other booth across the lab, alive and intact. At least that was the way it worked when they tested the guinea pig.

The score was lovely, lush and full of strings and the occasional buzz of a fly, loud enough to be heard, but nearly always ignored by the person who was supposed to hear it. This lets the audience know something is not right and that some small part of the white headed fly still retains part of Andre's brain and is trying to find someone familiar to help it return to the lab to be reintegrated. Not every one buys the idea, which could have been done more effectively in the film, that both creatures have part of Andre directing their actions. This battle of will Andre ultimately loses, along with his life, and that is the real core of his struggle in the film.

There were a very limited number of sets: The Delambre house, garden, and basement lab, the press area of the factory, Francois's house and a club that Charas belongs to, but all were used efficiently and effectively by Neumann.

There are very few exterior and no location establishing shots, the only way to actually know you are in Montreal is to see the stenciled name of the city on the police cars and ambulances. The basement lab is crammed with special equipment, which makes its' destruction all the more shocking; leaving Price's character to exclaim there was over $200,000 worth of equipment destroyed when he sees the ruin for the first time.

The fly head mask weighed 20 pounds. It was made from a plaster life mask of Hedison's head. It cost about $4,500 to manufacture — a large sum of money for those days. It was essentially a rubber foam rubber mask that zipped up the back and was covered by a specially knotted and trimmed Max factor hair wig and another specially made lace wig of dyed black turkey feathers. Stripped turkey feathers were used to make the front feelers. The golden eye cones were inserted into the rubber mask and cranked open on the inside to let some air in and let Hedison see out the bottom. The design evolved the entire time during pre-production. The first set of eyes made with pins did not look realistic through the camera and had to be scrapped. Hedison was in the mask for five days of filming. It was very hot and extremely uncomfortable for him to wear. Hedison meditated to get himself through the shooting of these scenes.

The construction was labor intensive. Ben Nye, the head of make-up at Fox received a call to read the script. Fox had limited experience with science fiction films; other than *The Day the Earth Stood Still* (1951), it simply was not what they were known for. The studio told Nye production was scheduled to begin in two months. He had no idea how to pull it off — this sort of thing had never been covered during his apprenticeship. But since Fox thought he could do it, Nye took the budget and met with the art director, to get his ideas. After several drawings, they could not agree on any one design, but it was a start. Nye said he relied mostly on his imagination creating the masking in a hectic month.

Once Hedison was cast, Nye and his assistant Dick Smith (not to be confused with famous make-up artist Dick Smith) brought him into their lab and made the plaster cast of his face. They agreed that they would have to create a rubber skin to fit tightly over the actor's head. On this skin, they would glue the various components to make a fly's head. They sculpted a head from the mold and began making latex foam rubber pieces. Once everything was glued on, they cut the rubber mask up the back and gave it to the Wardrobe Department to sew in a zipper. This zipper would then be hidden by a wig.

Six weeks before filming was scheduled to begin, they started to manufacture the eyes and the sucker. Nye decided on a beaded look for the multi-faceted fly eyes. They used 14mm pearl beads, inserted into wire frames, constructed for him by the Prop Department. The frames were covered in wire mesh, in a convex curve, to fit into the holes left in the mask for them. Nye and assistants Richard Blair and Richard Hamilton applied 14 mm beads to the mesh. He said they were a little like Laurel and Hardy in the beginning. After completing several pairs, he discovered, to his chagrin, the beads had been layered in conflicting patterns, so there weren't any matching pairs.

After all the beads had re-layered to match up properly and had been once again pushed down in place, they were sprayed with an airbrush using iridescent colors of beige, yellow and green. Two very hectic weeks later, the eyes were finally done, even though it required Nye to come in on the weekends. This was mostly because he had other responsibilities as Department Head, plus three or four other features were also being made on the lot at the same time. Hedison could see out through the mesh and the beads, which helped him to move around in what was a very confining mask, and the design let air in, which was a tremendous help.

Andre instructs Helene how to work the press.

Nye moved on to the other elements. The sucker was molded from clay. It had a V-shape look from the front, with the sucker tip on the end. There was a wooden support core that Hedison held in his mouth that enabled him to move it. The core was at the right angle and was comfortable enough for him to do this easily to great effect in the film. It was the only piece of the mask that could be moved. The exterior of the mouthpiece was sponge rubber.

Turkey feathers were cut in such a way to make them look unrecognizable, and were attached to either side of the headpiece as feelers. They were painted iridescent blue, green and black. At the top of the sucker, slightly melted little plastic rods were attached to the sponge rubber to give the appearance of hair. Nye said the finished design was what he thought a fly would look like.

However, since the scientist keeps his changed head covered by a black cloth for most of the film, very little of these creations were seen. Fox also was leery of scaring the audience too much, so the monster scenes were filmed with less light and a lot of the fine detail of this makeup has been lost on the screen.

Nye was very disappointed that this happened. He was very proud of what he had created, as it was the first time and last time he did something this detailed. He called it the most difficult make-up assignment he had ever done because he basically had nothing to start with. However, after he started making what his imagination had come up with, the concepts unfolded one by one and the completion of the mask and its components were very gratifying.

Before the first camera test, Nye painted with rubber head with metallic green, blue and black paint. He decided to define a jaw line by placing more black paint on the bottom. Over this he added plastic rods to simulate whiskers. With the eyes in their sockets, the sucker attached and the mask painted, Nye was ready to add the wig.

The wig was a special order from Max Factor. He sent them a plaster head of Hedison, so it would fit him perfectly and asked that the individual hairs be knotted three-eighths to a half inch apart. This was sparse and they could see through the netting when it arrived. Nye placed it on Hedison's head and trimmed it to fit right then, because they only had one more day left to do their camera test.

Everything looked great on film, except the eyes. They photographed exactly what they were. They looked like beads in wire mesh, not eyes. It took Nye another week or so to come up with a different idea for the eyes, which was convex plastic shells. After experimenting, he found if he used two very thin shells he could fit one inside each other and paint them to look right. He used light orchid on the inner shell and light green on the outer. Then he applied yellow and green paint around the eyes to heighten the effect. The mask was camera tested again and everyone liked the results, except for Hedison, who had to wear it.

Closing in the eye holes was not a good idea. Hedison got very hot inside the mask during the test, and they had to open the lower part of the shells to give him some air. Before continuing the test, Al asked if the lower shells could be opened a bit more and thus the studio found the right balance that looked good, yet allowed Hedison to breathe and see enough to move around without falling over set pieces. The shells also left a very small space open at the bottom of the eyeholes, so Hedison could look down at the floor and determine where he was and where he needed to go.

The plaster mold for the foam rubber mask weighed 25 pounds, which made lifting it into the oven quite a chore for the apprentices. But foam rubber was so much easier for the actor to wear than the older makeup methods of using putty or wax.

Nye decided to make the fly leg a claw-like appendage. The Special Effects Department made it and put in an opposable thumb, so Hedison could grasp and hold on to something with it if necessary. Nye made a rubber sleeve to fit over the end of the claw and painted it to match, using green, blue and black again. After hair was applied to this rubber sleeve, the "claw" became very menacing. In the movie, Hedison played it as if the claw had a mind of it own. There were scenes where Andre ended up wrestling with his fly appendage to keep it from stopping him from typing or writing with chalk and from going after his wife.

It's been said that this struggle of Andre's was copied by Peter Sellers in *Doctor Strangelove*, some six years later. The first *Terminator* film also has a very fly-like ending. The film has had dozens of parodies of its most famous scenes over the years as well. Hedison was offered the fly mask at the end of the shoot.

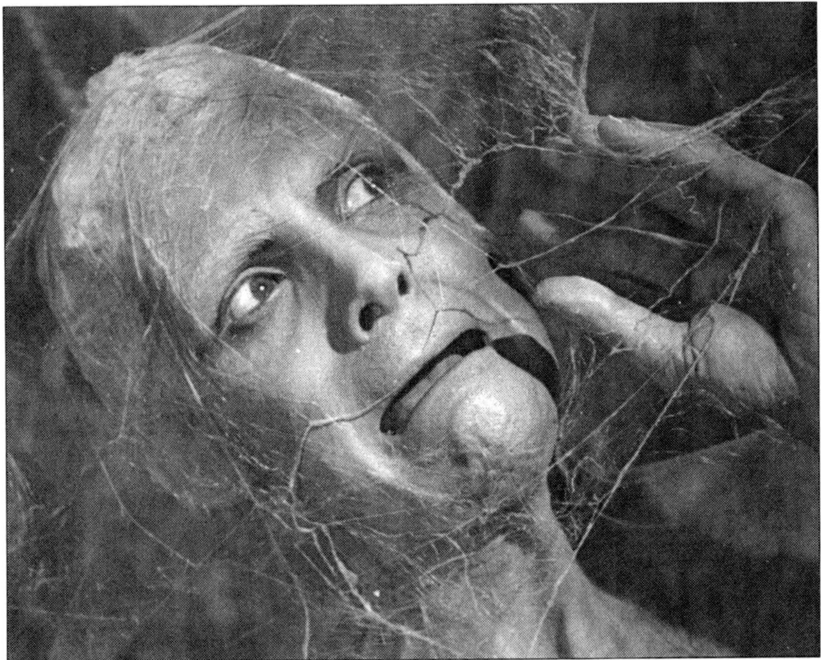

Al Hedison in white head makeup, covered in spider webs.
PHOTO COURTESY OF BEN NYE, SR. ARCHIVES, 2008

He said, no, that was the end and he never wanted to see it or wear it ever again.

The gaunt pale makeup used to make Hedison into the white-headed fly was merely a very effective use of highlight and shadow to give him that death's head appearance. It worked. Few who have seen this shot, ever forget it.

Nye was also concerned about the white glue he used in this now famous scene to simulate strands of the spider web. The glue would come off in long thin fibers that he then laid over Hedison's head. Ben was very concerned that the actor would suffer some in the removal stage. Luckily, at the end of the day's shooting, it slipped off Hedison's head completely. Nye only had to do this makeup once and was very pleased with the effect. Let it be noted that this was Hedison's last shot of the film. If the glue had not come off so easily and they had been forced to cut it out of his hair with scissors, at least the picture was over.

The spider used in the scene was a hollow facsimile of a spider that could be used a hand puppet. While the mold looked good, Nye said the prop people got in over their head when they tried to put hair on it. Nye took it over and had his apprentice, Dick Blair, layer crepe wool evenly with light to brown dark hair to give it a better look. They also glued the eyes in place. It looks good in the effects shot Abbott designed.

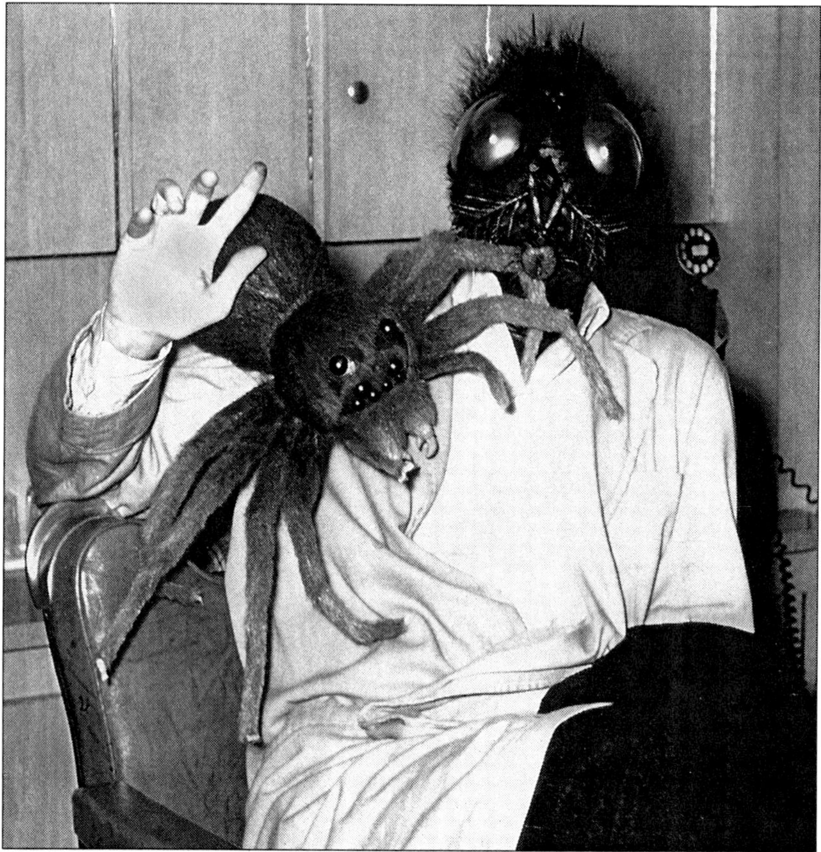

"The Fly" has a little fun with a prop spider during makeup.
PHOTO COURTESY OF BEN NYE, SR. ARCHIVES, 2008

The Fly made $34,000 on the opening day in Los Angeles. By the end of the week, the four hundred theatre West coast release had grossed almost a million dollars.

The movie was released on a double bill with *Space Master X-7*, another Lippert film about a blood rust fungus that came back on a satellite and infested Earth. *Space Master* was made under the Regal Films banner and profited quite handsomely from this shared bill. *The Fly* was one of the biggest hits Fox had in 1958, the other being *Peyton Place*. The movie earned over three million dollars at the box office by the end of the first year and box office was over five million a few years later after re-releases with the 1959 sequel.

Critics either loved or hated this movie. In more recent years, reviewers tend to pick the science of it apart, stating that Andre would not still have his brain inside the fly head and there was no way the fly limb could or would become human sized when the transference occurred.

For all the bad science which was far less obvious and not as important to the writers and audiences of fifty years ago, the film still works. Those who saw it on the initial theatrical release became caught up in the story and the acting; the whole tragedy that Andre has to die, because there is no way for him to be unscrambled. Viewers would have to wait for the 1959 sequel for that ending to happen.

The situation was noted as much for its pathos as its horror and the actors do a great job of making us care about these really nice people who get caught in this tragedy. The film is hair-raisingly suggestive without being gross and is comparable to the original 1951 *The Thing,* which was also far more subtle than its 1980's remake. This 1958 movie is well deserving of its place in the science fiction pantheon and is still being shown regularly in syndication.

Filming for *The Fly* was announced on March 25, 1958. Making a Science fiction movie was considered quite the novelty then for Fox Studio's ritzy stages as it was not that sort of movie, i.e. a rich, costume drama that the studio had made their reputation on. The film went into production in early April. The cast and crew filmed for 18 days — roughly three and a half weeks.

The first release of this film was in Los Angeles. On July 16, 1958 forty-five Los Angeles area theaters including *The Los Angeles, The RKO Pantages, The Uptown, The Academy* in Inglewood, and *The Crown* in Pasadena, plus thirty Southland theatres and nine drive-ins were the very first to show *The Fly.*

The official premiere; the one that was recorded and distributed via the Fox Movietone newsreel was in San Francisco on July 17. The studio sent a group of actors dressed as Frankenstein, Kong Kong, Dracula, the Hunchback and Mr. Hyde to open the film. The unnamed fellow in the spacesuit must have been there to represent *Space Master X-7.* The "Flight of the Fly" arrived via cable car to the Fox Theater in San Francisco and duly mugged for all.

According to the Fox Studio press herald for the film, movie theaters showing *The Fly* during this first run were strongly encouraged to put together their own group of monsters from what ever was available from the local costume store. Fox wanted the film to be represented by Dracula, Frankenstein, The Wolf Man, Dr. Jekyll, The Mummy, The Hunchback of Notre Dame and the Creature from the Black Lagoon as these were "the most terrorific screen monsters in 'scream' history." The Movietone newsreel footage of the San Francisco premiere can be seen on the 2007 DVD release on the bonus disc materials for *The Fly,* for those of you who missed the original newsreel in the theatre that summer of 1958.

This West Coast four hundred theatre opening was a gamble for the studio. It has been variously described as one of the largest simultaneous openings mounted and one of the biggest mass bookings to that date, according to 20th Century Fox.

The studio plugged the film on July 9, 12, 15 and 16, 1958 in *The Los Angeles Times* to make sure everyone knew it was coming out. *The Motion Picture Herald* ad — The Fly is Open! 400 theatres never saw business this big! — was pulled the day after it ran.

Fox made so much money that first day of release ($34,000) that they immediately sent out far less risqué trade ads and hyped the picture even more. Yet another publicity blurb was published in *The Los Angeles Times* on July 25. The film quickly racked up one million dollars in ticket sales.

The next major release of prints was in New York on August 29 to at least one hundred theatres in the New City Area and surrounding boroughs and counties. The film had a staggered release in July and August across the rest of the United States. The Fox press herald, also known as *The Exhibitor's Campaign Book*, was filled with all kinds of gimmicks the theaters could use to drum up attendance.

Anyone who wanted to watch the film alone had to (supposedly) sign a waiver. There was an ad campaign that stated Fox would pay $100.00 to anyone who could prove the film's premise couldn't happen. It was amended quickly to the first person after the Fox lawyers decided to change the offer to something more impossible to achieve. Fifty years later there is still no proof that teleportation is achievable, at least as demonstrated in his basement lab by Andre Delambre.

There were instructions in the press herald on how to build a box that moviegoers could put their hands into to shake hands with *The Fly*. They were actually touching a hairbrush — a Fuller Brush hairbrush would be fine, the copy said — but needed enhancements of sounds and light to work like the haunted house gag it was meant to be.

William Castle would take the promotion gimmick angle to its peak in 1960, but Fox used every trick they knew then to insure the success of *The Fly*. This included the calculated release in July, intense radio ad saturation and every fly tie-in gimmick the theatres would support; from huge plastic green flies hanging in lobbies to handing out fly swatters.

The Fly was released on a double bill with the aforementioned *Space Master X-7*. It was directed by Edward L. Bernds. The movie starred ex-cowboy star, Bill Williams, who later became more well known for being the husband of Barbara Hale (Della Street on *Perry Mason*) and the father of actor William Katt (*The Greatest American Hero*). The runaway success of *The Fly* also meant this co-bill was also a hit.

Neither Price nor Hedison was available to do any publicity for the first Fly film. Hedison had been sent to London to make the Fox movie, *The Son of Robin Hood* and Price was hosting an ABC television summer quiz show called *ESP*.

The Fly would go on to make a phenomenal three million dollars by the end of year, making it one of the biggest hits of 1958 for Fox. The Movie out-grossed *Peyton Place* in many markets. The overseas theatrical release in London was on October 3, 1958. The film was also released at that time in West German theatres by Centfox.

Herbert Marshall, Vincent Price, and Charles Herbert on a German program booklet cover, produced by Fox Studios.

The film had many different release titles around the world — here are a few: *L'esperimento del dottor K* (Italy); *Die Fliege* (West Germany); *Flugan* (Sweden); *Fluen* (Denmark); *Kärpänen* (Finland); *A Mosca* (Portugal); *La mosca* (Spain); *A Mosca da Cabeça Branca* (Brazil); *La Mosca de Cabeza Blanca* (Mexico); *La mouche noire* (France); *La mouche* (Belgium) and *De vlieg* (Flemish Belgium).

The Fly (1958) was released on 16mm film almost immediately after the first theatrical run and enjoyed immense popularity as a rental from 1958 to 1977, when the film was released on Betamax and then VHS. The movie is still rented in this format and is often advertised as a feature at myriad film festivals across the country. One of the more prominent festivals where it was screened recently was a large outdoor summer festival of classic films held at Bryant Park in New York City in the summer of 2005.

Most pre-recorded Betamax titles first cost anywhere between $29.00 and $89.00. *The Fly* was popular as both a rental and was purchased for home viewing until the Sony format was overshadowed and under-priced by VHS. Soon, like eight track tapes, the Betamax version of this film remained only with collectors who had a working Betamax machine to play it.

Inevitably, the film sold to television and was an ever popular addition to the syndicated *Creature Feature* ghoul-hosted programs that proliferated on the local stations beginning in the 1960's and into the 1980's. From Zacherley to Elvira, they all showed *The Fly*.

The first video release of *The Fly* was on Betamax. It was released first as a rental and then as the price was reduced, as a home video purchase. The same release pattern happened on VHS, a first high-priced tape, which sold as a rental and then the sell through home version at a much reduced price, particularly after the Betamax version was no longer available from retail stores.

A second VHS release of *The Fly* came on October 17, 1991 with new cover art. The last American release on VHS was in 1996. There was also a German VHS re-release that same year. Other VHS releases overseas were: a PAL version first released in 1987 and re-released on September 28, 1989 with Hi Fi sound added. Another VHS version was released in 1982 in Belgium by Starfix Video Productions. A third VHS version was released in France in 1991. There was a fourth Hi Fi PAL VHS version released by Key Video on June 30, 1998.

A CLV laserdisc version of both films (as a double feature) was released in the United States in 1996 and a Japanese Laserdisc was also produced. A Hi Fi CLV widescreen Dolby laserdisc version came out on August 31, 1999, but as the format was on its last legs at that point, it's doubtful this single film version had a very wide release.

The Region 1 North American VHS version was released again on September 5, 2000, when the first DVD version — which was also a double bill of *The Fly* and *The Return of the Fly* was released. This VHS version has remained in distribution even after it was allowed to go out of print, and is still available for purchase through some retail outlets. It was very common for the first two films be released as a double feature, a trend that started with the VHS versions and continued into the DVD releases. The first double release can be recognized by the Fox Double Feature banner on both VHS and DVD.

The latest DVD versions of all three films were finally released together as a set with a bonus disc of documentaries and audio commentary (for *The Fly* only) by David Hedison and film historian David Del Valle. The trilogy set went on sale September 11, 2007. This was the first time the third movie, *Curse of the Fly*, was released on DVD in North America.

There had been a previous release of a Region 2 (European) mega set of all five Fly films on May 26, 2006. The Region 2 European version of *The Fly* in this set includes subtitles in: Czech, Danish, Finnish, Hebrew, Hungarian, Icelandic, Norwegian, Polish, Portuguese and Swedish.

Fox released two versions of the film in Germany in 2007. The first *Die Fliege* has a purple cover and was (re)-released on March 19, 2007. The second DVD, released on September 3, 2007 is under the Studio Classics Banner and has the poster art, the same as the UK version, but is not angled. The French DVD currently available has the purple cover of the first German release, but of course is called *La Mouche Noire* and has a release date of October 24, 2001, so is probably the first region 2 release of the film that is still selling.

A VCD of *The Fly* was released on the DIVX format on December 22, 2006, but was only on the market for a very short time. Whether or not this film, or any of the other sequels, make it on to Blu-Ray disc like the 1986 version of *The Fly* remains to be seen. That event may occur sometime in 2008, most likely as a Halloween release.

The next release of *The Fly* is slated for June 2008. At that time Fox will release the latest versions of the 1958 and 1986 versions in a double pack to Canada only.

The history of *The Fly* on home video is long. Ampex offered the first consumer version of a videotape recorder for $30,000 in 1963. The first almost affordable VCRS included one made by Sony in 1969 that used one inch tape. Another version (the U-Matic) that used three quarter inch tape went on sale in 1972. For those television viewers who could afford to buy it, the U-Matic videotape recorder was mostly used to record programs off the air.

The AVCO CartriVision system was the first videocassette recorder to have pre-recorded tapes of popular movies (from Columbia Pictures) available to be played on the machine. These cartridges could either be bought or rented. However, this company went out of business a year later, in 1973, and no titles from Fox were ever made available.

Sony's Betamax VCR in 1975 with a price of $2,000 for a recorder and a recording time up to one hour; led to the first large scale real sales of these machines to the buying public. RCA introduced their first VCRs (based on JVC's system) in the United States in 1977. They were capable of recording up to four hours on half inch videotape. By the end of the 1970s, Sony's Betamax VCR sales had fallen well below that of VHS machines. Consumers preferred the longer tape time and larger tape size of VHS, over Sony's shorter tape time which was limited them to 1 hour recording.

In 1976, Paramount was first studio to authorize the release of its film library onto Betamax videocassettes. In 1977, 20th Century Fox would follow suit and begin releasing their films on videotape.

The first theatrical films were released by the Magnetic Video Corporation. They licensed fifty films from 20th Century Fox for $300,000 in October, 1977. Magnetic then began to market and distribute the half-inch videotape cassettes (both Betamax and VHS) to consumers. It was the first company to sell pre-recorded videos. The movie *M*A*S*H** (1970) was Magnetic's most popular title.

In 1977, George Atkinson began renting out his purchased Magnetic Video titles in Los Angeles and launched the first video rental store, Video Station, on

Wilshire Boulevard. He rented movie videos for $10 a day. Within five years, Atkinson had franchised more than 400 Video Stations across the country.

In 1978, Philips introduced the first optical disc storage media for the consumer market and Pioneer began selling home Laserdisc players in 1980. The laserdisc system would be replaced by the easier to use and less bulky DVD format in 1998. DVD prices started at $30 initially and dropped much sooner than VHS.

VHS video and laser disc players and the release of movies on videocassette tapes and discs increased dramatically as prices came down into what the average consumer could afford. This created a new industry and substantial revenue and profits came to the movie studios.

Fox was no exception; they kept *The Fly* available for purchase on VHS for thirty years. The DVD version has been available for eight years and the latest two versions of the DVD are still available for sale.

With the rise of cable television in the late 1970's *The Fly* found its way on to various cable movie channels. It has aired the most on the American Movie Classics cable channel, but it also has been shown on the more recent Fox Movie Channel. *The Fly* airs at least seven times a year on cable, making it the most seen of any of Hedison's films, although his two James Bond movies probably come in a close second.

Fox Studio publicity shot of Al Hedison, 1957.

CHAPTER 2

ALBERT DAVID HEDISON, JR.

Albert David Hedison, Jr. was born on May 20, 1927 in Providence, Rhode Island. He lived there until age two in a house on Byfield Street. His parents then moved to Medford, Massachusetts to open a small grocery/novelty store. It was the Great Depression and no one had any money to buy jewelry, which was what his father had been trained to make. Medford was a business disaster for his parents, so they moved to another store in West Roxbury and failed again.

His parents closed the second store and moved back to Providence when Al was 12. His father saw his brother Harry's jewelry business was doing better and opened his own shop called A. Hedison Enameling Company. As that business prospered, they moved into a house on 221Vermont Avenue.

Al was part of a very large, extended Armenian family. He had several older male cousins who, like him, were expected to come work in the various businesses that their fathers and uncles ran when they became adults. Most of his cousins did that, but Al had found a greener field he wanted to pursue.

Hedison decided at age twelve, he wanted to be an actor. No one took him seriously. Al would stand outside the Majestic Theatre, where the Warner Brothers studio movies were shown and dream about becoming one of their stars, like his cinematic heroes, Humphrey Bogart, John Wayne and James Cagney.

The movie that crystallized Hedison's ambition to be an actor was *Blood and Sand* with Tyrone Power in 1941. He made his cousin Harry sit through it twice. Al even cut class so he could watch the film over and over again. He loved the colors. He loved Rita Hayworth. He loved everything about this movie.

At summer camp in 1942, Al wrote a one act version of W. W. Jacobs' *The Monkey's Paw,* performed it and succeeded in scaring the living daylights out of all the junior campers. Hedison had started acting at Roger Williams Junior High — he played the Principal, Mr. Bradley, in *What a Life* and also did community theatre with the Benefit Street Players.

At age sixteen, he spent the summer as a student at the famed Rhode Island School of Design where he learned how to design jewelry, but as much as he loved what he was doing there; Al realized this was not the future he had dreamed about having. He taught Sunday school at Washington Park Methodist church, having also learned he had no patience for the four hour Armenian Apostolic masses his parents went to.

In 1945, Hedison followed the rest of his male cousins into World War II and enlisted in the Navy on the day he graduated from Hope High School. The war, however, ended while Al was in the midst of basic training in Sampson, New York.

Stationed in Jacksonville, Florida, Hedison typed up discharge papers and would trade prized day watch guard duty for the middle-of-the-night watches (midnight to 4:00 AM) so he could participate in the local community theatre productions of *Bell for Adano* and *The Philadelphia Story* in 1946. World War II officially ended in August of 1946 and the Navy declared his service done. Al was given an honorable discharge having achieved the rank of Seaman second class.

Hearing that John Ford was going to make a movie in Mexico; Hedison wrote the director and asked for a job, any acting job to get started. Al enclosed a photo of himself taken in his Navy Whites with his hat cocked on the back on his head. Ford wrote back, told him the picture wasn't going to made, but gave Hedison a list of contacts in California, if he ever made it out there. Ford closed the letter with the comment: "The next time you send your picture to an Ex-Navy four-striper, be sure to square your hat, sailor!"

Once home, Al announced again his intention to become an actor and go to New York City for professional training. His father, Albert, still hoped his only son would come into the jewelry enameling business with him. He wanted Al to graduate college as well, as he thought acting was no way to make a living. Hedison agreed to defer acting for a while and enrolled at Brown University to please his parents, whom he loved dearly.

College wasn't something Al enjoyed, but he became involved in drama department activities very early on and that almost made it bearable. Hedison was a member of the college theater group, The Sock and Buskin Players. It wasn't the same as being in a school in New York City where he only studied acting, but at least he could still perform and learn technique.

Hedison thought he met the right young woman at Brown, a blonde Swedish muse. He eventually proposed marriage, but she wanted to stay in Providence where she had family and roots. She would have no part of him leaving college early and getting married, and then heading to New York City together so he could pursue his dream of becoming an actor. The young bride-to-be insisted Al go into business with his now prosperous father and make money instead. She wouldn't budge and since both sets of parents also opposed his plan, this marriage never happened.

Al spent the summer of 1949 working at a summer stock theatre in Wellesley, Massachusetts. While there he appeared in the play *Moliere* that was broadcast over the Yankee Television Network. Hedison loved his time at Wellesley. Many big stars came there in the summer. Al met all kinds of people and liked what he saw. This was where he belonged, no matter what his parents thought of his crazy career choice. So Hedison chose acting over everything else and never looked back.

He dropped out of college in his junior year — over the vehement objection of his parents and was hired as an apprentice at the Newport (Rhode Island) Theatre in the summer of 1950. He worked with Lillian Gish and Zasu Pitts in *Miss Mabel* and *Post Road*. Two fellow apprentices that summer were Charles Nelson Reilly and Charles Pierce. Together they learned their craft as they helped build the sets for *The Velvet Glove, This Thing Called Love, Born Yesterday* and several other plays.

His decision made, Al sold Fuller Brushes and saved his money until he had enough funds to pay for one year's tuition at the Neighborhood Playhouse School of the Theatre in New York City. He packed up and left to study with Sanford Meisner. Hedison lived in a $5.00 a week room in a shabby brownstone at 341 East 50th Street and set about learning his craft. For Al, that brownstone was a palace. He was finally where he wanted to be.

At the end of his first year, Hedison auditioned for Frederic March. Mr. March was in New York appearing in *The Autumn Garden* by Lillian Hellman. March won the Barter Theatre Award for this performance. As the winner, March had the privilege of auditioning and selecting one male and one female actor to be hired for the 1951 season of the Barter Theatre in Abingdon, Virginia. Rosemary Murphy was the female chosen. Al recalled his audition number was 116 for the male award, which he won. There were over 250 applicants for these two slots. The plays Hedison did in Virginia during the Barter Theater 1951 season included *Harvey, See How They Run, Two on an Island, Mr. Thing and Broadway*.

Al returned to New York in 1952 and continued studying at the Neighborhood Playhouse, graduating in 1953 with a class that included Steve McQueen and Joanne Woodward. Hedison did two plays during this time, *Paris Bound* and *Much Ado About Nothing*. He also appeared on some New York based television shows including *Studio One, Goodyear Theatre, Armstrong Circle Theatre, Broadway TV Theatre* and *Crime Syndicated*.

Hedison lived with two very good friends, Don and Priscilla Morrow. They never charged him any rent or for food, content to support him until he made it. Hedison stayed with them until his graduation. Al kept track of all the money both his father and friends spent taking care of him and made sure he paid back every cent when his acting career finally did take off.

Unwilling to impose on his friends' generosity any further, Hedison took a part in the sprawling summer pageant in Ashville, North Carolina called *Thunderland*, where he played four parts during the 1953 summer season. Al supplemented his earnings there by being a DJ on the local radio station WWNC.

He did 14 plays in 15 weeks in the summer of 1955, as a summer stock player at White Barn Theatre in Irwin, PA. Hedison was the juvenile in two plays that starred Colleen Dewhurst: *The Rainmaker* and *Oh, Men, Oh Women*. Other plays staged that summer included *Picnic, The Tender Trap, King of Hearts, The Real Mr. Pennypacker* and *Sabrina Fair*.

He met a widow with a young child and seriously considered marriage again. Al knew having to support a ready-made family would put an end to his itinerant search for acting work and he would have to find more stable work doing something else. Hedison hated that he could not continue that relationship, but felt very strongly that being an actor was what he wanted for his life and if he continued to work hard, he would eventually become a successful one.

Fox Studio publicity shot of David Hedison, 1959.
PHOTO COURTESY OF THE PERSONAL COLLECTION OF DAVID HEDISON, 2008

In the fall, Al returned to New York. Broadway theater jobs were still not coming his way, so Hedison did live TV shows including *Kraft Television Theatre* and *Big Story,* as well as commercials. He worked as an assistant to the maitre d', in the Empire Room at The Waldorf Astoria, in order to pay his rent. This evening job, unlike one he had selling jewelry in a department store, worked out the best, as it left his days free to audition, and then rehearse and/or film the small parts he was able to obtain.

His father continued to send him money from time to time, unasked; usually after his mother would call and make sure he was eating regularly. If he wasn't,

Al would not tell them, but a check would show up anyway. Hedison was never happier when he finally was able to send his father a check (for Father's Day) out of acting wages. Not money from any other job, but money he was paid for acting! Theatrical productions Hedison appeared in at this time included *The Green Cockatoo*, Christopher Fry's *A Phoenix Too Frequent* and Clifford Odets' *Clash by Night*.

His long awaited theater break finally came in 1956 when he was cast in *A Month in the Country*, a play starring Uta Hagen and directed by Sir Michael Redgrave. Hagen was one of Hedison's acting teachers — by this time he had studied with Herbert Bergdorf, Sanford Meisner, Martha Graham and Lee Strasberg. Hagen recommended Al.

For his work on *A Month in the Country*, Hedison was one of 14 actors voted most promising in Daniel Blum's Theater World book of 1956. Some other actors who won that year were Andy Griffith, Anthony Franciosa, Susan Strasburg, Jayne Mansfield and Fritz Weaver.

Charles K. Feldman attended the play and submitted Hedison's name to be considered for a movie contract. A few other studios were also interested, but the only real offer came from Fox. Al caught a quick flight to Los Angeles, and screen tested with Terry Moore, who was very helpful. Hedison thought he had totally blown the test, but Fox seemed to like it and signed him to a studio contract on April 1, 1957.

His first Fox film was made in 1957, after he moved to California. The studio sent him to Hawaii to film *The Enemy Below* with Robert Mitchum. *The Fly* (1958) — his first starring role — was made at Fox with Vincent Price, but the *Son of Robin Hood* (1959) with David Farrar, entailed Al being sent over to London for the summer. Then it was back to Fox for *The Lost World* (1960) with Claude Rains. The Korean War film *Marines, Let Go* (1961) with Tom Tryon was filmed in Kyoto and Okinawa, Japan. Of these films Hedison is best remembered for the title role in *The Fly*.

The Fly was a huge hit and made so much money for Fox studios that they immediately commissioned *Journey to the Center of the Earth* to capitalize on the new found audience appetite for fantastic science fiction. *The Lost World* was another film green-lighted to capitalize on the success of *The Fly* and they made sure Hedison was on board to make that one a success, too.

The Fly very quickly became a Halloween staple. *Photoplay* put Hedison in a voodoo mask and had him terrorize a haunted house party in one publicity piece associated with the film. It was also reported that Al was given cans of DDT for Christmas by practical joking friends.

The film had amazing legs and kept right on making money. A sequel was quickly commissioned and dubbed *The Return of the Fly*. Brett Halsey played the son of Hedison's character and met almost the same fate. Al passed on the 1959 Fly sequel, which was filmed in B&W and not as good, but could not escape being cast in *The Lost World* in 1960, no matter how hard he tried.

Al was very popular with the ladies after he arrived in California and dated many studio starlets. He was linked with Chris Noel, Chris White and Susan

Oliver in the fan magazines, but found he enjoyed having parties of ten or twelve friends over more fun than these solo outings where his picture was always taken.

Hedison's recipe for the perfect party was to pack the refrigerator with food, as a reserve, put out a big buffet of cold cuts and turkey and lots of drinks. It was not necessary to provide entertainment, beyond recorded dance music. Al let people be people and a good time was had by all. If he did cook, they were served shish kabob, okra, Italian beans and rice, which were the only dishes he knew how to make.

He had a serious relationship with Gary Cooper's daughter, Maria, for a while, until she decided to marry pianist Byron Janis. Al discovered that he had a better time dating women who had been raised in other countries, including Venetia Stevenson, Valerie Varda, Simone Zorn and Luba (Otasavik) Bodine, who was a protégé of Cary Grant. France Nuyen was also of interest, until she left Los Angeles to return to New York.

Still not sure of the best use of their contract, Fox loaned Hedison to NBC for his first ever television series, *Five Fingers*, which aired on NBC in 1959-60 for 16 episodes, up against *Gunsmoke* and *Have Gun, Will Travel*. NBC decided their newest TV star needed a more elegant name than Al. After much discussion, Fox suggested they use his middle name. NBC agreed, so he changed his name and became David Hedison professionally. He enjoyed this series, thought they told some excellent stories and Hedison really liked his recently imported from Rome co-star, Luciana Paluzzi.

He had great hopes the series would make him a bigger, more well-known star, and that better roles would come his way, like a remake of *Blood and Sand*! Hedison learned to bull-fight, as one of the many classes he took while at the studio. David also learned to scuba dive and found Catalina Island to great place to relax and enjoy the sea, fishing and lazing on the beach, when he wasn't working. The hours were very long on *Five Fingers*, but David felt the dramatic stories they were doing on the series were worth it.

The cast of *Five Fingers* was informed during their Christmas break from filming that there was no need to return, their show had been canceled. David made a few more television appearances, one on *Bus Stop* and another on *Hong Kong* — series, like *Five Fingers*, that were based on other Fox owned film properties — that also had short runs.

In those very early days of television the studios were throwing everything they had against the wall and very little of it stuck. David persuaded Fox to loan him out for a Fourth of July 1961 summer stock appearance in *King of Hearts* at the Theatre-by-the-Sea in Matunuck, Rhode Island, and was also was in the sixth season Halloween episode of *Perry Mason* in 1962.

Joseph Papp, of the famed New York City Shakespeare in the Park -- wanted David, whom he had directed in *The Green Cockatoo* a few years earlier, to come to New York and play the lead in *Henry Five* in the Park. Fox nixed David's participation in this project saying they had a film for him to do — which never happened! That film became a musical for Elvis Presley instead.

Five Fingers was sold overseas as 48 minute feature films and aired in England in early 1961 and other places around the world through 1963. It was at a 1963 television festival showcasing *Five Fingers* in Egypt where David first met Roger Moore and made another friend for life. This TV series had a brief revival in syndication on US television in the summer of 1962 on ABC.

The disaster of a film that was *Cleopatra* brought an end to Hedison's contract with Fox in 1962, along with every other actor who still had one. David began free lance acting and found the freedom to choose what he wanted to do very exhilarating, even if it wasn't the steady paycheck his contract had been.

He enjoyed being out on his own, but David's hiatus didn't last. He was signed by United Artists for a part in *The Greatest Story Ever Told* in early 1963. He was cast in one of the plum Apostle roles, which became a showcase for most of the young male talent at that time, including Gary Raymond and David McCallum.

Hedison spent nine months in Page, Arizona, making this epic film. The first cut was six hours long. The picture was not released until 1965, when they were finally able to edit down all the footage into a three hour road show. David was still in the movie, but his part as the Apostle Philip had been drastically reduced. Sharing a dormitory with nine other bachelor Apostles for almost a year made him more friends and netted Hedison an invitation to be a groomsman at his co-star Jamie Farr's wedding, biblical beard and all.

David spent the next few years as the co-star of the hit television series, *Voyage to the Bottom of the Sea*. Hedison played Captain Lee B. Crane for four seasons, a science fiction television series run record that was not broken until 1992 by *Star Trek: the Next Generation*. His second season hiatus found him playing a hilarious Captain Fisby in *Teahouse of the August Moon* at the Carousel Theatre in West Covina, California, and his third season hiatus found him scouting locations in Italy for a feature film to be made after the fourth season hiatus began.

David was more than ready to move on, both in his professional and personal life, by the time the *Voyage* series ended. He knew the kind of woman he wanted to marry. Finding her was another matter. He told a reporter in 1967 that a man ought to think twice before proposing, and then amended it to three times. Hedison knew that demanding and/or denying one's own preferences could be frustrating. He wanted a relationship where the couple shared as equals, each contributing joyfully and sympathizing instantly when things went wrong. One that would provide a foundation that would last.

David believed in the true love his parents and some of his friends had. Hedison had never lacked companionship or felt he had to be with only one woman. He was never lonely. He liked kids and wanted his own. He was sure they would come when he found the right woman. David would marry only once. He wouldn't be rushed into it, but would continue to follow his own plan and heart in this very important matter.

During the fourth season hiatus, before he knew whether or not the TV series would be renewed for the fall, Hedison was filming a movie in Italy called

Kemek, a psychological thriller about love and money and stolen pharmaceutical drug formulas.

Hedison had scouted the film the previous spring during the third season break. When David finally found his location manager in a small dinner club in Positano, the Buca di Bacco, it was the gentleman's dance partner, one Bridget Mori, who caught his attention. He could not keep his eyes off her — wanting only to be with her. For David, it was four lovely days of discovery, until it was cut short by a cable summoning him back to Los Angeles to resume filming on his TV series.

However, his pursuit of Bridget Mori had only started. As soon as Hedison was sure he was totally in love, he didn't want to stay single any longer. He courted Mori by letter and transatlantic phone calls. It was to be the first and last marriage for both of them. They were certain of their feelings for each other, because neither had ever felt like this before. Bridget was all he had searched for and David was determined to be a good husband. Hedison managed five days off in February, and after taking care of business in Rome, he spent the other three days in London having a great visit with Bridget.

It was back to Los Angeles to film the rest of the TV series fourth season and then make a movie during the spring hiatus. David saw Bridget again when he was filming *Kemek*, but you wouldn't know it from the fan magazine reports. They had him dating his Canadian co-star, Alexandra Stewart, a nameless Italian heiress and even the (married) Brigitte Bardot, who was promptly whisked back to Paris by her jealous millionaire husband. The Bardot story is true, but it happened on another visit to Italy, long before this one.

David only had eyes for his Bridget, who came to Positano on May 12, after he had written her several notes asking her to come see him while he was there filming. On May 14, Hedison turned to her as they were walking down the Ramp Teglia to the beach and asked her to marry him. She said yes. A few days later he gave Bridget an engagement ring and the film crew threw them a party.

Mori had a job in a London advertising agency where she met many actors, so she wasn't naïve about them. David had impressed her with his charm and intelligence. She found herself thinking about him constantly and wondering if he truly was the one. Turned out, he was.

A year and a month later, after filming wrapped on *Kemek*, he married Bridget, in London, at the Brompton Oratory, on June 29, 1968. The combined Roman Catholic Armenian Apostolic ceremony came as a surprise to his *Voyage* co-stars and many fans, even though it had been reported in February that David had mentioned on the *Voyage* set that he would be married "within the year." When he cabled his friend, Richard Basehart, with the news, his co-star could only shake his head in disbelief that Hedison was finally getting married. An assortment of Los Angeles based ladies of the silver screen felt the same way.

Their wedding reception was at the River Room at the Savoy Hotel and the honeymoon was spent traveling to Amsterdam, Paris and Madrid. Fox wanted David to make personal appearances in those cities to help overseas sales of

Fox publicity shot of Andre Delambre — make up test, April 1958.

Voyage, which he did, with Bridget proudly by his side. Forty years later, they are still married. Bridget has always been his willing partner, sounding board and biggest supporter.

Hedison brought his new bride back to California at the end of the summer. The fan magazines claimed Hedison pulled a fast one, when they finally reported his marriage in October and December and some still had him single into 1969. With his series cancelled in the United States during their honeymoon, David now had to look for other acting work. He turned down the part of the father in *The Brady Bunch* and did a *Love, American Style.* He traveled to England (as a last minute fill-in for Lloyd Bridges) to do an episode of *Journey to the Unknown.*

Hedison went on a three month theater tour of *Under the Yum Yum Tree* in the spring of 1969 with Edd Byrnes. He played the lead role of the scheming landlord. After the birth of his first daughter, Alexandra, in 1969, David was back on stage in *Funny Girl*. He played Nicky Arnstein in two different California productions, the first in Sacramento and the latter in Los Angeles in 1970.

After accepting a job in a West End production of James Leo Herlihy's *Bad Bad Jo Jo*, David packed up his family and moved to England. His second daughter, Serena, was born shortly after they arrived on January 22, 1971. He had wanted two girls, close together, so they didn't wait to have children and that is what they ended up with. David wouldn't have it any other way.

Hedison acted on British television during his two year stay in London, including the BBC presentation of Tennessee Williams' *Summer and Smoke* in the role of John Buchanan opposite Lee Remick in 1972. He was in several ITV and Anglia TV movies. The first one had his wife and family Doctor plotting to kill him for the insurance by telling him he's terminally ill, so they can continue their affair (*A Kiss is Just a Kiss*) and another had him end up dissolved (by a vengeful husband) in a vat of acid. (*Man about a Dog*). Other TV movies done at this time were *Man in the Wood* and *The Complement* and their plots were equally as cheerful. One of these had him locked in the basement of a deserted country house at the end, left to starve to death.

Hedison's final job in London before moving back to the States was to costar with Sean Connery in the eighth James Bond movie, *Live and Let Die*. David was cast as Felix Leiter with the help of screenwriter Tom Mankiewicz, who wrote the role with David in mind. Mankiewicz arranged a meeting for David to be seen and he was hired.

The next thing Hedison knew, Connery was out of the picture and Roger Moore had been signed for the role of Bond. Roger was a dear friend and it made playing buddies very easy. David's scenes for this movie were filmed on location in New Orleans and New York City.

David returned to Los Angeles after completing the film and immediately began working as a television series guest star. Quinn Martin liked his work and would regularly send David scripts, whenever he thought Hedison was right for a part. David would get a call from John Conwell, Martin's casting assistant. He did two episodes of *The FBI* with Efrem Zimbalist in 1972 and 1973, three episodes of *Cannon* with William Conrad in 1973, 1974 and 1975; an episode of *Manhunter* in 1974 and an episode of *Barnaby Jones* in 1977. The *Barnaby Jones* was David's favorite of these shows, even if he did end up murdering his cousin.

Hedison also did several TV movies, some televised plays and many pilots during this time including *Cat Creature, Murder Impossible, The Lives of Jenny Dolan, The Art of Crime, and Murder in Peyton Place.* PBS Television Theatre's production of Oliver Hailey's *For the Use of the Hall,* directed by Lee Grant in January of 1975 remains his favorite U. S. television appearance.

David's parents came to Los Angeles in late 1977 and visited the set where their son was filming *Murder in Peyton Place*. Sadly, it would be the last time his father would come to the West Coast. Albert had a massive heart attack at age 83 and did not survive it.

Impressed by his work in *Family* in 1976, David was offered the role of the Captain in *The Love Boat,* a new series Aaron Spelling was developing. Hedison did not like the script and turned it down — much to his dismay after the show became a monster hit. Ditto for the father role he was offered on *The Brady Bunch* in 1968.

Spelling hired him to guest on *Love Boat* during its first season in 1977 and for *Fantasy Island's* fourth episode in 1978. David made two appearances on *Charlie's Angels, Hotel,* and *Dynasty,* with five more on *Love Boat* and a total of six on *Fantasy Island.* His most appearances on a Spelling show came as a semi-regular on *Dynasty II: The Colbys* in 1985. David was in nine episodes, playing a British Lord who was the current husband of Katherine Ross' character.

David made a conscious decision to go back on stage in 1979, declining a role that would made him a regular on the sitcom *Benson.* Coming in to replace Jerry Orbach as the lead actor, David toured in the National Company of Neil Simon's *Chapter Two,* first with Barbara Anderson and then Anita Gillette, through 1980. He worked with three different companies during this road show run. Hedison did another theatre tour in the summer of 1981 in *Marriage Go Round* with Jane Powell. All the plays were very well attended.

David spent Christmas of 1979 in Detroit. He flew his wife, daughters and mother in to be with him and they decorated their hotel rooms for the holidays. Being together was all that mattered.

Hedison appeared in two more Roger Moore films after *Live and Let Die.* He made *ffolkes* in 1979, a North Sea oil rig kidnap thriller filmed in Ireland and *The Naked Face* in 1983. The latter was made in Chicago. They played doctors who were related by marriage, trying to figure out who is trying to kill Roger. The film was based on the novel by Sidney Sheldon.

1985 began with the airing of the NBC mini-series *A.D.,* directed by Stuart Cooper. David then appeared in Los Angeles in the West Coast premiere of Alan Bowen's *Forty Deuce,* and in the Allan Miller production of *Are You Now or Have You Ever Been* playing Larry Parks in the spring and summer. All this took place during the first and second seasons of ABC's *Dynasty II: The Colbys.*

Some other Spelling shows that Hedison guest starred on were: *Hart to Hart,* the *T. J. Hooker* pilot, *Matt Houston* and *Finders of Lost Loves.* David also worked on NBC and CBS as well, in *Simon and Simon, Crazy Like a Fox, Trapper John, M. D., Knight Rider and A-Team,* as well as *Murder, She Wrote* and *The Law and Harry McGraw.*

He was back on stage again with Elizabeth Ashley in 1988. They did a four city preview tour of Joseph Hayes' new play, *Come into My Parlor.* David was also in the world premiere run of Bernard Slade's *Return Engagements.*

It was during *Parlor* that David was cast for his second James Bond film, 1989's *Licence to Kill* with Timothy Dalton. The sixteenth Bond began filming right after the run of *Return Engagements.* Hedison worked on sets in Key West and Mexico, making him the first actor to play the role of Felix Leiter twice.

In 1990, David went to Poland to make the film *Undeclared War* and then was on back on stage in Hornchurch, England, for the play, *Catch Me if You*

Can, where he is trying to murder his wife. Theatre has always been important to Hedison; he enjoys being on stage more than anything else he's done in his seven decades long acting career.

After that, Hedison moved to New York City, when he was signed to play evil businessman Spencer Harrison in the NBC daytime drama *Another World*. David appeared on this show from July of 1991 until June of 1995. Spencer's schemes never seemed to work out for him, but it was a good, long run.

Al Hedison welcomes a visitor to the set, April 1958.

PHOTO COURTESY OF STEVE IVERSON, 2008 (WWW.CULTTVMAN.BIZ)

The summer of 1992, David received an offer that he felt he couldn't refuse; to play the non-singing Pasha Selim role in the Cincinnati Opera's performance of Mozart's *Abduction from the Seraglio*. Hedison took a July weekend off to go to Ohio. The Opera had a special screening of *The Fly* the day before his debut, and handed everyone a small red fly swatter urging them to "Catch the Fly" at the Cincinnati Opera. When asked, Why an opera? David replied he had never done one and he wanted to see what it was like.

In 1996, Hedison went back to the stage, embarking on a long run of summer plays, mostly in New York and the Northeast. The New York City plays he did that year — continuing his affiliation with the Actors Studio — were *Eighteen, Eleanor, The Benefits of Doubt* and *Marriage Play*. He enjoyed working and teaching at the New York Studio.

David auditioned for and was accepted into the Actors Studio in 1955. He was inducted the same night as Steve McQueen. Hedison would teach in New York in the spring of 2003. David began working and teaching at the Actors Studio West in Los Angeles in the late 1960's and still monitors classes and performs in plays there on a regular basis.

In June of 1996, Hedison was in *Rough Crossing* with the Lincoln Nebraska Repertory and in August he played the lead male in *Social Security* at playhouses in Maine and Massachusetts. In May of 1997, director Kent Paul asked him to do *Blithe Spirit* at the Woods Theatre in New Jersey with Juliet Mills playing his lovely, if addled wife. In addition to appearing in A. R. Gurney's *Love Letters* with Anita Gillette in 1998 in Connecticut, David also appeared in *Alone*

Together, again at playhouses in Maine and Massachusetts. In 1999 he was back in New York doing *First Love* and his final summer stage appearance of this period was as the long-suffering husband in *The Tale of the Allergist's Wife,* at the Cape Playhouse in Dennis, MA in 2002.

That summer David lost his mother, Rose, who had always kept up with whatever he was doing. She had attended as many plays as she could, until old age kept her from traveling. She was 97.

In 1998, Hedison began making more frequent appearances at various Science Fiction conventions around the country. He did his first convention in 1989 in California and had done a Star Trek Convention in Georgia in 1993 up to this point. Some of the places he appeared were Chiller Theatre in Arlington (1998) and New Jersey (1998; 2000; 2002; and 2004); Dragoncon (Atlanta) in 1999 and 2003; Frightvision in Ohio in 2000, and The Memphis Film Festival in June of 2003 — celebrating the 45th anniversary of *The Fly,* with 'his son' Brett Halsey.

Hedison also attended Wonderfest in Louisville and FX in Orlando in 2005 plus several other shows in Las Vegas; Dallas, New York City, Cleveland, Maryland and Toronto during this three year period. David also traveled to the United Kingdom, where he did two shows on each trip: Autographica and Birmingham in 2003, and Swindon and Basildon in 2005.

Some of David's more recent films include *Fugitive Mind* (1999) with Michael Dudikoff and Gil Gerard, *Mach 2* (2000) with Brian Bosworth and Michael Dorn, and the popular *Megiddo: The Omega Code 2* (2002) with Michael York and Michael Biehn in which he played three different ages, 40, 60 and 80. Hedison loved the challenge of that.

In January of 2004, David debuted on the CBS Daytime drama *The Young and the Restless* as Judge Arthur Hendricks, an old flame of Katherine Chancellor. Soon after his arrival in Genoa City, Arthur was revealed to be the biological father of Katherine's new found daughter, Jill Foster Abbott. Arthur proposed marriage to Katherine. When Arthur's bitter stepson, Harrison, learned of their plans, he came to Genoa City, told Katherine Arthur was responsible for the death of his mother and planted fake insurance papers that Jill found. Heartbroken his new-found family would believe a stranger over him, Arthur broke the engagement and left town. David's last airdate was November 29, 2004.

David's most recent film, *Spectres* was shown at several film festivals before being released on DVD in April of 2005 and had its cable premiere on the Lifetime Movie Network as Soul Survivor in June. His last film *Death by Committee* failed to find a distributor in the United States, despite a name change to *Reality Trap* and a showing at the Avignon Film Festival in France in June of 2005.

In the early part of 2006, David appeared at the Hollywood Collectors Show in Burbank, CA and was in demand for interviews prior to the first release of *Voyage to the Bottom of the Sea* on DVD, February 21, 2006. The 2nd *Voyage* DVD was released on July 11, 2006, with David's interviews from the 1995 *Fantasy Worlds of Irwin Allen Special* included on the DVD, plus a Blooper reel. Hedison did another round of web interviews for that release.

The third *Voyage* set was released on October 24, 2006 (Season 2, vol. 1) and he was interviewed again, mostly on the radio. The fourth *Voyage* DVD release came on February 20, 2007 (season 2, vol. 2) and David did more radio interviews. The fifth DVD release (Season 3, vol. 1) was June 19, 2007 and included in the extras even more clips of David's interviews from the *Fantasy Worlds of Irwin Allen.* The 6th DVD release (Season 3, vol. 2) came out on October 23, 2007 and also has interview clips from the Irwin Allen Special.

David appeared on stage in Los Angeles in November of 2006 at the first ever play reading series sponsored by the Armenian Dramatic Alliance. He was in the first of three productions, *The Scent of Jasmine.*

In the summer and fall of 2006 and into 2007, David worked on four audio books. The first, *McKnight's Memory* was released in November of 2007. The second, *The King, McQueen and the Love Machine* was released in May, 2008. The third project was a 12 minute introduction to the reissue of the *James Bond Lifestyle* which went on sale in June of 2007. His fourth audio book, a joint project with Edd 'Kookie' Byrnes, Alan Young and Henry Silva, called *My Casino Caper,* was released in August.

He attended the Megacon convention February 18-20, 2007 and then staged *Uncle Vanya* for the edification of the master class at the Actors Studio West the next week. He recorded an audio commentary in May for *The Fly Collection* DVD release on September 11, 2007, which was also the release date of the first ever DVD of *The Lost World.* He appeared in the play *Love Letters,* this time with Nancy Dussault, at Monmouth University in New Jersey, on August 3, 4 and 5, 2007.

Hedison had an extremely busy October with two back to back con appearances in Denver and one in Los Angeles. He and Bridget attended the World Magic Awards, a UNICEF Feed the Children event at Barker Hanger on October 13. David gave a wonderful speech and helped Roger Moore unveil his star on the Walk of Fame on October 11 and celebrated with Roger on his 80th Birthday at the Regency Club in Westwood on Oct. 14.

2008 has David out on the road again. He made two appearances in England in March, one in Soho and one in Birmingham, where he was very popular and signed many autographs. David plans to continue to do appearances all year to celebrate the 50th anniversary of *The Fly*! Look for reports on all his 2008 appearances on his web site *www.davidhedison.com.*

Al Hedison in full makeup waits patiently for the next camera set-up with Karl Struss and the camera crew.

PHOTO COURTESY OF THE PERSONAL COLLECTION OF DAVID HEDISON, 2008

CHAPTER 3

STARRING AL HEDISON

David Hedison: I'm so used to David now. This all started in 1959, when NBC asked me to change my name to something "more elegant" to star in their continental espionage series, *Five Fingers*. Since I was still under exclusive contract to Fox, they simply substituted my middle name, David.

I remember one evening in early 1959, sitting in Romanoff's restaurant in Beverly Hills with Abe Lastfogel, head of the William Morris agency, his wife, Stan Kamen, a William Morris agent, and Maria Cooper. I happened to mention my dilemma with the name change that was about to take place. I turned to Mrs. Lastfogel and said, "Please tell me — what you think?" There was a moment of silence. She closed her eyes, opened them and said, "Al. There is no other choice!" But Fox thought differently, and lo and behold David Hedison was born. What do you suppose would have happened to my career if I had stuck with Al?

When did you make this film?

DH: It was shot in 18 days. I made *The Fly* in April of 1958 and it was released that summer. The movie premiered on July 17 in San Francisco, while I was in England filming *The Son of Robin Hood.*

How did you get this role?

DH: At first, it was offered to one of the other contract players, Rick Jason. He turned it down because he didn't want to wear a cloth on his head for one third of the film and then be out of the film for another third of it. I didn't realize I was up for the part. Jason turned it down because he wanted the Vincent Price part, but Vincent was already cast. I'm sure Rick Jason would have been a very fine André. I probably could have talked him into doing it, but I'm glad I didn't! Michael Rennie was offered Charas — he also turned it down. He was a good choice for Charas, but Herbert Marshall was dead on.

Do you have any script notes on your original script that you can share?

DH: I had so many notes in my original script of *The Fly* that by the time the film ended, my script was totally battered. There were all kinds of notes, even phone numbers of friends and a market list for groceries, and I just dumped a whole lot in the trash bin. Gone forever. I wish I'd known then what I know today. Don't we all?

Luckily I had a fresh copy of the script and had it leather bound with several photos of the film which I included. It's sitting on a shelf in my library along with leather bound copies of some of my other films, *The Enemy Below, The Son of Robin Hood,* and *The Lost World.* I also have four scripts bound from my first TV series, *Five Fingers.* They are the episodes: *Dossier, The Moment of Truth, Unknown Town* and *Epitaph* — five leather bound copies in all. My scripts after that didn't get the leather treatment, metal brads were all *they* got. Pity though. There were some good ones.

Kurt Neumann was a good director?

DH: He was very pleasant. He was easy to work with — he let you alone. With him, as long as he got the shot and he got it done quickly — that's what mattered. I was more used to working with theater people and theater directors who like to dig deeper and come up with something more honest and truthful. That's why Theater is so wonderful. No one can mess with you, except yourself. You're up there and that's it. I've always envied those actors who have worked on superlative film scripts with heavyweight directors, who sit around a table for a week and work on every detail of production until filming starts. Such a glorious way to work.

Do you like a director that leaves you alone?

DH: I like it when the director and I are in tune — a director who really works with me and knows when I need help and is able to make clear suggestions. Not to give a line reading, but to give you a glimmer of what he wants. To whisper a key phrase in your ear, like, "Why don't you try this as if you were ... ?" Some of the best directors, I feel were actors at one point like Sydney Pollack and Mark Rydell and so many others. They know actors, understand them, and help them.

There was a disagreement with Kurt Neumann?

DH: One day on the set I had a huge fight, with Kurt Neumann — one of the very few I've ever had. There is a shot of Andre turning a timer knob — a simple close-up of the hand. Well, as I walked onto the set early one morning before my actual call (I was always early); the crew had just finished shooting that close-up. I said, "What was *that?*" I was told it was only Andre turning a knob. Kurt did it.

I turned to Kurt and said angrily, "How could you do it, Kurt? Why would you do that? That's not my hand! Kurt, you have a fat little hand — I don't have a hand like that! I've got long fingers! Look at my fingers, they are not like yours! That's not my hand!" Kurt said, "It doesn't matter. It's going to be a quick shot. Nobody's going to know the difference." Well, I was furious! What I should have done is say, "I am not going to shoot today unless we redo that scene." But I didn't and they kept it in.

Next time you watch *The Fly*, there is a scene where Andre turns a knob and you see a fat hand. That's Kurt Neumann's hand. There is also a close-up

Andre and Helene in "the garden scene."

of a typewriter. A message is being typed as if it were being written by a very healthy person. Steady typing. Nothing to do with the character typing it, who was by then suffering. It was done one day when I wasn't working. Probably Neumann again!

Did you think then Neumann was too old for this project?

DH: Not at all! He was only 50. In those days that was considered elderly but in fact it wasn't old at all. He died right before the film was released, which was a shame. *The Fly* would have done a lot for his career.

Who thought of you for Andre?

DH: Billy Gordon, the head of casting at Fox came to my house to bring me a script. I was supposed to do a screen test for a film Robert Evans was set to do — it was called *The Fiend Who Walked the West*, only at that time it had another working title — *Enough Rope*. Many contract players in those days did screen tests for other people. I was the other actor in a lot of first screen tests; Ann-Margret, Stella Stevens, Tommy Sands, and Capucine. Terry Moore was partnered with me for my first test in 1957.

Anyway, Billy had left his wife in the car, so I invited both of them in for a drink, and we sat and talked — his wife was from Providence, Rhode Island, where I grew up. Later he must have mentioned me for *The Fly*. When the studio sent me the script, I was very enthusiastic — after all, the screenplay was by James Clavell, who was a great writer. I thought it was fabulous and I knew that the film was going to make money. Plus, it would be a wonderful acting challenge, so I jumped on it.

You read the *Playboy* magazine short story?

DH: Yes, I did. I read the script and then I went right to the short story. I thought, this is really good stuff!

You had your own ideas about *The Fly*?

DH: I wanted to make it more real, in terms of how Andre is taken over by the fly. I went running to Buddy Adler, who was head of production then. I said this picture is going to go through the roof, but we cannot use a fly mask. Using progressive makeup will be much more effective. When the wife first pulls the cloth off, what you see is part of his face and part of the fly. As his situation worsens, as the fly continues to take over, you would still see perhaps one eye and his expression and his pain. Adler thought this was interesting, but it was eventually turned down. Probably the budget had something to do with that.

Ben Nye, the make-up man, agreed with Adler's decision. He wanted to put me in a plaster cast (called a life mask) and make the fly head from that. He said, "Al, you don't want to have to come in at 4:00 in the morning for make-up, do you?" I said, "I'd come in at three!" I put my case to him as well, but I lost. They put me in plaster and got the size of my face and made the mask. One of my favorite films was the 1931 version of *Doctor Jekyll and Mr. Hyde* with Frederic March. The make-up was incredible and terrifying. That was the effect I wanted. I tried to convince them I had the right idea, but I could not persuade them. I felt — and I still do, that it would have made a big difference.

Like a good soldier, I dutifully went into makeup and they got the plaster cast of my head made that they wanted. I went through that procedure for hours — with all the time they spent doing it their way, we could have as easily done it the other way. I think the mask could have been the final stage, but in the beginning it would have been wonderful if they came up with something half and half that was really frightening.

My issue was that I wanted to have the ability to show more emotion with the progressive makeup. For instance, as I mentioned to Buddy Adler, when his wife pulls off the cloth, Andre is not yet insane. But slowly, as the fly takes over, he becomes more frightened — terrified that he might in some way harm his wife — and he realizes he must destroy himself and then it makes sense that he gets her to help him by putting him under the press.

They had everything arranged for making the mask head, so that was that. I guess the scene was horrifying, but I still think the film would have been

Andre destroys his final transportation device.

so much better with progressive makeup — so that every time Andre was "revealed" he would be more fly than the time before — if you could see he's only partially turned into the fly, with a real eye and a real ear, I think that would have been a great moment. Maybe one time, his eyeball would have popped out and rolled down his face! Now *that* would have been cool!

Many years later, that wonderfully talented director, David Cronenberg, did that and Jeff Goldblum was spectacular. It wasn't an eyeball, but his ear fell off. In any case, my film turned out well with the mask — which I couldn't take off between takes. Once that mask was on, it was on for most of the day, and was very uncomfortable — suffocating.

The cloth over your mask didn't bother you?

DH: Not for a moment. It gave me a chance to use my body — to act with my body — and I was very excited about the role. I was improvising as I went along. The cloth was thin enough for me to barely see through. I could figure

Andre shares his breakthrough with Helene.

out what objects were close by; find the blackboard and the papers and the bin to burn them in. It was my second film — the first was *The Enemy Below* — but this was my first starring role. I thought this was a really good story — believable. I believed it and I hope I made the audience believe it, too.

Could you see with the mask on?

DH: Not well — it was rather blurry. In one scene towards the end I had to tear the lab apart with an axe. I swung that axe all over the place. After one of the scenes, a crew member said, "Al, you swung once and I thought you were going right through your leg!" I had barely missed, because I really couldn't see that well. I was swinging that axe all over and knocking things about, but I had no idea what I was doing, except to tear that damned lab apart!

You said you wore it for five days. One of the makeup men said you lost 10 pounds!

DH: I suppose I wasn't eating that much during the shoot. 10 pounds sounds a bit excessive! I'll give him five.

How long did it take to apply everything to the mask?

DH: It took maybe an hour and a half, and between takes I'd sit there and wait. I was very patient that way. It gave me a chance to prepare, to meditate, and to get ready for the next scene. I wasn't into having coffee and talking with the crew, because I was really doing a lot of preparation, and my thinking terrified me. I'll lose my wife, my child. What do I do?

How did you get the sucker thing on the front of the mask to move?

DH: The piece was rubber on the outside with hairs on it. It was connected to a wooden core they stuck in my mouth. I could move it with my teeth. I saw the film again last spring to do an audio commentary. A few people around me seemed horrified by that mouth thing, because when she screamed, I not only pulled back, but I really made that sucker quiver. It was a great movement on my part and was very effective. When I saw it again, I laughed. I thought it was great!

Did you find it difficult not being able to speak?

DH: Not at all! Just believing it in my head — I was paranoid, which resulted in plenty of body language. I watched myself some time ago when it was on the AMC cable channel and I thought, well, that's not bad. I felt good — but when she pulled the cloth off, I said (and here we go again): Oh, what it could have been with progressive make-up! And then at the end with the spider web — it would have been such a gloriously horrific, painful scene. And it wasn't. I'll explain why later. Stay tuned.

You were 30 and looked younger — is that why they put grey in your hair?

DH: They got me into makeup and put gray in the sides. They did everything they could do to play down my youthfulness. I thought it looked pretty good — we got away with it.

Were you sure you would?

DH: Oh, yes, no doubt about it. My best work was under that cloth. In those scenes, I was really feeling something. I felt the pain of Andre; what he was going through. I made it my pain to show what was going on in him in that kind of situation. I made it real.

James Clavell's girls saw it and the film made them cry because it was basically a love story. When the fly has the chalk in his hand and writes 'love you' on the blackboard — that is very effective. When Michaela and Holly Clavell were 10 or 12 their father showed to them in London. They were in tears. Then the next time they saw me in person; it was, Oh My God, more crying —

Was that you in every shot?

DH: Yes. Everything the fly did was me, including the very end when he's in the spider web. I covered my teeth with my lips. They told me they did not want to see my teeth. So I started screaming and going, "Help me, Help me!" Now that's another thing that would have been more effective. In that final scene, they cranked up the speed of my voice, so it comes out in a high squeaky voice, which doesn't sound right. As the camera closes in, you should hear a man's voice screaming. I was screaming my lungs out, like a spider was really going to devour me. I was really terrified. Then I saw the movie, heard the squeaky voice and I thought what are they doing? That's not horror, that's funny. You should be hearing Andre screaming for his life!

What was the rig for the "help me" scene?

DH: I was on an interior set, up on a platform in a net, a large blue screen in the background. It was my final scene in the film, I'm pretty sure. They painted white all over my face because people talk about the white-headed fly throughout the movie. There was no spider there. Lying in the web, I had to look in a certain direction and imagine something crawling towards me. It's called acting. They put white glue between two 2 by 8 boards and then pulled them apart to make the spider web strands that covered me. The spider was a hand puppet.

That glue covering you couldn't have been pleasant, did it feel sticky? Was it hard to get off after filming?

DH: Yes — and I couldn't get into that shower fast enough.

Was that an actual metal press?

DH: Oh, yes. That was the metal press they used at Fox. We shot that scene in the studio machine shop, where the machinists worked — that press was really there, they used it on the metal to build sets. That wasn't a set, it was an actual place. They brought in lights and the actors and the director of photography and the director, and we shot it.

The press scene looked dangerous. Was it?

DH: They had the press blocked so it didn't crush me completely. I wasn't the least bit afraid. I wanted the scene to work. It didn't bother me. They tested it and I could see it stopped at a certain point. I even told them to make it a little lower, because there was too much space over my head, so they dropped it another inch to make it look more realistic.

How and where did you meet screenwriter James Clavell during the making of the film?

DH: We met three or four days before filming started. He and his wife April, invited the director, Kurt, and his wife, Patricia Owens and me for a drink — this was also the first time I met Patricia. From the start we became good friends. He was, of course, a very intelligent man, but very much an introvert. We lost touch after a few years — they moved back to London — but we ran into him after we went to London in the early 70's, and saw a lot of them for years after that. They had a house here for a while, and then moved back to London again and finally to Switzerland where he died. Either my wife or I

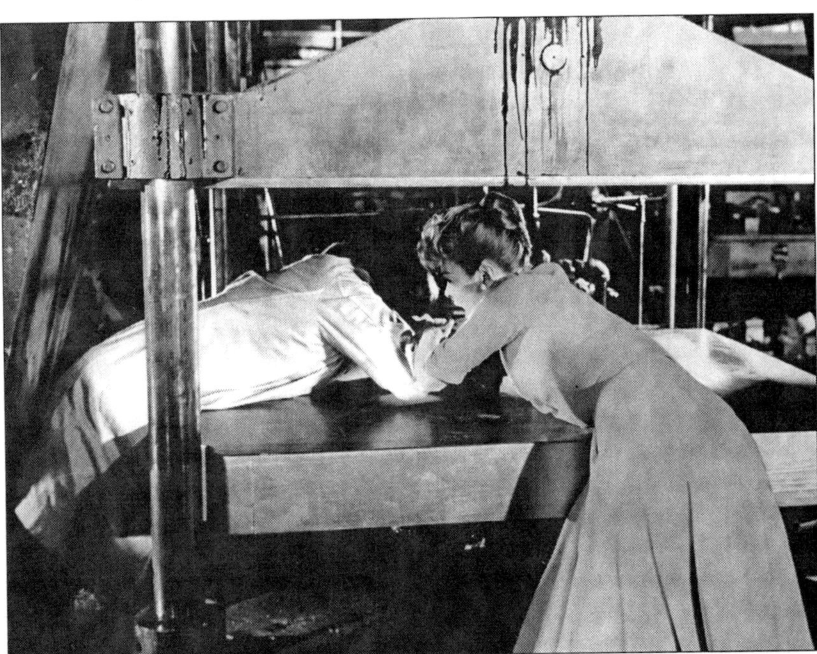

Andre throws Helene clear of the press.

took the photo of him on the cover of the first hardcover edition of his book, *Noble House* in 1981 — we both shot the roll of film and we don't know whose photo it was — so it credits "Hedison."

Did you tell James Clavell about your ideas for the film?

DH: I told him. He thought the ideas could have been interesting, but he didn't care one way or the other. The one thing he liked was that optical spot, that shows a fly's point of view looking at the wife. They were like eight interfaces in a honeycomb pattern. He liked that. I liked that scene, too — thought it was great and very effective on the screen. The audience always reacts to it. So many times, at various functions, people always comment on that one scene. I was good and never answered, "Yes, but don't you think it would have been better if ..." Not a word. I smiled and simply said, "Oh, Thank you!"

Did *any* of your ideas make it into the film?

DH: That whole business of scribbling on a blackboard to tell my wife I love her — that wasn't a direction, but I figured that was the way he would have done it. I think the director wanted me to write "help me" or "kill the fly." But this guy is going through a struggle: the fly is taking over his brain. He wants to be killed. People ask, "Did you do all that stuff in the mask when you break everything in the lab." Of course I did! You think a stunt man could move like that and do the things that I did? No way!

Tell us about your process — how did you get "under the skin" of this scientist who means so well and then has everything go so terribly wrong?

DH: I really bought it, that whole thing with the atoms breaking down and coming together in another room. I really believed that there could be an end of hunger in the world, that you could transport food and medicine to starving nations, break down the atoms and send it over. I really believed that! To me, it made sense, having a realistic premise made acting it so much easier.

Clavell's script was a very sympathetic story of two people very much in love who have this horrible tragedy happen to them in pursuit of the greater good. I played Andre as a conscientious scientist, not an obsessed fanatic. He discovered something marvelous; he wants to do wonderful things for humanity; to transport food to anywhere in the world it is needed, instantaneously — he had all these wonderful ideas. I thought that was the most important point James Clavell made in that script.

Else Schreiber was a mentor in those days?

DH: She was a wonderful acting coach, used to work with Gregory Peck on all his films. She had her own house up on Doheny Drive and she worked there with certain actors at Fox and all over Hollywood. You would go there with a script and you'd work on it together and read certain scenes and so on. She was marvelous.

How did you approach this film?

DH: At that point, I was terribly earnest. Terribly boring. Took it all very seriously. I remember one scene where I was going through some explanation. When the scene was over, makeup started coming over to freshen my face, and I pushed them away. Patricia Owens said, "You have dark circles under your eyes," and I said, "Patricia, shouldn't he? Wouldn't the scientist in this horrible situation? Of course, he would have dark circles. He's exhausted. I don't want this powder on my face."

I was upset with the way they made Patricia Owens look in some of her more dramatic scenes. She had to run around looking for the fly and she's frantic. She almost catches it and it gets out through the screen and she's going crazy. Well, at the end of every take, makeup and wardrobe would come running in and fix her hair, powder her face and fluff up her costume. I kept saying, "What are you doing? Pull her hair down. We know she's beautiful, but she's looking for this fly — she's in this manic state — she should be bruised; her head should have hit the window. Her whole face would have been bruised. Her hair should be down!" If it had been more realistic in that way, *The Fly* could have been so much better. It's a cult film today, but it could have been a true classic.

What was it like to work with Vincent Price?

DH: When people ask me, I have to tell them we never worked the same days on *The Fly*. I never worked with Herbert Marshall, either. All my scenes were with Patricia and my little boy, Charlie Herbert. I had seen Price many times on the lot. He was under contract to Fox before I did *The Fly*. He knew the studio really well. I talked to him a few times and we were together at the final wrap party.

Although we didn't have too much to do with each other on *The Fly* and I didn't get a chance to know him then, some nine years later he was a guest star on *Voyage to the Bottom of the Sea*. We did a fourth season episode together called "The Deadly Dolls." I was kidding around on the set constantly, doing all kinds of nasty pranks. Vincent looked at me in shock and said; "I don't recognize you. You are so *funny*! When we were doing *The Fly*, you were so *earnest*!" Those were the exact words he used.

I admitted to him that I took everything more seriously in those days. We had a lovely time on *Voyage*. I was such a cut up and we're having so many laughs that he invited me to his house for dinner. It was Richard Basehart and his wife, Diana, and me and my date. Anne Baxter was there and some of the other Fox people, it was really nice. Vincent was a great chef and to sample some of his cooking was a treat. He had a beautiful house and, of course, there was his incredible art collection.

You were billed over Vincent Price?

DH: Let's face it — that was embarrassing. On *The Fly* it was Al Hedison, Patricia Owens, Vincent Price and Herbert Marshall. It was nothing I had anything to do with. It was the studio building up their new stars. I didn't even want to look at the credits the first time I saw it. Look at Herbert Marshall's body of work! And Vincent Price's! It was the first time I had star billing in a film and with those proven champions, it seemed so ludicrous.

It has been reported that Vincent Price didn't take this film seriously.

DH: Absolutely! He made a lot of fun of it; he thought it was the most ridiculous thing.

And if you watch his performance — slick as it was — you could tell. He and Herbert Marshall had to look down at that tiny fly in the web and they kept breaking up laughing.

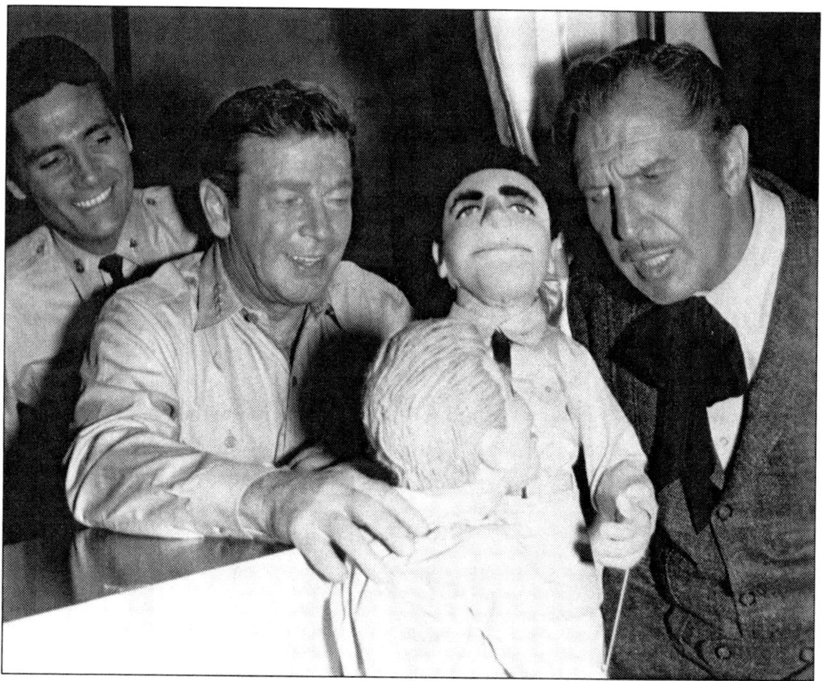

David Hedison, Richard Basehart and guest star Vincent Price mug with the Admiral Nelson and Captain Crane puppets in a publicity shot from the *Voyage to the Bottom of the Sea* episode "The Deadly Dolls".

Patricia Owens says the three of them got sent home by the director one day (after about fifty takes) because they couldn't stop laughing and that it was Vincent's fault.

DH: I heard about that scene. Fifty takes? I don't think so. Maybe seven? Vincent and Herbert sent home because they couldn't stop laughing? No way. Not on our schedule.

You knew about Vincent's Price's bisexuality?

Well, I knew Vincent had this sort of light touch, but no one ever said to me — as we said in those days, "You know, he's queer." No one ever said anything about anyone to me, but there were a lot of people I worked with who were gay. Looking back it must have been horrible for someone who was homosexual, being pushed into a loveless marriage and ruining their own and the woman's life. How much healthier it is today, when a young person can say, "Oh, yeah, I'm gay and this is my partner." That's the way it should be — but back then it was kept under wraps. Perhaps sometimes it still is today — which is ridiculous.

Where was the last time you saw Vincent Price?

DH: I ran into him at the Fox commissary and we had lunch together. Strange — but I can even remember what I ate: a Rueben sandwich with a glass of Fresca. I can't remember Vincent's choice. I do miss that man — always so knowledgeable and amusing — and a great friend. He gave us his cookbook for our wedding (more than 39 years ago) and we still use it and think of him when we do.

You and Patricia Owens worked well together — were believable as a loving couple. How did you get to that chemistry?

DH: She was good to work with, a sweet and lovely girl. I loved her. She would come up to me when I was in the mask and say, "Can I get you something? Is there anything you want?" I would tell her, "No, sweetie, I'm fine," and go back to meditating, preparing for my upcoming scene.

The first time I met Patricia was at the home of James Clavell. He and his wife invited us all before the film started. It was a lovely evening and we toasted each other, vowing to have a good time as we made the film. The first scene I played with Patricia was in the garden, right before I turn into the fly when I do the experiment. The studio was very nervous because they thought I was too young for the part of the scientist. That was the very first day — I remember that distinctly. And the reason I remember it is because when the dailies came out the next day I sensed a sigh of relief from everyone, that the scene had worked because I felt very good in the scene; I felt in tune with Patricia. The love scene, I thought, worked quite well. It was a wonderful scene, until they decided it had to be dubbed, because of the birds in the background. I never saw Patricia again after the Fox days. I believe she retired and moved away from the Los Angeles area.

What was the first scene filmed?

DH: The garden scene. When we did it originally, it was very effective. Then Fox decided it had to be dubbed. I didn't understand dubbing very well, or how to go about doing it. I had to catch a plane that day to London to go do *The Son of Robin Hood.* So that scene has a very sterile quality, because it's dubbed. It was very disappointing to me. I did it with Kurt Neumann and we only had an hour. It was my first dubbed scene. My voice is totally wrong, it sounds strained. They kept telling me to lower my voice. And I'd lower it, but I kept thinking, why am I doing this? This is not a human sound. It's a dubbed sound; it's hollow and unfortunate. When Patricia saw the picture, she said, "Whose voice is that? That's not Al! What is that sound?" Big mistake. I'd love to go back to Fox and re-dub that whole sequence.

Did you watch any rushes during filming?

DH: No. I have never enjoyed watching myself — because that person on the screen was always a stranger to me. Who is he? Where is Al David Hedison? I suppose if I ever had the opportunity to get involved in an incredible character role, I might check out the dailies to make sure I was on the right track, but that would be the only reason.

Where did you see *The Fly* for the first time?

DH: I came back from filming in London and found the film was a big hit. I went to see it at the theater in Westwood. I went by myself, sat in the last row, saw it and left. I was disappointed in a lot of it ... disappointed that my ideas for the progressive makeup didn't work out, disappointed by that "help me, help me" voice — the dubbed garden scene — all that bothered me. I was disappointed and yet I thought most of it was quite good. At least the audience I was sitting with seemed to be having a great time.

Did you do any publicity?

DH: No, I was in London filming. Fox opened the movie at four hundred theaters simultaneously, but they had no idea of the business it was going to do. After that amazing opening, there was a big double-page ad in *The Motion Picture Herald* that said in bold print, *The Fly* Has Opened — 400 Theaters Never Saw Business This Big! Back then, that was shocking — Fox had to pull it and couldn't use it again. That ad came out once, in one issue only. Today they'd leave it in.

Fox hired airplanes to tow banners over all the Santa Monica beaches before the film's opening, telling people — *The Fly* Opens Tonight! — back and forth all day long. We were much more innocent in those days! There was a health club in Los Angeles at the time called Vic Tanney's where a lot of actors went to keep fit. The story I heard goes: After those planes flew by with the *The Fly* Opens Tonight! banners, a few minutes later another plane flew by with the slogan: Keep it firm at Vic Tanney's.

Did you do any publicity for the overseas double bill re-release of both films? "See them together but not alone!"

DH: I wasn't asked to do any. The most recent DVD re-release includes *The Fly, The Return of the Fly,* and *Curse of the Fly* in a four disc set called *The Fly Collection*. My film is the only one with any commentary. I was interviewed about the film in London in May of 2007 and shortly after that, here in Los Angeles, I sat with David DeValle and we both made comments during a screening which was recorded for an audio commentary track, but not filmed.

What did your parents think of your first major film success, after supporting you through lean times a few years earlier in New York City? I understand your mother kept a scrapbook of all your work?

DH: My parents absolutely loved my first film — a great film — *The Enemy Below* with Robert Mitchum and Curt Jurgens. The Providence Rhode Island newspapers did a write-up about me and my mother marched down to the Albee Theatre. She talked the manager into putting up some pictures in front of the theater of Al Hedison — the local boy! The surprised manager did as he was told! *The Fly*, however, did not impress them that much. Not their cup of tea! Was that your voice in the garden scene?" asked my Mother. "Yes," I said. "Funny," she answered, "sure didn't sound like you!"

Why has *The Fly* lasted?

DH: It was in color. It had a good look and a lovely score. It was well-mounted. At its center, it is a very tragic love story. Fox had never taken on a project like that. It was one of their very first science-fiction films, so they were very hesitant about it. We had an 18 day schedule and it was made for practically nothing. I received my contracted $750.00 week, or whatever it was.

Do you think the screenplay is what made it last?

DH: Some of it definitely belongs to James Clavell because he stuck to the story and gave us a good screenplay. I think it's due to all of us. We had something that we thought might be successful. I originally felt it was going to be major. It was an A minus, but it could have been an A plus.

I knew it would be wonderfully amusing and entertaining — and maybe make some money — but I certainly didn't think it was going to become the cult science fiction film that it has. What I should have done, maybe during one of the anniversary years (1998 or 2003), was try to remake it myself. It's amazing — I got so many calls in 1984-1985, from New York and even Europe, because people had gotten wind that *The Fly* was being remade then.

Now for every anniversary or DVD release they try and find me again. They tracked me down in 2003 for the 45th anniversary and in 2006, for the 20tæ anniversary of the 1986 remake. I did DVD commentary in for the 2007 re-release and am involved in this and other projects for the film's 50th anniversary in 2008. They are even planning to do an opera of *The Fly* here in Los Angeles in September of 2008. I would ask for the leading role, but I don't sing opera! I have no doubt they will track me down in 2011, for the 25th anniversary of the 1986 film. Talk about a project having legs!

I saw the film some years ago on Channel 5 in Los Angeles and all the things I felt when it came out and have mentioned here stood out even more. It all comes back to the story when you say something is a classic. The basic story is wonderful, and that worked. It goes to show, the story's the thing. Get a good story going, and sometimes even if it's only in competent hands, it'll be successful.

Did the film help your career?

DH: I don't know that it did one way or the other. A lot of people enjoyed it and thought, he's a good actor, or whatever, but I don't think it helped that much. In those days I don't think being under exclusive contract helped anybody's career. It was easy going and you got paid every week -- 40 weeks of the year. I think now it was the worst thing I could have done -- to be under contract to a studio. I had to turn down so many good parts.

I remember -- Joe Papp wrote me a letter, he thought it would be wonderful if I would come back to New York and do *Henry V* in the park. I went to the studio head, Buddy Adler, and they wouldn't let me do it, they had a picture in mind for me. That picture ended up being given to Elvis Presley. I wish now I had waited awhile, done more theater in New York, and then maybe a two picture a year deal like so many other actors did. They were wise. They stayed longer in New York. I did that one play with Uta Hagan (*A Month in the Country*) and, next thing I knew — whoosh — I was off to Hollywood, which was not a good career choice.

I remember being in New York at the Neighborhood Playhouse with Steve McQueen. We both got in at the same time and he told me after we had done one of our school plays that we were going to be "big stars." Fast forward five years, we both have made it to Hollywood and I drive past this movie marquee on Sunset Boulevard that is advertising Steve McQueen in *The Blob* and Al Hedison in *The Fly*. Yes, sir, really big stars!

You didn't want to do the 1959 sequel?

DH: In those days, when they made sequels, they were pretty awful. Not like today — when they get better and better. I didn't want to do two *Fly* pictures. My career was getting started and I wanted to do something totally different. So I did *The Son of Robin Hood* in London. Talk about bad career choices!

What did you think of the 1986 remake? You and your wife were invited to the LA premiere and she left to go sit in the lobby after Brundle's ear fell off, but you stuck it out?

DH response: I stayed until the end because it was directed by a champ and I appreciated the performances. I do like the story of the original better than the other versions, however.

You were Al in *The Fly* and now you are David.

DH: My father was naturalized in 1917 as Albert David Hedison. I was born Albert David Hedison, Jr. in 1927. When my grandfather, David, came to this country he changed our name from the Armenian Heditsian because he thought it would be easier to use Hedison, so that's what we became. One of my grandmothers called me Ara as a nickname. It's a traditional Armenian name. There was an ancient king; called Ara the Beautiful. I guess my grandparents thought I was easy on the eye. Even my Dad called me Ara — but only in the family.

One of those silly 1950's fan magazines asked if I had a nickname and then suddenly my "real name" was Ara Heditsian. This fiction was picked up by other magazines and was printed all over the place. I guess what was actually on my birth certificate wasn't "exotic" enough to match the way I looked in those days. Those fan magazines were voracious, always taking my picture when I was at events with my various girlfriends and asking for interviews, almost as bad as the tabloids today, but with thankfully with more restraint and far more decency than they show now.

Does it bother you genre roles never get any recognition, particularly from the Oscars?

DH: The thing is people never recognize science fiction performances as good. They relate to the fellow playing the guy next door and who is playing a real emotion to a situation they understand; he's lost his child and he's grieving. Someone who is trying to kill a giant cockroach about to blast off for outer space in the New York World's Fair Monument [*Men in Black*] is not something they understand. Jeff Goldblum should been nominated for the 1986 remake of *The Fly* and so should have Jeremy Irons in David Cronenberg's *Dead Ringers*, but no one at the Academy or elsewhere wants to recognize that kind of role. And while I'm at it, what about that brilliant actor Richard Basehart in that submarine series he did!

They show *The Fly* about three times a year on cable and always at Halloween.

DH: I always know when it's airing in October. My friends call and tell me it's on. Roger Moore will ring and then harass me with a falsetto "help me" on the other end of the transatlantic line.

Do you watch *The Fly* since it plays so often?

DH: No, I don't. It's strange. I don't like to look at work I've done, over and over. I don't know why. There was a good American Movie Classics documentary called *The Fly Papers* that aired in 2000. It was very interesting. It was released on the FLY II DVD in 2006. Right after that, AMC showed *The Fly* and that's when I flicked off the TV. I don't want to go home again. I've seen it, talked about it and that's enough.

David Hedison
July 2007

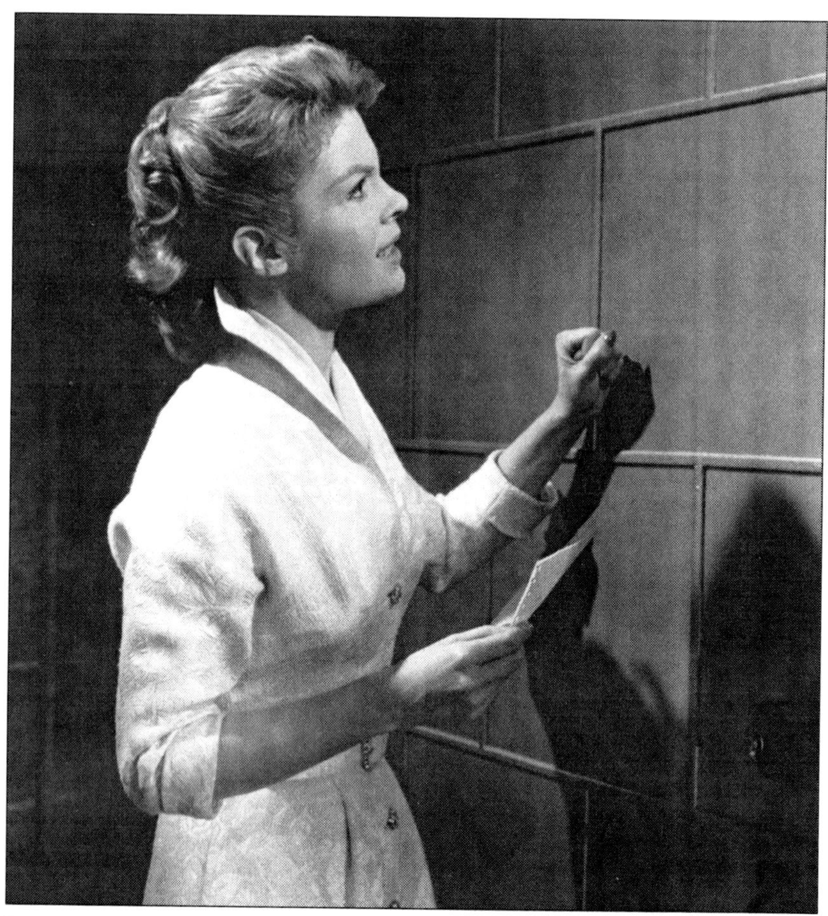

Patricia Owens – Helene asks Andre to explain his note.

CHAPTER 4

MAIN CAST

PATRICIA OWENS
HELENE DELAMBRE

Patricia Molly Owens was born in January 17, 1928 in Golden, British Columbia. Her family moved to London when she was eight. Patricia had always wanted to be an actress and she persuaded her family to send her to the Central School of Dramatic Arts when she was 14. Her first role was Rosalind in Shakespeare's *As You like It.* In 1943, she began to get uncredited bit parts and small roles in British movies. Her first film was *Miss London Limited* (1943).

Her first real theater notice came in 1952 in *Second Threshold* with Clive Brook. She played a pert American teenager named Thankful Mather. The role caught the attention of Writer/Producer Sydney Bartlett, whom Owens would marry four years later. Because she was Canadian and had a different accent, Owens was often cast as "the American" in British productions. She played sweet young girls, usually the daughter or a family friend.

Other roles of note during her time in England were *The Inward Eve* on the BBC, where she played a blind girl, *Winter's Journey* (the British version of *The Country Girl*) at Kew Theater and a run in *Sabrina Fair* — also at the Kew Theatre. This performance brought her to the attention of James Pattinson, a scout who worked for Basil Litchfield in Fox Studio's London Office. Litchfield pronounced her the girl who should be sent to America and she was. For her Fox screen test Patricia did a scene from *The Country Girl* and was signed to a seven year contract in 1956.

They put her to work immediately in *Island in the Sun* with James Mason. She was then loaned out to Warner Brother's for *Sayonara* with Marlon Brando. She enjoyed filming in Japan with Joshua Logan, until she was stricken with appendicitis and had to have an emergency operation in a Japanese Hospital. Owens returned to the Fox lot and was cast in *No Down Payment* with Jeffery Hunter and then appeared in *The Law and Jake Wade* with Robert Taylor.

She took to America right away and after only two years here, she could not see ever returning to England. The thought of living without an automobile was unbearable. She also had to put her foot down not to have her name shortened to Pat. She happened to like Patricia and was determined not have a nickname, so much so, that she even stood up to her director, Joshua Logan, about it and won.

With her red hair and elegant manner, she was groomed to be a younger version of Deborah Kerr, who was a very popular female star at this time. Her resemblance served Owens well through a series of pictures where her character often suffered, but remained strong and resolute and ever the dutiful wife.

She married Sidney Bartlett on April 7, 1956, even though he was more than 20 years older. She was his third wife and she spent most of the first year of their marriage on various locations making films. They divorced on April 16, 1958; after a second incident of him striking her when he was drunk. The then 49 year-old Bartlett would later lose a fourth wife over this.

Owens continued her film career after the divorce with *The Fly, The Gunrunners, These Thousand Hills* and *Five Gates to Hell,* which was written and directed by James Clavell. Owens also began to appear on television, as part of her Fox contract, in *Alfred Hitchcock Presents, Adventures in Paradise, Alcoa Theatre* and *Follow the Sun*. She also appeared on Mervyn Leroy's *This is Your Life* tribute in 1960.

Patricia re-married on July 10, 1960. Her new husband was a Palm Springs Realtor named Jerry Nathanson. She gave birth to a son, Adam, in the spring of 1961. Patricia made three more films: *Hell to Eternity, Seven Women from Hell,* and *X-15,* before her second child was born. *Tales of Well Fargo* and *Bus Stop* were her last two TV appearances before Fox ended everyone's contract in 1962.

Her first free lance TV appearance was for the Desilu Studios on *The Untouchables* in 1963. She also guest starred on *Gunsmoke* in 1964. Increasingly having to choose between her growing family and her career Patricia made two films in 1965; *Black Spurs* and *Walk a Tightrope* and two TV appearances in 1966 on *Burkes Law and Perry Mason.* Her last two acting performances came in 1968, when Patricia made what would become her last film *The Destructors* and then appeared in an episode of the TV series, *Lassie.* Patricia announced her retirement in 1968, telling the press she was quitting show business to concentrate on raising her children.

She left Hollywood and never looked back. Patricia Owens died in Lancaster, California on August 31, 2000. She was cremated and her ashes were given to her family in Palmdale, CA, in accordance with her wishes.

Owens was interviewed during the filming of *The Fly* for a beauty column, so she doesn't really say anything about the film she was currently working on, but she does give some answers about her impressions of the United States to date and the California lifestyle in particular.

Americans eat too much because the portions served them are way too large. Owens thinks we should eat less more often. Also Americans need to walk more and stop taking their cars to go around the corner. There are too many labor saving devices now present in American homes, like dishwashers, washing machines and TV dinners. She also thinks American women are more independent, but they should never let it go so far as to make the man feel not needed.

Patricia is enjoying her new look for this film. They lightened her hair, thinned her eyebrows, altered her lip line and used much less make-up. She is very pleased with the result. Now if she could only get used to American practice of mixing business and pleasure. The British very distinctively separate their jobs from their social life, but Americans don't, which can lead to tension headaches. The best cure for that is a properly brewed cup of tea, poured over leaves, not made with a bag dunked in luke-warm water.

And if one can't get tea, take deep breaths and soon relaxation will come. At least until one is called back to the set to find out her husband had been turned into a fly!

Reporters once again caught up with Owens a month into the release of the film and asked her to make comments on the atomic age storyline. She replied she was more concerned on the effect on her male co-stars than herself. While she was not adverse to some innovation, it seemed to her that the men had gone gadget crazy during the making of the film. That they had all kind of electronic equipment on the set and these men spent more time messing around with dials and diodes, and making lights flash, than paying attention to any female on the set. She thought she heard a wolf-whistle one day and turned around to be appreciated, only to find it was merely a howl from some miserable machine being operated by Al Hedison.

While she hoped it was only a temporary aberration on the movie set, she could see where women might face a real problem if and when electronics take over people's lives. It happened to her screen husband. If Andre had not been so wrapped in his scientific experiments, he would have noticed the fly in the booth with him and not been transformed, but if he hadn't been, there would have been no reason to make the film, she concluded.

VINCENT PRICE
FRANCOIS DELAMBRE

Vincent Price was born Vincent Louis Price, Jr. in Saint Louis, Missouri, on May 27, 1911. He came from a wealthy family, thanks to his grandfather, Dr. Vincent Clarence Price, creator of the first commercially manufactured baking powder in the United States. His father was president of the National Candy Company which specialized in jaw breakers and jelly beans.

Young Vincent had three older siblings and was first educated at the elementary school where his mother, Margaret, was a teacher. He attended St. Louis Country Day High School and was then accepted to Yale University, where he earned degrees in art history and fine art. He wasn't interested in the Drama School then, but enjoyed touring with the Glee Club.

Price became interested in stage acting in the thirties in London after first trying to be an artist and a teacher. He made his first professional appearance on stage in 1935. Vincent Price became a major Broadway star in *Victoria Regina*. He made his film debut in 1938 in *Service de Luxe*, and played Joseph Smith in *Brigham Young* in 1940 but did not really did not make a name for himself in film until 1944 with the release of *Laura* and *Keys of the Kingdom*. Price told a hair-raising tale of being nailed into a full cask of wine by his co-stars in during the filming of *Tower of London* in 1939, their idea of a really good (and dangerous) practical joke.

He was married with a young son during World War II so he did not serve. Price was married three times. He had a son in 1940, Vincent Barrett Price, with his first wife, Edith Barrett, who he married on April 23, 1938 at the height of his Broadway career. Barrett was from a famous stage family and he saw the match as another Lunt and Fontaine, but then Price went to Hollywood and found success as a film actor. Edith did not and that put a strain on their marriage and hastened its end, but not before they appeared in two films together, *Song of Bernadette* (1943) and *Keys of the Kingdom* (1944). His son became a poet and a teacher in his own right.

Vincent met costume designer Mary Grant and found her to be a much more compatible and companionable partner for all of his interests. Price divorced Barrett and married Grant on August 25, 1949. His only regret was that his son, whom he loved dearly, moved away to New York City to live with his mother. In 1962, a second child, his daughter, Mary Victoria, was born.

Victoria had a good relationship with him, saying Price would often take her deep-sea fishing, which was one of his passions and that he was always fun to be with. Her father loved his life and all the things he found to do in it, his cooking, his art, giving lectures and doing readings. He remained married to Mary Grant for 25 years.

After assaying the villainous Mr. Manningham in *Angel Street* in 1942, he carried that slick villainy into the films *The Long Night, Rogues Regiment* and *The Bribe.* On the flip side, he became Simon Templar, The Saint, on radio from 1947 to 1951 for three different networks. This may have been the start of folks thinking Vincent was British. Price certainly had the voice and manner for it and was often referred to as a "younger" Karloff.

The most famous film he appeared in the 1950's was the 1956 version of *The Ten Commandments,* playing, of course, a villain. Price's first foray into horror was as the voice of The Invisible Man in *Abbott and Costello Meet Frankenstein. House of Wax* in 1953 was the first 3-D film to be top ten at the box office and he sealed his life-long connection to horror film with his appearance in *The Fly* in 1958 and *The House on Haunted Hill* in 1959. He also did *The Bat* and *Return of the Fly* in 1959.

This led to a contract with Roger Corman and American International Pictures that included his famous "Poe" films; one a year. Fall *of the House of Usher* (1960), *The Pit and the Pendulum* (1961), *Tales of Terror* (1962), *The Raven* (1963), *The Masque of the Red Death* (1964) and *The Tomb of Ligeia* (1965).

He played Egghead eight times in the 60's *Batman* TV series and ended up being one of their best loved villains. According to series stars West and Ward, Price started an egg fight on the set, simply because the artillery (eggs) was at hand. Yvonne Craig loved him as a foil to her Batgirl. He started appearing on *Hollywood Squares* in the late 1960's and by the mid-seventies was a semi-regular. His voice and manner were well suited to the show's format. Price was a popular guest making several hundred appearances during the show's long run. He loved an audience of any kind and referred to himself as "an old ham." He also liked to work and had a habit of going on any television program that would ask him. A Red Skelton appearance in 1968 with Boris Karloff is considered a classic now. Price said he did the show because he realized Karloff wasn't going to be around much longer to work with.

Price made *The Abominable Dr. Phibes* in 1971 and did several other pictures in this vein until about 1975, when horror films went out of vogue for a while. The most important film of this period was *Theatre of Blood* — not only did the plot strike very close to home for Price, who was sensitive to the fact that

Vincent Price – Francois begs Helene to tell him the truth.

the quality of film he was being offered had declined over the years, but also because the film had an Australian female co-star named Coral Browne that Price (at age 60) fell madly in love with.

He divorced Mary Grant and married Coral Browne, on October 24, 1974 and they were inseparable until her death from cancer in 1990. They always told everyone that they were lucky to have found each other so late in life and they loved every moment they had together.

Price became a member of the road company of *Oliver!* for six years from 1970-1976. He filled in any other spare time with voice work on albums and radio and commercials. He did *Tales of the Unexpected* for a year on syndicated radio, was heard in Alice Cooper's first solo album, *Welcome to my Nightmare* and plugged Milton Bradley's Shrunken Head Apple Sculpture, amid dramatic readings of Poe and many art exhibitions.

In 1977, Vincent put together a one man show, *Diversions and Delights,* where he played Oscar Wilde sitting in a Parisian theater, a year before his death, reminiscing about his life and his love for Lord Alfred Douglas. Price toured the play all over the United States for the next six years and consistently made money with it. He would eventually take the show worldwide doing at one count over 800 performances. His daughter, Victoria, considers this one man show some of the best acting he ever did.

From 1981 to 1989, Price was the host of the PBS Series *Mystery*, until his Parkinson's disease progressed to the point where it was too noticeable for him to remain on screen any longer. Price also suffered from emphysema, but he continued to do a variety of things, mostly voice work. He was in Tim Burton's *Vincent* in 1982, the same year he recorded the "rap" to the mega hit *Thriller* by Michael Jackson, reinventing Price as a MTV music video star.

His favorite role of this era was the voice of Professor Ratigan in Disney's *The Great Mouse Detective*. His performance in *The Whales of August* in 1987 brought him critical acclaim late in life and his last major film role was as the inventor of *Edward Scissorhands* in 1990.

In 1990 Price was also hired by Walt Disney Imagineering to voice the role of the phantom narrator in "Phantom Manor," the Euro Disney version of Disney's iconic "Haunted Mansion" being built outside Paris. The French language and Price were a bad combination and the takes were deemed unusable; when an English language version was substituted, Price recorded the entire piece in two takes. These English recordings were placed in the attraction, but after a few months of use, Euro Disney, suffering from poor attendance, felt it was because there was not enough French in the park. So in 1993, Price's narration was removed from the attraction and replaced by a French language version recorded by Gérard Chevalier. His narration can be found on *Disney's Haunted Mansion* CD. Today the park is known as Disneyland Resort Paris and although his narration is long gone, one part of Vincent's performance remains: his laugh. Although the narration of the Phantom was changed, Price's original recordings of the Phantom's evil laughter still echo through the attraction.

Price died of lung cancer on October 25, 1993, leaving behind a very eclectic legacy of film, art and cookbooks. From 1962 to 1971, Sears offered *The Vincent Price Collection of Fine Art* and sold about 50,000 pieces of fine art to the public through select Sears Stores. East Los Angeles College has an endowed Vincent and Mary Price Art Gallery. The Gallery was started in 1951 with 90 pieces, and the now world class collection has over 2,000 pieces and is valued in excess of five million dollars. The works of art can be viewed for free on the ELAC campus. He loved ELAC and they loved him, often having Price in as a guest lecturer to talk authoritatively about the many works in his gallery.

His cookbooks were done in collaboration with his wife Mary. *The National Treasury of Cooking* came out in 1967 as a multi-volume set; and the *Come into the Kitchen Cookbook* was also published in 1969. The first edition of his *Treasury of Great Recipes* first appeared in 1965, with at least three more editions being re-printed through 1995. His first cookbook covered European cuisine, his second American regional cuisine and his last one — having covered everything — was a collection of his personal favorites that were easy to make.

Price was also a frequent contributor to audio books with *Tales of Terror* and the poems of Percy Bysshe Shelly two of the more popular and lasting titles of all the recorded books that he did.

Victoria Price wrote a biography of her father in 1999. Lucy Chase Williams authored *The Films of Vincent Price.* Williams was a consultant on the A & E biography *Vincent Price: the Versatile Villain* which has now been released on DVD and most recently included as bonus material on the September 2007 release of *The Fly Collection* DVD set of all three Fox films.

Price was a great raconteur and was well liked in the Hollywood community, with frequent appearances on *The Tonight Show* to plug his films and whenever he had a new cookbook out. Johnny Carson was always game to have Vincent cook him anything.

Price's home town of St. Louis honored him with a place on their Walk on Fame. There is a black box theater named for him at his alma mater, the private St. Louis Country Day High School. There is a character on *Sesame Street* named Vincent Twice, he played the voice of Vincent Van Ghoul on *Scooby-Doo* and he was once parodied on *The Simpsons* in the episode *Sunday, Cruddy Sunday.* Price was on *The Muppet Show* and *The Love Boat,* in the *Tiny Toon Adventures* and on *The Critic.* There was very little Vincent wouldn't do and he liked to say that he got away with it, because the audience could see that he was having fun. Price is remembered fondly by all who knew him. Vincent Price was cremated together with his favorite gardening hat per his wishes and his ashes were scattered in the Pacific Ocean off Point Dume, California.

HERBERT MARSHALL
INSPECTOR CHARAS

Herbert Brough Falcon Marshall was born May 23, 1890 in London, England. He was educated to be a charter accountant, but after he fought in and survived World War I, Herbert — who liked to be called Bart — decided he would become an actor instead. The fact he had lost a leg in an accident during the war, did not deter his ambition. Herbert was rehabilitated with a wooden leg and taught himself to walk without a limp, so no one could tell.

Marshall started acting on stage in London and his mellow baritone voice and crisp English diction made him a natural when sound movies were introduced in 1929. He worked steadily in movies through the thirties and forties and well into the fifties. His first film, *Mumsie,* was made in England in 1927 and was silent. Some of his more famous films include *Murder!* (1930), *Trouble in Paradise* (1932), *Blonde Venus* (1932) *The Dark Angel* (1935), *Angel* (1937), *The Letter* (1940), *Foreign Correspondent*(1940), *The Little Foxes* (1941) and the lead role in 1946 version of *The Razor's Edge,* the same year he also appeared in *Duel in the Sun.*

He played everything from the leading man to the betrayed husband. He specialized in priests, doctors, diplomats, prime ministers, and any manner of civil servants. He was on the radio as a British Intelligence agent Ken Thurston, known as *The Man Called X,* from 1944 to 1952, first on the CBS network and then later on NBC.

His other science fiction films, in addition to *The Fly,* include *Riders to the Stars* and *Gog,* both made in 1954. After *The Fly,* he was supposedly too ill to be in the 1959 sequel, but then later worked in the films *Midnight Lace* (1960),

Herbert Marshall – Charas takes a call from Francois to come investigate Andre's death.

Five Weeks in a Balloon (1962) and *The List of Adrian Messenger* (1963). His final film, *The Third Day,* was released in 1965.

Stories vary on why Marshall didn't do *Return of the Fly.* One explanation could have been his wife's death. Boots Mallory died on December 1, 1958. The other theory was that the sequel budget wasn't robust enough for Marshall after they signed Vincent Price.

Marshall began supplementing his movie work with appearances on television in 1950. His first appearance was on *Nash Airflyte Theatre* in 1950. He appeared on *Robert Montgomery Presents* in 1951 and *Ford Television Theatre* in 1952, the same year he was the host of *Times Square Playhouse.* In 1954, he did "The Philadelphia Story" on *The Best of Broadway,* had a role on *The Elgin Hour* and made the first of three appearances on *Lux Video Theatre.* He would appear the next two summers on this program, doing "The Browning Version" in 1955 and "Now, Voyager" in 1956.

He guest starred on The *Loretta Young Show, Playhouse 90* and did his first *Alfred Hitchcock Presents* in 1957 and followed that with an appearance on *Studio One* in 1958 and a second role on *Alfred Hitchcock.*

In 1960, he was in two episodes of *Adventures in Paradise,* one episode of *Hong Kong* and an episode of *Michael Shayne.* Marshall's final two television appearances were on *Zane Grey Theatre* and in a historic five part episode of *77 Sunset Strip.*

Marshall's eldest daughter Sarah became an actress starting with *Hallmark Hall of Fame* in 1954. Sarah worked steadily as a guest star in the television medium until 1995, but the only show she was in where her father was also cast in was the "Colonel Cat" episode of the Fox series *Hong Kong* where they played father and daughter. Some of Sarah Marshall's later TV appearances include roles on *Mannix* and *Ironside.* Her last role was in the movie *Bad Blood* in 2006.

He died of a heart attack on January 23, 1966 in Los Angeles and worked until the end of his life. Marshall would marry five times, and have one child each with Edna Best, Lee Russell and Boots Mallory. He was three times divorced, was made a widower by the death of Mallory and was survived by his fifth wife, Dee Ann Kaufman. Marshall was buried at The Chapel of the Pines Cemetery in Los Angeles.

CHARLES HERBERT
PHILIPPE DELAMBRE

Charles Herbert Saperstein was born on December 23, 1948 in Culver City, California. A very well known child actor for almost a decade, Charles Herbert's career began in 1952 at the age of age of 4 on the television series, *Half Pint Panel.* His last appearance was in a 1968 episode of the television series, *Julia.*

During his time in Hollywood, Herbert made twenty feature films, including *The Fly* and fifty television show appearances, but his parents put very little of the money he earned away for him to have when he was twenty-one. His father had a heart condition and Charles supported his family until he outgrew the child roles that made him famous. Herbert received no studio education and only sporadically attended public schools. He was kept so busy acting, that when he became too old to be employable as a child anymore, he was basically left with nothing to fall back on.

Charles had a very good run as a child actor. In addition to *The Fly,* he is remembered as the harmonica playing youngest son in *Houseboat* (1958). Herbert was also in *Gunfight at OK Corral* (1957), *Colossus of New York* (1958), *The Five Pennies* (1959), *Please Don't Eat the Daisies* and *13 Ghosts,* which were released in 1960.

His first film was supposed to be *The Long, Long Trailer* in 1954, but his scenes were cut. He did make it into the films *The View from Pompey's Head* (1955), *The Night Holds Terror* (1955), *These Wilder Years* (1956), *Man in the Net* (1959) and *The Boy and the Pirates* (1960). Some other films he appeared in, but did not receive credit, were *Ransom!* (1956), *He Laughed Last* (1956),

The Tattered Dress (1957), *The Monster That Challenged the World* (1957), *Gun Glory* (1957), *No Down Payment* (1957) with Patricia Owens, *The Reluctant Debutante* (1958), and *The Seventh Commandment* (1960).

Television show appearances were the bulk of his career, beginning with *The Bob Cummings Show* in 1955 and *The Ford Television Theatre* in 1956. It was his 1956 appearance on *Science Fiction Theatre* that helped cement his status as a

Charles Herbert – Andre explains his work to his young son.

science fiction icon. In this Christmas episode, he plays a blind boy whose wish is granted to see the holidays in "The Miracle Hour." Herbert also appeared on *Jane Wyman Presents the Fireside Theatre, The Jack Benny Show, The Gale Storm Show, M Squad* and *Goodyear Theatre.*

Herbert was also on *Alfred Hitchcock Presents* in the episode "The Night the World Ended" in 1957 and the original *Twilight Zone* series in "I Sing the Body Electric" in 1962. Charles appeared in four episodes of *The Donna Reed Show* in 1958 and 1959 as David Barker and was a series regular, Rickey Selby, in the series *The Clear Horizon* for the only season (1960-61).

Other shows Herbert made multiple appearances on were *The Loretta Young Show* (4 episodes), *Men into Space* (4 episodes), *One Step Beyond* (2 episodes), *Wagon Train* (5 episodes), *Lassie* (2 episodes), *Going My Way* (2 episodes) and *My Three Sons* (3 episodes).

Additional Television shows Charles guest starred on were *Screen Directors Playhouse, Celebrity Playhouse, The 20th Century Fox Hour, It's a Great Life,*

Tombstone Territory, Riverboat, The Millionaire, The Ann Sothern Show, Wichita Town, Klondike, The Eleventh Hour, The Best of the Post, General Electric Theatre, Rawhide, The Fugitive, The Farmer's Daughter and *Family Affair.*

In more recent years, with the help of former co-stars Paul Peterson (*House-boat, The Donna Reed Show*) and Susan Gordon (*The Boy and the Pirates, The Man in the Net*) Herbert has been appearing at Science Fiction conventions and enjoying his status of a 1950's science fiction icon — based largely on his appearances in *The Fly, The Colossus of New York and 13 Ghosts. The Boy and the Pirates* recently was released on DVD to cash in on the Pirate mania spawned by the mega-hit Disney *Pirates of the Caribbean* series. Herbert holds no bitterness toward his parents for the mismanagement of his earnings or his career, and is currently living in the American Southwest.

Kathleen Freeman — The white headed fly escapes out the window.

CHAPTER 5

SUPPORTING CAST

KATHLEEN FREEMAN
EMMA

Emma is the Delambre cook and housekeeper. She does not always approve of what is going on, but is dedicated to the family and always tries to help.

Kathleen Freeman was born February 17, 1919 in Chicago, Illinois. Her parents were vaudeville actors, and she danced in their act as a child. Kate — as she was known — came to California to study music at UCLA, but found the pull of acting to be stronger, and began working on the stage. Her first screen role was in 1948 and she worked steadily on both the stage and the screen and in television until her death in 2001.

Kate was a gifted character actor who became quite well known playing a certain type of female in films during the 1950's. Her most famous role is probably that of the exasperated dialogue coach in the classic *Singing in the Rain* (1952).

She is also remembered for appearances in ten Jerry Lewis films. Her first appearances was in *Athena* in 1954, but Kate is most remembered for playing the Studio Boss' wife in *The Errand Boy* (1961), Millie Lemon in the original *The Nutty Professor* (1963) and as Nurse Higgins in *The Disorderly Orderly* (1964).

Some of the more famous films she has appeared in include *No Man of Her Own* (1950), *A Place in the Sun* (1951), *The Greatest Show on Earth* (1952), *Monkey Business* (1952), *The Far Country* (1955), *Houseboat* (1958), and *Support Your Local Sheriff* (1969) as well as nearly one hundred more films.

Her appearance in *The Fly* was contract work. Kathleen is seen in the background of many shots, offering strong support to Patricia Owens. She even has a scene with Vincent Price.

Freeman had a very substantial post *Fly* career. Kate is probably best known for her roles in the *Blues Brothers* films (1980 and 1998) where she played Sister Mary Stigmata and as the never seen (but often heard) mother-in-law who terrorized Al Bundy on *Married... with Children*.

Other sitcoms she had recurring roles in were: *Topper*, where she was Katie, the maid; *Hogan's Heroes*, where she played General Burkhalter's sister, who longed to marry Col. Klink and *It's About Time* where she was cast as Mrs. Boss. One role she considered for (and did not get) was as Alice the housekeeper on *The Brady Bunch*. This was a Fly reunion that never happened, as David Hedison turned down the role of father Mike Brady at the same time.

Fans of her excellent work in the Jerry Lewis films would hire her for work later in life, with cameos in Dragnet (1987), *Innerspace* (1987) and *Gremlins 2: The New Batch* (1990) and *Naked Gun 331/3: The Final Insult* (1994). Thirty seven years after her appearance in *The Nutty Professor,* she would be cast in *The Nutty Professor II: The Klumps* (2000).

Freeman also did voice work; her biggest roles were in *As Told by Ginger* and *Duck Tales,* with smaller roles in *Hercules (1997)* and the original *Shrek (2000).* She was the voice of Madame Xima in the video game *Curse of Monkey Island.*

A trouper to the end, Freeman was cast in the Broadway production of *The Full Monty.* She played the role of piano accompanist Jeannette Burmeister, until she was too ill from lung cancer to continue. She was nominated for a Tony and received a Theatre World Award for this role. Freeman died five days after her last performance on August 23, 2001. Freeman is buried in the Hollywood Forever Cemetery and remains a fan favorite. Never married, Kathleen was survived by her long-time life partner, Helen Ramsay.

EUGENE BORDEN
DR. EJOUTE

Eugene Borden plays family physician Dr. Ejoute. He is called in to examine Helene when the murder of Andre is first discovered. He has one scene where he reports on Helene's condition to a very concerned Francois.

Eugene Borden was born March 21, 1897 in Paris, France. He immigrated to New York in 1914. He had a very long film career, beginning in such East Coast silent films as *Haunting Shadows* (1917) and *The Slacker* (1917). Even as the film industry began to aggregate in southern California, Borden remained in New York, working on films and an occasional play. He appeared on Broadway twice in *The Better 'Ole,* October 1918-October 1919 and *The French Doll,* February-June 1922.

1929 saw the advent of sound and Borden finally joined the westward migration to Hollywood. His Parisian background came in handy and he worked steadily in films for nearly twenty five years, mostly playing Frenchmen. He is probably best remembered as Gene Kelly and Oscar Levant's landlord in *An American in Paris* (1951).

Borden made over 160 films from 1917 to 1964. One of his last roles was as a Frenchman in the TV series *Combat*! Some of his more famous films, besides *The Fly,* include *On the Town* [French Waiter] (1949), *All About Eve* [French Cocktail Party Guest] (1950), *Titanic* (1953), *The Far Country* (1954), *To Catch a Thief* [French Waiter] (1955), *The Spirit of St. Louis* [French Gendarme] (1957), *Silk Stockings* (1957), *Can Can* (1960), *The Devil at Four O'clock* (1960) and *What a Way to Go!* (1964).

He did a two television appearances in 1952 and appeared (as a French Chef) in the 1954 TV version of "Casino Royale" on *Climax!* with Barry Nelson as James Bond. Borden was kept sufficiently busy with film work as an extra that he rarely appeared on television more than once a year through 1958.

Borden began to do more TV after *The Fly*, following the work as television began to dominate the entertainment industry. His last credited appearance was on *The Donna Reed Show* as a headwaiter in 1964. Eugene Borden died July 21, 1972, in Woodland Hills, California and is buried in Woodlawn Cemetery, Santa Monica.

TORBEN MEYER
GASTON, THE NIGHT WATCHMAN

Gaston is the most memorable of the minor characters in the film. He is the one that discovers Andre's body in the press and calls the police. His best line in the film is when he stuns Francois with his suspicion that the murderer was Madame!

Torben Meyer — Gaston tell Charas and Francois he thinks it was Madame he saw running away.

Torben Meyer was born December 1, 1884, in Copenhagen, Denmark. He had a long career as a supporting character, mostly playing German, Swiss and Dutch characters. Meyer began working as an actor on stage in Denmark and made his first silent film there in 1912. Over the next fifty years he would appear in over 180 films. Torben made twenty silent films before achieving international fame in a 1926 version of *Don Quixote*.

In 1927, Meyer came to Hollywood and landed his first role in 1928 in a Conrad Veidt film called *The Man Who Laughs*. Torben appears primarily in uncredited supporting cast roles through the 1930's, but managed to win parts in *Murders in the Rue Morgue* with Bela Lugosi in 1931 and *What Price Hollywood* in 1932. In 1935, he was strangled by Boris Karloff in *Bride of Frankenstein*, had a role in *The Prisoner of Zenda* with Ronald Colman in 1937, appeared in *The Saint in New York* in 1938 and ended the decade in *Topper Takes a Trip* in 1939.

Meyer found steady work with Preston Sturges in 1940 beginning with *Christmas in July* and ending with *The Beautiful Blonde of Bashful Bend* in 1947. His best known Sturges role was Dr. Kluck in *The Palm Beach Story* in 1942.

Some of his other better known film appearances include a Dutch banker in *Casablanca* (1942) and roles in *The Great Dictator* (1940), *The Lady Eve* (1941), *Sullivan's Travels* (1941), *Miracle of Morgan's Creek* (1944), *Yolanda and the Thief* (1947), *The Great Lover* (1949), *Call Me Madam* (1953), *Houdini* (1953), *The Caddy* (1953), *The Conqueror* (1956), *We're No Angels* (1955), *Anything Goes* (1956) and *This Earth is Mine* (1959).

Aside from *Casablanca*, the other role Meyer is most famous for came when he was 76 years old and was put on trial in *Judgment in Nuremberg* in 1961. He played Werner Lampe, a guilt ridden Ex-Nazi judge. He was also in the *Playhouse 90* TV episode in 1959.

He is the second Fly cast member, after Vincent Price, to be a guest star on *Voyage to the Bottom of the Sea*. Meyer appears in the first season as a Danish proprietor in the episode, "The Village of Guilt." Torben was not particularly known for appearing in science fiction films, besides this one. He did one other horror film besides the two mentioned above, *Frankenstein Meets the Wolf Man*, in which he played a gypsy. His last two films were *GI Blues* in 1960 and *A New Kind of Love* in 1963.

Aside from being on *Voyage*, Meyer did few television appearances. He was guest star on *I Love Lucy* in 1956 and in one episode of *Telephone Time* in 1957. Meyer's other television appearances came in 1965 on *Burke's Law* and he was a guest star on *I Dream of Jeannie*, in 1966, which was his last documented credit.

Torben Meyer died in 1975 of pneumonia at the age of 90. He is buried in the Chapel of the Pines Cemetery in Los Angeles.

BESS FLOWERS
ARTS MATRON AT THE BALLET

She is the woman sitting on Andre's right at the ballet when he starts writing scientific formulas on his program until Helene makes him stop.

Bess Flowers was born November 23, 1898 in Sherman, Texas. She was known as the "Queen of the Hollywood Extras" and worked in over 740 films from 1923 to 1964. Her first film was (appropriately) *Hollywood* (1923) and her last film was *Good Neighbor Sam* (1964) with Jack Lemmon.

She married Cullen Tate in 1923. Tate was an assistant director for Cecil B. DeMille, which no doubt helped start and sustain her career as an extra. They remained married until his death in 1947. Then Bess married William S.

Holman, the studio manager at Columbia Studios and continued her film work. Aside from being married to men with pull in the casting department, another thing that may have contributed to her success was she was tall for an actress of this era (5'8") and thus could stand up to most any man. She was cast as a bossy matron throughout her career.

Flowers' films are much too numerous to attempt to list here, but she was in seven Alfred Hitchcock films, *Mr. and Mrs. Smith* (1941), *Notorious* (1946), *To Catch A Thief* (1955), *Dial M for Murder* (1954), *Rear Window* (1954), *The Man Who Knew Too Much* (1956), and *Vertigo* (1958). Three of the above films starred James Stewart, who was in nine other films Flowers found extra work in, starting in 1936 and including *Ziegfeld Girl* (1941), *Magic Town* (1947) and *Strategic Air Command* in 1955. Flowers also made nine films with Director Frank Capra; *Broadway Bill* (1934), *Mr. Deeds Goes to Town* (1936), *Meet John Doe* (1941) and *Pocketful of Miracles* (1961).

Bess supported The Marx Brothers in *Monkey Business* (1931), *A Night at the Opera* (1935), and *A Day at the Races* (1937). She was in films with The Three Stooges and Leon Errol. Flowers appeared in dozens of short comedies with Laurel and Hardy.

Flowers holds the record for being in the most films that won the Academy Award for Best Picture. The films are *It Happened One Night* (1934), *You Can't Take it With You* (1938), *All About Eve* (1950), *The Greatest Show on Earth* (1952) *and Around the World in 80 Days* (1956).

Flowers was in two more films that David Hedison also worked on. In *Rally 'Round the Flag, Boys,* she was an extra, he provided the voice over narration and she attended the Zoological Institute Forum in Hedison's *The Lost World* (1960), two years after that.

Bess Flowers died on July 28, 1984 and is buried in the Chapel of the Pines Cemetery in Los Angeles.

BETTY LOU GERSON
NURSE ANDERSONE

Gerson plays the nurse who comes to the Delambre house to look after Helene after she is judged to be insane.

Betty Lou Gerson did more work in television than she did as a movie star, but she will always be remembered for her voice work for Disney in 1961 as the odious Cruella De Vil.

Gerson was born April 20, 1914 in Chattanooga, Tennessee and raised in Birmingham, Alabama. She began her career in Chicago as a radio actor in 1935 and went on to earn the nickname, "Soap Opera Queen of Chicago" as a mainstay of radio melodramas, appearing on *Arnold Grimm's Daughter* (as the titular daughter, Constance Grimm), *Road of Life (as Nurse Helen Gowan),* and the attractive but world-weary radio star Charlotte Wilson Brandon in the radio version of *The Guiding Light* (where Gerson met her first husband, radio producer Joe Ainley). She was the first choice for romantic leads and breathy ingénues on such romantic anthologies *First Nighter* with Don Ameche and June Meredith, *Curtain Time* and *Grand Hotel.*

She moved to Los Angeles in the 1940s when the Chicago radio industry was dismantled and the program production was split between New York and California. She made a few additional radio appearances on and *The Lux Radio*

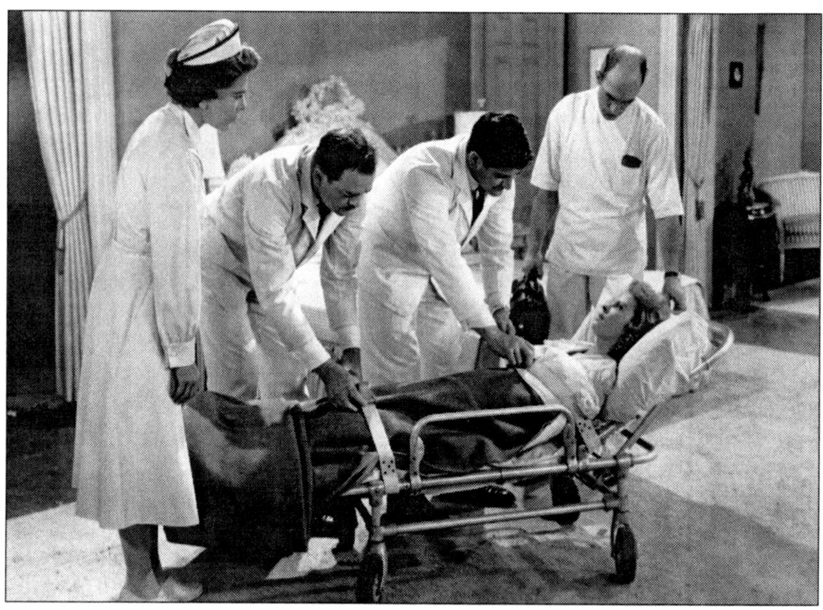

Betty Lou Gerson, Harry Carter and William Tannen — The medical team prepare Helene to be transported to the sanitarium.

Theater, but she easily transitioned into television and movies. Her first film appearance was as an uncredited extra in *Nightmare Alley* (1947) but was a principle in her next film, the socialist cautionary melodrama *The Red Menace* (1949).

Her first voice job for Disney soon followed as the narrator of *Cinderella* (1950). She would seamlessly work in both television and film through the 1950s. In 1958 she appeared on for the first time on *Perry Mason* and was called back for a second role in 1959. That year Betty also made and an appearance as herself on *The Bob Cummings Show,* and was on *Death Valley Days* and *The Untouchables,* with a second appearance on *The Loretta Young Show.* She guest starred in 1960 on *The Rifleman, Coronado 9, Checkmate and Wanted: Dead or Alive.*

In 1961 Gerson got the signature role of her career as the voice of Cruella De Vil in the original animated version of *101 Dalmatians.* Gerson was back on television after that, appearing in her third *Perry Mason* in 1961, along with a guest star role on *Target: the Corruptors.* In 1962, she was on *Ripcord!* and *Hazel.*

Betty made two appearances on *The Dick Van Dyke Show* in 1963 and was on *The Twilight Zone* and *The Farmers Daughter* in 1964. Her final TV appearance was a second guest star role on *Hazel.* Her last film role was a cameo in the Disney film, *Mary Poppins* (1964) as an old crone on the docks who frightens Michael and Jane. She was inducted as a Disney Legend in 1996. Gerson did one final voice over in *Cats Don't Dance* in 1997 and died on Jan. 12, 1999 in Los Angeles.

CHARLES TANNEN
DOCTOR

Charles Tannen is the head of the medical team that shows up at the end of the film to take Helene to the sanitarium.

Charles David Tannen was born October 22, 1915 in New York City. He was the son of actor Julius Tannen and the brother of actor William Tannen.

His recorded credits show him working as an uncredited extra for 23 years from 1935 through 1958, starting out as clerks. His first film was *The Dark Angel* in 1935, which also starred Herbert Marshall. In the 1940's, he was often cast as pilots and sailors, with the occasional stint as a reporter. He often found voice work as various radio announcers in movies, the most famous of these being the radio reporter in *The Day the Earth Stood Still* (1951).

One is his better known roles was as CPO Gleason in the 1961 film *Voyage to the Bottom of the Sea* (with Robert Sterling as Captain Lee Crane). Tannen was also in the very famous "cookbook" episode of *The Twilight Zone* aka "To Serve Man," which runs a very close second to *The Fly* for being parodied in later films.

At the end of his career, Tannen served as a script consultant on eight episodes and wrote four scripts for the series, *Gilligan's Island.* His last credit was as a writer on the 1972 comedy series, *Temperatures Rising.* Charles Tannen died December 28, 1980 in San Bernardino, California. His remains were cremated and scattered at sea.

HARRY CARTER
ORDERLY

Harry Carter is one of the team who shows up to take Helene to the sanitarium. He helps put her in the stretcher.

Harry Benjamin Carter was born February 27, 1906 in Montana. He worked at 20th Century Fox Studios as an extra and contract player from 1941 to 1961. Harry became friends with Richard Widmark and appeared in many of his films. Carter had appeared in 175 films by the time he was cast in *The Fly* and was in 25 more after that.

Some of his more famous films include *Roxie Hart* (1942), *Crash Dive* (1943), *Four Jills In a Jeep* (1944), *Wing and a Prayer* (1944), *Smoky* (1946),

Captain From Castile (1947), *Down to the Sea in Ships* (1949), *It Happens Every Spring* (1949), *Broken Arrow* (1950), *Halls of Montezuma* (1950), *Monkey Business* (1952), *Hell and High Water* (1954), *Girl in Red Velvet Swing* (1955), *The Tall Men* (1955), *Carousel* (1956), *and Peyton Place* (1957).

After *The Fly*, Carter was in *Compulsion* (1959), *One Foot in Hell* (1960), *Wild in the Country* (1961), *The Manchurian Candidate* (1962), *Dear Brigitte* (1965) and the remake of *Stagecoach* in 1966.

One of his more interesting post Fly roles was as a stunt/double for Guy Williams in a *Lost in Space* episode, "The Antimatter Man." It was one of only four television shows he ever did, the other three being *Margie, The Virginian* and *Great Adventure.*

His last credited film was *The Mephisto Waltz* in 1971. Harry Carter died in Los Angeles on April 1, 1996.

ARTHUR DULAC
FRENCH WAITER

The waiter brings a telephone to Inspector Charas' table and plugs it in so he can take the call from Francois to come investigate Andre's murder.

Arthur Dulac was born Arthur DeRavenne on May 13, 1903. He was a child actor in French films who came to Hollywood in 1916. He had three acting siblings, Ray DeRavenne, Charles DeRavenne and Nina Borget. Arthur changed his name to Dulac for American films.

In addition to being an uncredited extra in *The Fly,* Dulac appeared in *Casablanca* (1943), *Action in the North Atlantic* (1943), *Berlin Express* (1948), *The Snows of Kilimanjaro* (1952), *Little Boy Lost* (1953), *Around the World in 80 Days* (1956) *and The Buccaneer* (1958).

Arthur Dulac died on September 18, 1962 and is buried in the Hollywood Forever Cemetery.

FRANZ ROEHN
POLICE DOCTOR

He tells Francois and Inspector Charas that Andre has been dead for about half an hour when the body is found in the press.

Franz Roehn was born Franz Friedlaender in Berlin, Germany on October 6, 1896. The son of internationally known music historian and scholar Max Friedlaender, he dabbled in German silent films for *Universum-Film Aktiengesellschaft* [UFA], adopting the name Franz Roehn. His father died in Berlin in 1934, two years after Franz received his PhD in art history.

With the situation deteriorating in Germany, he began making arrangements to emigrate to the United States with his mother and his siblings. The family had previously lived in Cambridge when his father was an exchange professor at Harvard in 1910. After a brief career in New York as a professional photographer specializing in fine arts, he and his mother returned to Cambridge in 1936. As finances dictated, Roehn and his mother sold off parts of Max Friedlaender's personal collection of original music manuscripts by Bach, much to the annoyance of music scholars who were refused access to the documents prior to their sale to private collectors. He began teaching English to German

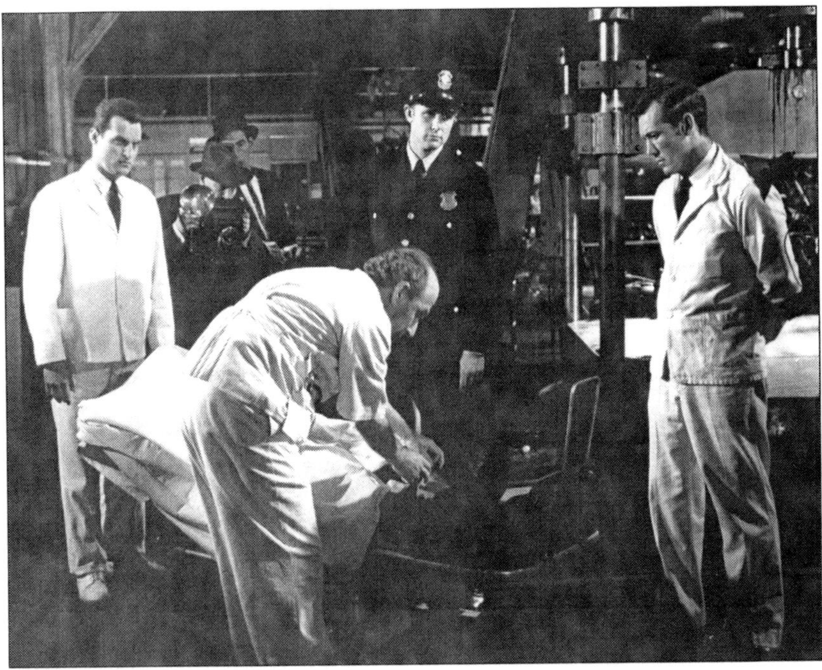

Franz Roehn — The Police Doctor examines Andre's corpse.

immigrants in Cambridge, a position which led his joining the German Language department at UCLA.

His career in America began as an extra for director William Dieterle in *Miracle of the Bells* in 1948, which the RKO press department lauded as a reunion between Roehn and Dieterle, who had given Roehn his start in German films. His association with Dierterle did not help Roehn's career - although he would appear in five films for Dieterle, all these roles were uncredited roles, barely above the status of an extra.

Even as he maintained his position as a German linguist with UCLA, Roehn continued to garner work in both television and films, making appearances as a German scholar in such TV shows as *Biff Baker, USA, Captain Midnight, The Adventures of Rin Tin Tin, The Adventures of Jim Bowie, The Adventures of Superman, Mike Hammer* and *Bourbon Street Beat* with film roles such as *Knock on Any Door* (1949), *Dark City* (1950), *Francis Goes to West Point* (1952), *Salome* (1953), *Tobor The Great* (1954), *Omar Khayyam* (1957), *The Deep Six* (1958) and *The Blue Angel* (1959), but his career never rose above minor characters roles. He appeared in the 1958 war comedy *Me and the Colonel* starring Danny Kaye and Curt Jürgens with fellow T*he Fly* alumni Eugene Borden. Both had minor roles, but both were actually credited.

An uncredited appearance as a gravedigger in William Castle's *Mr. Sardonicus* (1961), and a 1960 appearance as a janitor on *Father Knows Best* ended his career.

He would garner publicity one last time he sold off the last of his father's estate — an unknown fragment of a Schubert composition, again refusing to allow scholars to study the document prior to the sale. It apparently generated enough of a nest egg that, when added to his social security pension, it allowed Roehn to return to Germany in 1961 where he died October 12, 1989.

Many other players in this film remain unidentified due to Fox's crediting practices in 1958. They include several policemen and two orderlies at the murder scene, members of Charas' men's club, Francois' servant(s), the second orderly in the scenes where Helene is about to be take to the sanitarium, as well as three people seated behind Helene and Andre in the box at the ballet.

These unnamed extras may have been as well known then as the extras we profiled above. The people in the audience who grew up watching these unsung seasoned veterans of the silver screen knew them by sight. Their identities may now be lost to posterity, but *The Fly* had a remarkable supporting cast with incredible experience in motion pictures.

Cortlandt Hull and Vincent Price, Autumn 1985.
PHOTO COURTESY OF CORTLANDT HULL, THE WITCH'S DUNGEON, 2008

CHAPTER 6

THE BUZZ ON VINCENT PRICE AND *THE FLY*

BY CORTLANDT HULL
WITCH'S DUNGEON CLASSIC MOVIE MUSEUM

I was twenty when I first met Vincent Price in September 1973 through our mutual friend, Barbara Rowlands, who had worked with Vincent on several of his British films. Vincent was a great inspiration in so many ways, due to his interest and knowledge of art. We remained friends until his passing in 1993.

Vincent's conversations and witty humor were unforgettable. Whenever talking about his career, he always had an interesting anecdote to tell. Vincent saw very little of David Hedison during production on *The Fly* because of the shooting schedule. Several years later, he greatly enjoyed re-teaming with David, on *Voyage to the Bottom of the Sea*. Vincent played the puppet master, in "The Deadly Dolls" episode. As Vincent put it, "I was the evil "Geppetto from Hell" — such fun, tormenting David and Richard (Basehart) — it was delightful."

Vincent had a number of scenes in *The Fly*, with child actor, Charles Herbert. He recalled that "Charles was remarkable; many scenes relied on his delivery of the dialogue. For his age, to carry as much of the picture as he was given, which really goes to the heart of the story, shows he was a very talented young actor."

During production, on *The Fly*, there was a scene between actor Herbert Marshall and Vincent observing the climactic sequence of David Hedison as the small fly, trapped, and being devoured by a spider. Director Kurt Neumann described to both actors before shooting the scene, detailing exactly what they were supposed to be witnessing.

Vincent said, "We approached the "spider web," simply made of string, which looked rather unconvincing, but when the prop men tried a finer thread, it just would not show up on camera. As Herbert and I began to say our lines, it went though our minds what we were watching — a fly, with David's head and arm, screaming "Help me! — Help me! All I can say is we got the giggles and we blew take after take."

"After the shoot, we both had misgivings about the end result, as what makes a horror or science fiction film work for the audience is the actor's ability to make the unbelievable believable — Karloff, Chaney and Lugosi were masters at this!"

"Evidently, our fears were pointless; the film was a huge hit for Fox studios obviously, as I was called back for a sequel! But, more amazing to me, the scene

Francois Delambre places the remains of the white headed fly in a matchbox and buries it in a deleted scene from the end of the movie.

we were most worried about (with the spider web), is the sequence people seem to remember! David will always be famous for repeating those two words — "Help me — Help me!" (Vincent imitated the high-pitched tone of the Fly).

Price loved to visit a movie theatre playing one of his films, to see the audience reaction. Once, after the sequence when Patricia Owens removes the sheet, revealing David Hedison as "The Fly," Vincent leaned forward to a row of high school girls, and said, "Is that a fly in your popcorn?" The girls shouted — "It's HIM!" Popcorn went everywhere as the girls screamed — he loved it.

Years later, Vincent wondered what modern publicity would do if the film was released in the 1980's. "Imagine if the *National Enquirer* announced the premiere of *The Fly* today — the headline would scream "Price opens Fly in New York!" That was Vincent's great sense of humor.

We decided to re-create a figure of David Hedison as "The Fly" in The Witch's Dungeon Classic Movie Museum. Artist Kelly Mann sculpted the most accurate headpiece for our figure, which was partially based on original pieces from the movie mold. My uncle Louis Gagnon and I designed elaborate gizmos for the laboratory set using old computer parts, with lights going on and off at intermittent patterns, using a motor hitting various light contacts. The machines are called the "Teleportation Transmitter" and "Re-integration Electronometer" — at least, they sound impressive!

Knowing *The Fly* was celebrating its 50th anniversary in 2008, we decided to honor the character again in the Halloween 2007 exhibit. In our "Graveyard of Classic Ghouls," I designed a tombstone for "Andre Delambre," with images of the fly, a spider web and the atomic symbol. The fabrication was done by Jim Wieloch of In-Motion, who also recently automated the museum tour.

The Fly is definitely one of the last great classic monsters, an unforgettable film, which has obviously inspired characters and plots in more recent productions.

Charles Herbert with the Fly figure, Summer 2006
PHOTO COURTESY OF CORTLANDT HULL, THE WITCH'S DUNGEON, 2008

Andre's grave at the Witch's Dungeon.
PHOTO COURTESY OF CORTLANDT HULL, THE WITCH'S DUNGEON, 2008

The Fly tableau at the Witch's Dungeon.
PHOTO COURTESY OF CORTLANDT HULL, THE WITCH'S DUNGEON, 2008

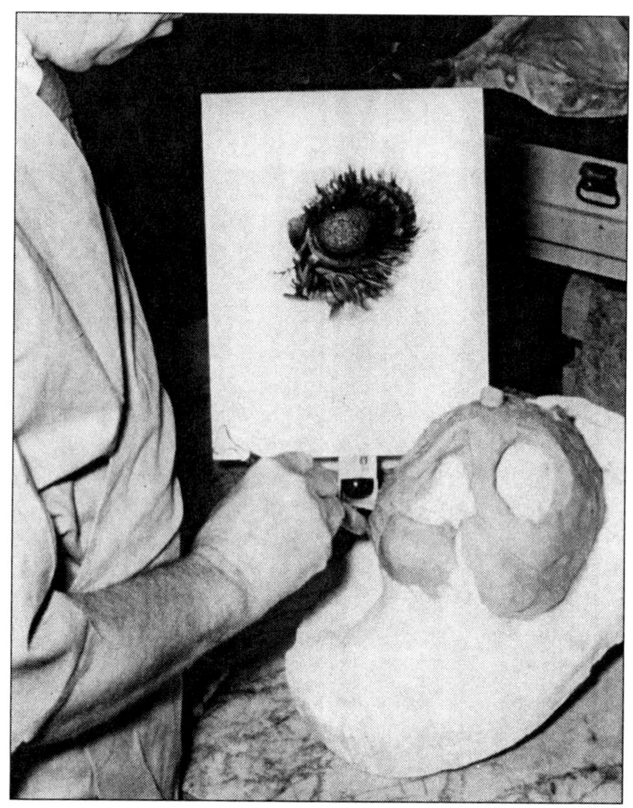

Making the Latex fly mask off the plaster life cast of Hedison.
PHOTO COURTESY OF BEN NYE, SR. ARCHIVES, 2008

Construction of Fly claw in progress.
PHOTO COURTESY OF BEN NYE, SR. ARCHIVES, 2008

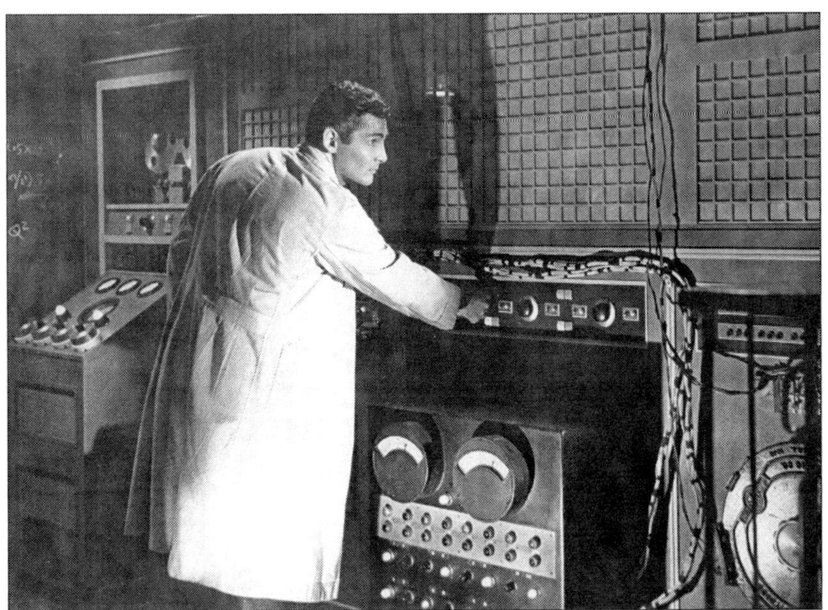

Andre in his basement lab.

Andre working in his lab.

Andre modifies his process to support larger transport booths.

Andre's first teleportation device.

Andre transports champagne after a night out at the ballet.

$100 REWARD FOR PROOF

The scientific premise of "The Fly," that man will be able to transmit matter in a manner somewhat similar to the way television transmits images, is an advanced idea, but by no means is it beyond the expectations of scientists.

As a matter of fact, this will probably be accomplished within the next decade, according to Dr. Frank Creswell, technical adviser on the film.

In this well-founded statement, you have the necessary support to remove any suspicions you may have entertained about using the "$100 If You Prove It Can't Happen" statement in your advertising. This line is a great come-on and should be prominently used not only in the ads but in special posters and signs around your theatre in advance and during your engagement of "The Fly."

YOU CAN'T SEE
The Fly
ALONE
UNLESS YOU
SIGN THIS
WAIVER

In consideration of my being allowed to see **The Fly** alone, I hereby agree to enter this theatre at my own risk, blaming no one but myself for whatever startling, shocking effects this picture may have upon me. In witness whereof, I hereby set my hand and seal.

Fox Studio Publicity 1958 Exhibitors Manual.

Patricia Owens, Herbert Marshall, Kurt Neumann, Vincent Price, Al Hedison, and several crew members at the wrap party.

PHOTO COURTESY OF THE PERSONAL COLLECTION OF DAVID HEDISON, 2008

CHAPTER 7

THE CREW

KURT NEUMANN
DIRECTOR AND PRODUCER

Kurt Neumann was born April 5, 1908 in Nuremberg, Germany and died August 21, 1958 in Los Angeles. Neumann came to Hollywood in 1931. After starting his career in German Cinema, he immigrated to England and gained some success as a London theater director. In 1928, he was hired by Universal to direct German language versions of Hollywood films.

After doing three of these, he moved on into *The Shadow* series for the second film *Trapped* and stayed through 1932 to complete the fifth film *The Red Shadow*. On August 1, he married Irma Ely. They would have two children, a son, Kurt, Jr., and a daughter, Mary Anne.

Neumann did a series of Mickey Rooney circus pictures when Rooney was 12 and 13 and soon established himself as a good utility man, doing any kind of project from Musicals to Westerns to Fantasy Adventures. Neumann produced many of his features after 1943 and was always quick and got the job done. One of his first low budget films to garner attention was *Secret of the Blue Room* (1932) with Paul Lukas and Gloria Stuart. Other thirties films of note he was involved in were *It Happened in New Orleans* (1936), *Open Faces* (1937) with Joe E. Brown and *Ellery Queen, Master Detective* (1939), with Ralph Bellamy.

When director James Whale refused to do a sequel to *Frankenstein* in 1933, Carl Laemmle, Jr. gave Kurt Neumann the director's chair, announcing the sequel would team Universal's two greatest monsters together in the same film — Boris Karloff as the monster and Bela Lugosi as the mad scientist Dr. Pretorius. The project stalled and Universal moved Karloff and Lugosi over to *The Black Cat* (1934). By this time, James Whale's *The Invisible Man* (1933) became an unexpected hit. Universal finally convinced Whale to return to the direct the sequel, but Lugosi was no longer available; he had switched over to Sol Lessing's Principal Pictures for the opportunity to finally play a hero in *The Return of Chandu* (1934). Ernest Thesiger took over the role of Dr. Pretorius.

Considering Neumann's deft handling of other genre films such as *Rocketship X-M* in 1950 and (of course) *The Fly*, the Frankenstein sequel with Lugosi would have been a very different film. It could have delayed Lugosi's slide into low-budget film obscurity and may have given Neumann the option of keeping the Universal monster franchise alive into the 40s, a task instead given to Curt Siodmak, who arguably may have brought a premature end to the genre films.

Neumann did *Hold Them, Navy* in 1937 and then found himself consigned to do Service Academy movies. Always trying to avoid being stuck as a niche director, Kurt did *Touchdown, Army* and then quickly found another place to work that offered him wider opportunities.

Neumann was signed by Hal Roach in 1941 to direct a series of 45-minute second features, known then as streamliners. These films were used to fill out short double bills and were mostly four reel comedies, such as *About Face* in 1942 and *Yanks Ahoy* in 1943.

Kurt began working for Sol Lesser in 1945 during the Johnny Weissmuller Tarzan run, beginning with *Tarzan's Desert Mystery*. In the next Neumann helmed film, *Tarzan and the Amazons*, Brenda Joyce was brought in to play Jane. Neumann remained with the series through 1954, which included a film with Gordon Scott. These films were made for RKO. He worked with another Tarzan, Lex Barker in a 1957 remake of *The Deerslayer*. Neumann also did *Hiawatha* and *Son of Ali Baba* in 1952.

One of Neumann's most famous films was *Rocketship X-M* in 1950 which he made for Robert Lippert. Rushed out to ride on the publicity generated by the making of *Destination Moon*, this film was released before the film it was emulating. It made a million dollars, even though they had to change their destination to Mars to avoid being sued.

Neumann liked making small movies and putting the deal together himself, even when it was low budget non-studio work. By the late 1950's he was working steadily for Robert Lippert and his "Regal" pictures company, where he made *She-Devil*(1957), *Kronos* (1957) and *Watusi* (1958). Lippert liked Kurt because he was fast and didn't waste money. Neumann kept a project moving, as soon as he would get the shot he wanted, he would move to the next set-up. Some of his non-science fiction films of the 1950's include *The Ring* (1952) with Rita Moreno and *Carnival Story* (1954).

Neumann brought the June 1957 *Playboy* magazine with "The Fly" short story to Lippert, hoping to get a job out of it and Lippert was immediately interested in optioning the film. Fox didn't mind Lippert securing the option, because he could get it cheaper. Most of the time, the studio let him make his own deals for what he wanted to make, but *The Fly* was such a good prospect, Fox took the project over.

Neumann made three more pictures after filming on *The Fly* was completed, *Machete, Watusi and Counterplot. Watusi* mostly served as vehicle to reuse stock footage from *King Solomon's Mines*. All were released after his death.

Kurt also received writing credit on *Rocketship X-M* (1950), *Carnival Story* (1954), *Circus of Love* (1954), *They Were So Young* (1954), *The Desperados are in Town* (1956), *She-Devil* (1957), *Apache Warrior* (1957), *The Deerslayer* (1957) and *Machete* (1958). He is credited with the Screenplay on *She Devil* and *Apache Warrior*. Neumann liked to be involved in all facets of making a film.

Neumann's wife died on July 12, 1958, 10 days after completion of filming of *Counterplot* and just before *The Fly* premiered.

Kurt Neumann died unexpectedly on August 21, five weeks after his wife's death. He was only 50. His family physician reported hemorrhaging, abdominal pain and kidney problems. The initial autopsy indicated kidney and liver damage consistent with ingesting carbon tetrachloride (dry cleaning fluid) and his death was initially ruled a suicide. A second autopsy was ordered because of possible homicide. There were inconsistencies with the suicide diagnosis — there was no evidence of carbon tetrachloride in the house, there was no suicide note and family friends said he was upbeat over his daughter's impending marriage and considering a trip to Europe.

The Fly continued to open in staggered release with the next largest theater opening (over 100 venues in New York City) on August 29, 1958, so Kurt Neumann never knew what a hit this film would become.

In September, the Los Angeles coroner's office released their final report — Kurt Neumann had died of natural causes brought on by acute hepatitis. Less salacious than a suicide, the final report was buried on an inside page of the *Los Angeles Times* beneath an ad for sewing patterns for children's jumpers. To this day, most biographies of Neumann list his death as a suicide.

Neumann's cremated remains are inurned in the Chapel Mausoleum at Home of Peace Memorial Park in Los Angeles.

JAMES CLAVELL
SCREENWRITER

Charles Edmund Dumaresq Clavell was born on October 10, 1924, in Sydney, Australia, the son of Richard Clavell, a captain in the British Royal Navy. His father had been stationed to Sydney help establish the Royal Australian Navy but the family returned to England while the future author was still an infant.

Clavell joined the Royal Artillery in 1940. He was trained for desert warfare, but when Japan entered the war he was among the hastily assembled troops sent to the tropical jungles of Malaya to defend Singapore, the impregnable "Bastion of the Empire." It took the Imperial Japanese Army barely six days to force the British surrender in the Battle of Singapore, one of the worst defeats in the British Empire's military history. On February 15, 1942, Clavell and the other surviving soldiers became prisoners of war and were sent to the infamous Changi prison nearby, where only 1 in 15 prisoners survived. "Changi became my university instead of my prison," he later told an interviewer. "Among the inmates there were experts in all walks of life — the high and the low roads. I studied and absorbed everything I could from physics to counterfeiting, but most of all I learned the art of surviving." Clavell credited his survival to an American POW, who later became the model for the lead character in his 1962 novel *King Rat*.

On his return to England, the newly promoted captain suffered a motorcycle accident that left him lame in one leg, a British lorry doing what a Japanese interment camp could not — ending Clavell's military career.

Through his soon to be wife, ballerina/actress April Stride, he became interested in directing films. The two married in 1951 as Clavell worked around London in film distribution. The family moved to New York City in 1953 when he landed a television production job, a glorified job title for a set carpenter. Seeing the television industry beginning to aggregate in Hollywood, he moved his family to California, padded his résumé and essentially bluffed his way into a job as a screenwriter.

Clavell had been anonymously working on script rewrites for Regal Pictures when Robert Lippert began assembling a production staff for *The Fly*. When Universal took over the production, Neumann kept Clavell as screenwriter based on the strength of his first draft, which required so few revisions that if was practically already in final shooting form. This was Clavell's big break and the leap from anonymous to credited scriptwriter was so sudden and atypical that years later, Lippert's story editor Harry Spalding didn't recall Clavell as a Regal Pictures employee and credited Neumann with hiring the unknown writer.

The Fly was Clavell's first film credit. He then did the screenplay for Kurt Neumann's *Watusi* (1959) and *Five Gates to Hell* (1958), the latter of which was his directorial debut and reunited him with Patricia Owens. Clavell also wrote and directed *Walk like a Dragon* (1960) and was starting to dabble in television, directing an episode *The Rifleman* when a writers' strike shut down Hollywood. When the strike ended, he did an additional episode of *The Rifleman* and an episode of *Ripcord* but his momentum as a director was lost. He continued to work on screenplays for such films as *The Great Escape* (1963), *633 Squadron* (1964) and *The Satan Bug* (1965).

During the strike, Clavell found himself with enough free time to finally begin writing his first novel, something he had been thinking out loud about doing as early as *The Fly*. *King Rat* was his first novel, published in 1962. The novel was semi-autobiographical and told of British and American POWS in Japan during World War II. It became both a best seller and a successful motion picture in 1965, starring George Segal, Tom Courtenay and John Mills.

Clavell was not allowed to adapt his own book into a screenplay, an early indication of his growing dissatisfaction with show business. Instead, he directed *To Sir, With Love* (1967) and *Where's Jack* (1968). He wrote and directed two more films, *The Sweet and the Bitter* (1967) and *the Last Valley* (1970) before finally leaving Hollywood for good to concentrate full time on his now flourishing career as a best selling novelist. A minor scandal in 1970 certainly didn't discourage him leaving California — he fathered a child with Caroline Barrett. Barrett would subsequently become Marlon Brando's personal assistant for 25 years, and Brando would adopt Petra Barrett Brando. This indiscretion on Clavell's part would return in 2004 when Brando, after a spat with Caroline, cut Petra out of his will right before his death, bringing her parentage back into the media spotlight.

Clavell had become a naturalized citizen of the United State in 1963, but as his writing career flourished, he began moving his family to a variety of homes: England, California, British Columbia, the south of France, and finally Switzerland. Clavell would eventually settle in Gstaad, a wealthy mountain resort in Switzerland near his friend, actor Roger Moore.

The Asian stories which Clavell began writing in 1966 became his best sellers. In the order they were written, it was *Tai-pan* (1966), *Shogun* (1975), *Noble*

House (1981), and *Gai-Jin* (1993). The hero of *Tai-Pan* was Dirk Struan, whose descendants would show up in later books. *Tai-pan* and *Noble House* were about Hong Kong and *Shogun* and *Gai-Jin* were set in Japan. They were all historical fiction basely loosely on real-life figures in Japanese and Hong Kong history.

Shogun and *Noble House* were sold to TV in the early 1980's. *Shogun* became one of the most successful miniseries ever produced. *Tai-Pan* was made into a movie in 1994. There was a TV movie of his 1980 cautionary novel of blind patriotism, *The Children's Story*, produced in 1988. Clavell's last novel, *Whirlwind*, was set in Iran. A shorter version was reissued posthumously in 1994 under the title *Escape*. Clavell also did a translation of Sun Tsu's *Art of War* in 1983 and wrote another children's book, called *Thrump-o-Moto* in 1986.

Clavell was nominated in 1964 (along with W. R. Burnett) for a WGA award for Best Written American Drama for the Screen for *The Great Escape*. He was nominated for a DGA award in 1968 for his directing of To *Sir, With Love*. He won the Outstanding Limited Series Emmy for *Shogun* in 1980.

James Clavell died September 7, 1994 in Vevey, Switzerland, overlooking Lac Léman and the French border, from complications from cancer. He was 69.

KARL STRUSS
CINEMATOGRAPHER

Karl Struss was born in New York City on November 30, 1886. He was a successful photographer in New York, where he studied under noted photographer Clarence H. White at Columbia University. Struss embraced Pictorialism, a late 19th-century style that emphasized expression over depiction. The Pictorialist style used soft-focus lenses coupled with elaborate printing techniques that created poetically blurry images. By 1909, Struss developed a type of soft-focus lens that bears his name, the Struss Pictorial Lens which gave the image a diffused, dreamlike look. He soon joined Alfred Stieglitz's Photo-Secession. Photo-Secession was a hand-picked group dedicated to promoting photography as an art form.

In 1914, he took over his former mentor Clarence White's studio on West 31st Street. He was well-established commercial photographer with clients such as *Vogue, Vanity Fair* and *Harper's Bazaar*. In 1916, he co-founded the Pictorialist Photographers of America [PPA], a group dedicated to promoting Pictorialism with exhibitions, lectures and workshops.

When the United States entered WWI in 1917 Struss shut down his gallery and enlisted, working on a project developing infra-red photography. Struss realized that with his shop closed for the duration, it would be difficult to rebuild his client base. He decided to try his luck in Hollywood. As soon as Struss was discharged from the army in 1919, he headed west.

He immediately found work taking photographs on the set of *Male and Female* (1919), and he was put to work as a cameraman. His camera work was good enough to him to be hired for *Something to Think About*, directed by Cecil B. DeMille that same year. DeMille liked him and kept him on for three more films. Struss would film a total of 28 silent movies before the switch to talkies. His most familiar silent film was the 1925 version of *Ben-Hur* for which he developed a colored filter system for the healing of the lepers scenes. Struss later calculated that he shot nearly 60% of the finished picture even though René Guissart received the credit for the cinematography.

One of his last silent films was F.W. Murnau's *Sunrise: A Song of Two Humans* in 1927, a film that not only one the very first Oscar for Best Picture but gave Struss the first Oscar for Cinematography. He shared the award with co-cinematographer Charles Rosher for that film but had also been nominated for the D.W. Griffith film *Drums of Love* (1928). Strauss would be nominated three more times: the 1931 version of *Dr. Jekyll and Mr. Hyde, Sign of the Cross* in 1932 and *Aloma of the High Seas* in 1941.

He was never out of work and made the transition from silent to sound with four more films for D. W. Griffith, the most famous of those films being *Abraham Lincoln* in 1930 as well as his Oscar-nominated work on *Sign of the Cross* in 1932. One of his more interesting jobs was as an uncredited Director of Photography on the Technicolor tests for *Gone with the Wind* (1939).

Some other well known films Struss worked on were *The Great Dictator* (1940), *Caught in the Draft* (1941), *Happy Go Lucky* (1943), *Bring On The Girls* (1947), *The Macomber Affair* (1947) and *Hello Out There* (1949). He was also the cameraman of choice on *Tarzan's Magic Fountain* (1949), *Tarzan's Peril* (1951), and *Tarzan's Savage Fury* (1952).

Struss made his first film with Kurt Neumann in 1939. It was called *The Island of Lost Men*. They would reunite with *Tarzan and the Leopard Woman* in 1946, and continue to work together on *The Dude Goes West* (1948), *Bad Boy* (1949) and *Rocket Ship X-M* (1950).

Always looking for new ways to push the boundaries of cinematography, Struss continued to develop new techniques that elevated black and white film; His graduated red-green filter, when used in conjunction with certain makeup applications, allowed a seemless transition from Dr. Jekyll to Mr. Hyde as well as the aforementioned healing of the lepers in *Ben-Hur*. His Oscar was in no small part due to the graduated gauze filters which allowed better lighting effects in *Sunrise*. When the Stereo-Realist Camera came on the market in 1947, it was no surprise that Struss would become one of the pioneers of the 3-D filming process, actually leaving Hollywood to do four movies in Italy, three of which were stereoscopic (3-D) in 1953 and 1954. Struss worked as a stereoscopic cinematographer on *Il Piu Comico Spettacolo Del Mondo, Il Turco Napoletano* and *Cavalleria Rusticana* starring Anthony Quinn and May Britt. The third film was released in the United States in 1963 as *Fatal Desire*, but not in the 3-D format.

Struss was not particularly impressed with *The Fly*, which is not surprising in a career that started with legendary directors like Murnau, Chaplin, DeMille and Griffith and stars such as Mary Pickford, Charles Laughton, Fredric March and Cary Grant. In a 1972 interview, Struss remarked that although he liked working with Kurt Neumann, he was convinced one scene was so over the top that the audience would be in hysterics. The scene? None other than the fly in the web shrieking "Help me, help me!"

Karl worked mainly in television from 1955 to 1957, filming seventeen episodes of *My Friend Flicka* and then moving on to do 13 episodes of the series *Broken Arrow*.

Struss returned to Neumann when there was work until Kurt's last film, *Counterplot* (1959). Starting in 1956 they worked together on *Mohawk* (1956), *She-Devil* (1957), *Kronos* (1957), *The Deer-Slayer* (1957), did *The Fly* in April of 1958 and *Machete,* also in 1958. Four of these collaborations were written by Neumann.

Struss' final film before his retirement was another human transformation film. Instead of insects, this time it was reptiles. *The Alligator People* was filmed in 1959 and ironically released on a double bill with *Return of the Fly*.

Karl Struss died in Santa Monica, CA on December 16, 1981 and is buried in Woodlawn Cemetery in the Bronx.

MERRILL G. WHITE
EDITOR

Merrill G. White was born on December 13, 1901 in California. He died on March 21, 1959, so *The Fly* was one of the last films he edited. He was nominated for an Oscar in 1957 for his film editing on *The Brave One,* for which he also helped write the screenplay. The film did win the Oscar for Best Story, given to writer Robert Rich, who, much to the embarrassment of the Academy, turned out to be screenwriter Dalton Trumbo, one of the "Hollywood Ten" who were blacklisted during the McCarthy era.

White was the supervising editor at Fox Studios from 1952 to 1959, where he did one other genre film, 1953's *Robot Monster,* memorable for the image of Ro-Man, an alien played by George Barrows in a gorilla suit with a diving helmet and antenna. It should not be considered a high point in White's career, even if it did introduce the word "psychotronic" to the world.

White worked with Neumann on three different Tarzan films, starting in 1948. Other Neumann projects Merrill edited included *The Ring* (1952) and *Carnival Story* (1954). White began his documented film career in 1927 with *The Broken Gate*. The last film he worked on was *Crime and Punishment USA* (1959), an Americanized version of the Dostoyevsky novel featuring Los Angeles beatniks.

THEOBOLD HOLSOPPLE
ART DIRECTION

Theobold (Ted) Holsopple began his career in 1947 as a set decorator on the film *High Tide* in 1947. His first job as a production designer came in *Bomba, The Jungle Boy* in 1949. It was not uncommon for him to do both jobs on some of his films.

He was the Art Director on six of Kurt Neumann's films. He got his start with Neumann in *Bad Boy* (1949). He continued to work with Kurt on *Bad Men of Tombstone* (1949), *Rocketship X-M* (1950), where he was promoted to Production Designer; *The Ring* (1952), *The Deerslayer* (1957) and *The Fly* (1958). Holsopple was also the Production Designer on *Desperados are Back in Town* (1956), *She-Devil* (1957), and *Kronos* (1957). His change in status seems to hinge on whether or not the picture was made as a studio film or as a B movie feature under Lippert's control.

Additionally, he was a set decorator on *Once Upon a Honeymoon* (1956) and the production designer on *Park Row* (1952), *Captive Women* (1952) and *Daughter of Dr. Jekyll* (1957). After *The Fly*; Holsopple worked as an art director on *The Wizard of Baghdad* (1960), *Three Blondes in his Life* (1961), *Hands of a Stranger* (1962), *Patty* (1962) and *California* (1963).

His last recorded projects were an art director on the Barbara Streisand film, *For Pete's Sake* and as a Production Designer on *The Bamboo Saucer* in 1968. Ted Holsopple died in April of 1975 in Sherman Oaks, California.

PAUL SAWTELL
COMPOSER

Paul Sawtell was born in Glive, Poland on February 3, 1906 and died in Los Angeles, August 1, 1971. Before immigrating to the United States in 1923, he received his musical education in Munich and was a violin soloist with various symphonies in Europe. In the 1920's he conducted music for silent film screenings, working for theaters, radio and musical halls. In 1935, he moved to Hollywood and worked as an arranger.

Sawtell composed music, conducted orchestras for soundtracks and was a musical director and supervisor for over 300 films during his career. Sawtell's first documented job in Hollywood was *Glimpses of Argentina* in 1938. He was hired to conduct the soundtrack orchestra. Paul began composing stock music for westerns in 1939 and never looked back. He became Music Director for RKO and Universal in 1940. Paul scored the occasional horror or detective film in the 1940's and began to do selected film series like Sherlock Holmes (*Pearl of Death, Scarlet Claw*), Boston Blackie and Blondie. He also did Abbott and Costello monster films.

Sawtell moved gradually into television work with *Schlitz Playhouse* in 1951 and the western series *Cheyenne, Maverick* and *Bronco*, before moving on to *Surfside Six, 77 Sunset Strip* and finally *Hawaiian Eye*, where he was music supervisor for 133 episodes from 1959 to 1963.

He would work with David Hedison again, first on *The Lost World* (1960) and the starting in 1964, he worked on *Voyage to the Bottom of the Sea*, with his work appearing in 73 episodes.

His last series was *Here Come the Brides*. Sawtell wrote music for eight episodes in 1968. He worked for Russ Meyer in 1965, doing the scores for *Faster Pussycat! Kill! Kill!* and *MotorPsycho*. Sawtell scored two more films before his unexpected death in August of 1971; *The Christine Jorgenson Story* (1970) and *Emiliano Zapata* (1970), his last collaboration with composing partner Bert Shefter. Paul Sawtell is buried in Forest Lawn Memorial Park in Glendale, California.

BERT SHEFTER
CO-COMPOSER

Sawtell's long-time partner Bert Shefter was born in Russia in 1902 and first came to the United States for his education. He was a concert pianist and toured for many years as half of the piano duo Gould and Shefter. He tried his luck in New York with limited success. He worked as a solo pianist and accompanist in relative obscurity until 1949, when he was hired as Musical Director of *Blackouts of 1949*. The musical revue barely lasted a month before closing on Oct 15, 1949, but it was pivotal in his career direction. He headed to Hollywood and within month was working as the Musical director for *One Too Many* (1950). He received more notice and film experience as the conductor of Michel Michelet's score for the remake of the classic film *M* in 1951. Bert credits his experience on this particular film with helping him learn the genre and for shaping the tone of his later Fly scores.

Sawtell first heard Shefter play in Las Vegas. They decided to become scoring partners in 1957, the year before *The Fly* was made and were tried out as a team for the first time on *The Black Scorpion*. The collaboration was a success because they complemented each other, often finishing each other ideas by being able to compose in the same style.

They were more efficient as a team; Shefter would do orchestration which Sawtell disliked and Sawtell would often finish off pieces Shefter would start. Their total lack of commitment to any style other than one that would advance their work output, made the duo very popular with producers of low budget films. They could produce 20 minutes a day with this seamless method and have a full score done in a week.

They would collaborate until Sawtell's death in 1971. They scored two of the Fox Fly films together: *The Fly*, and *The Return of the Fly* and Shefter provided the score for *Curse of the Fly*. They also worked together on the films *Kronos* (1957), *It: The Terror Beyond Space* (1958), *The Lost World* (1960), *Voyage to the Bottom of the Sea* (1961) *and Jack The Giant Killer* (1962). Shefter did two solo scores after Sawtell's death; the first for *The Gatling Gun* in 1973 and his final film was *Revenge of the Fists of Fury* in 1975. Bert Shefter retired from the movie business in 1975 and died on June 29, 1999 at the age of 97.

EUGENE GROSSMAN
SOUND

Eugene F. Grossman was born in Davenport, Iowa on January 19, 1896. He worked in sound in a career that spanned three decades, from 1930 until 1960, with over 100 films to his credit.

Some of the films he recorded sound for were *Stand Up and Cheer* (1934), *Curly Top* (1935), *Young Mr. Lincoln* (1939), *Dressed to Kill* (1941), *Heaven Can Wait* (1943), *The Keys of the Kingdom* (1944), *My Darling Clementine* (1946), *The Beautiful Blonde from Bashful Bend* (1949), *Fixed Bayonets* (1951), *Hell and High Water* (1954), *She Devil* (1957), *No Down Payment* (1957), *Rally 'Round the Flag, Boys* (1958), *Compulsion* (1959) *and Wild River* (1960).

He worked on *The Rifleman* for 16 episodes in 1959 and recorded one episode of *The David Niven Show* before retiring in 1960. Grossman died in Woodland Hills, California on February 16, 1982.

JACK GERTSMAN
ASSISTANT DIRECTOR

Jack Gertsman was born in November 1904. He married in 1931 and began working as a script clerk in 1935 as a way to support his growing family. He worked his way up to unit manager and then production manager, before becoming an assistant director in the late forties. He worked as a film AD until 1960, doing several movies including *Bungalow 13* (1948), *The Secret Garden* (1949) *Wyoming Mail* (1950), *The Lady from Texas* (1951), *Flight to Hong Kong* (1956), *Rally 'Round The Flag, Boys* (1958), and *The Story on Page One* (1959).

Gertsman also did assistant director work in early television programs such series as *Sky King, Highway Patrol, Sgt. Preston of the Yukon* and *The Third Man.* It was to television he returned as he headed toward retirement, working as assistant director on *Peyton Place* and the James Michener created series *Adventures in Paradise.* He retired in 1969, finishing his career as an assistant director on episodes of *The Brady Bunch* and a unit manager on *Gilligan's Island.* He died in May, 1981 in San Juan Capistrano, CA.

L. B. ABBOTT
SPECIAL EFFECTS

Lenwood Ballard Abbott, Jr. was born June 13, 1908 in Pasadena, CA. Known as "Bill" to all who worked with him, he was the son of Lenwood Abbott, one of the first Los Angeles portrait photographers and a well know adventurer who photographed expeditions across the globe and who dabbled as Director of Cinematographer on several early silent films.

In 1924, Lenwood Abbott was hired to photograph an expedition to Tibet. He ended up stranded in Singapore and sued the expedition backers when he finally arrived back in Los Angeles. The story was popular in the news, so his son started using his initials to differentiate between him and his famous father.

As L.B. Abbott, Bill landed his first job (at $4 a day) in 1926 as an assistant camera man on *What Price Glory* for Fox Film Corporation, marking the beginning of an affiliation with Fox that would last until his retirement in 1970.

L.B. Abbott continued to work as an assistant until 1937, when the Fox Special Effects Department was overwhelmed by the workload of *In Old Chicago.*

Abbott spent several months lending a hand, his first taste of special effects and miniatures. Abbott was hooked and tried to land jobs in Special Effects until 1943 when Fred Serson, head of Fox's Special Effects department, asked him to join the staff full time.

Abbott became head of the Special Effects Department at Fox in 1957; the same year that Al Hedison was given his first contract with the studio. Abbott is the crew member who shares the most credits with Hedison, beginning with *The Enemy Below* in 1957, continuing with *The Lost World* in 1960 and on to the *Voyage to the Bottom of the Sea* television series in 1964. He quickly became known as one of the best special effects cameramen in the industry, winning Academy Awards for his work on *Doctor Doolittle, Tora! Tora! Tora!, The Poseidon Adventure* and *Logan's Run*. This work is more remarkable when it is remembered that this was long before digital effects rendered tidal waves and squadrons of airplanes commonplace effects.

Although retired, Abbott continued to heed the call, working on the TV series *MASH* and all of Irwin Allen's disaster films: *The Poseidon Adventure* (1972), *The Towering Inferno* (1974), *The Swarm* (1978) and *When Time Ran Out* (1980). Additionally, Abbott worked on Allen's TV movies *City Beneath the Sea* (1971), *Flood*! (1976), *Fire!* (1977) and *The Return of Captain Nemo* (1978).

In addition to his Oscars, Abbott also won four Emmys for his work with Irwin Allen; two for *Voyage to the Bottom of the Sea* and one each for *The Time Tunnel* and *City Beneath the Sea.*

Abbott worked on all of the "Planet of the Apes" movies and several of the TV series episodes. Some of the better known films Abbott did effects shots for were: *The Day the Earth Stood Still* (1951), *The Sound of Music* (1965), *Fantastic Voyage* (1966), *Butch Cassidy and the Sundance Kid* (1969) and *Patton* (1970).

In 1984, he published *Special Effects - Wire, Tape and Rubber Band Style,* a combination biography and how-to book that showed how elaborate and sophisticated film effects were done, as the title suggests, by low-tech, low-budget techniques and imagination.

L. B. Abbott died in Los Angeles, September 28, 1985 after a 55-year career that saw him working on 300 motion pictures and hundreds of television episodes. His ashes were scattered at sea.

In March of 2008, UCLA celebrated the centennial of his birth with "Wire, Tape and Rubber Band Style: The Effects of L.B. Abbott," a three-week film festival.

BEN NYE
MAKE-UP

Benjamin Emmet Nye, Senior was born January 12, 1907 in Fremont, Nebraska. He went to Hollywood looking for a career in the arts, but found himself working as a clerk at Fox Studios in 1932, making photostatic copies of sheet music. In 1935, he became an apprentice in the makeup department at Selznick International Pictures, working for David O. Selznick on such films as *Rebecca* and *Gone With the Wind.*

As an apprentice, Ben Nye was working primarily as a hair stylist for the hundreds of extras on *Gone With the Wind.* His older brother Carroll Nye, a successful silent movie actor, had auditioned for the part of Frank Kennedy

Ben Nye begins applying the make up to transform Al Hedison into The Fly.
PHOTO COURTESY OF BEN NYE, SR. ARCHIVES, 2008

but was turned down because he was considered too young for the role (the character is in his forties). Ben put his brother into the make up and added the whiskers the character called for and Carroll Nye landed the role of Scarlett O'Hara's second husband.

In 1944, Ben Nye was again hired by Fox, this time for make-up. He would remain there until retiring as head of makeup from 20th Century Fox in 1967. His work for Fox has him credited on such diverse films as *Five Weeks in a Balloon* (1962), *Von Ryan's Express* (1965), *Fantastic Voyage* (1966), *Hombre* (1967) *Miracle on 34th Street* (1947), *Gentlemen Prefer Blondes* (1953), *The King and I* (1956) and *Planet of the Apes* (1968). Although merely credited as a technical advisor for *The Mudlark* (1950), it was his prosthetics that transformed Irene Dunne into Queen Victoria.

Nye is credited with makeup or technical advisor in over 400 movies and several television series over the course of his impressive career. He officially retired from Fox Studios in 1967 and started his own makeup company, which is now run by his son Dana. His other son, Ben Jr. and his grandson Ben III worked as make-up artists.

The Fly co-star he worked on the most was Al (David) Hedison as Nye supervised the makeup on *The Enemy Below* (1957), *The Lost World* (1960), *Marine's Lets Go* (1961) and on forty three episodes of the television series *Voyage to the Bottom of the Sea*. Nye also supervised makeup on multiple episodes of *Lost in Space, Time Tunnel, Batman* and *Green Hornet* before his retirement.

Ben worked on films through 1968, took a break and then came back. He worked on two TV movies in 1974 and the films *Marathon Man* in 1976 and *Heaven's Gate* in 1980. His last job was a TV movie in 1982 called *The Wall*. Ben Nye died in Santa Monica, California February 9, 1986.

ADELE BALKAN
COSTUME DESIGNER

Born August 27, 1907 in Alameda County, California, Adele Balkan was a costume designer and sketch artist, working with design icons such as Travis Banton and Edith Head at Paramount and Charles LeMaire at Twentieth Century-Fox in a career that spanned four decades. Her first job was with Paramount Pictures as a sketch artist, working on Cecil B. DeMille's 1934 epic *Cleopatra* with Claudette Colbert.

Her credits as costume designer or part of the wardrobe department range from *Alfred Hitchcock's Notorious* (1946) and *Mighty Joe Young* (1949) to *The Blue Angel* (1959) and *Flaming Star* (1960). Much of her work was not credited, such as her wardrobe work on *The Ten Commandments* (1956) or her costume designs for *There's No Business Like Show Business* (1954).

Not one to slow down, Balkan continued to work until her retirement in 1972 and then became a full-time professional artist. She participated in the Academy of Motion Picture Arts and Sciences Oral History Project; her taped interviews about her career, costume design, sketch artistry and specific films ran over 320 pages when transcribed. She died on November 20, 1999, at the age of 92.

ROBERT L. LIPPERT, SR.
ORIGINAL PRODUCER

Born in San Francisco March 31, 1909, Robert L. Lippert was adopted by Leonard and Eleanor Lippert of Alameda, CA. Always fascinated with the movies, Lippert began his career doing odd jobs in the local movie house, such as playing the pump organ, sweeping up after the show and eventually worked his way up into the projection booth. Something of an innovator, he made many improvements to the projectors of the day and developed new variations.

From 1936 to 1940, to attract movie goers during the Depression years, Lippert introduced "Dish Night" and "Book Night," touring the country with the promotion. He also installed the first popcorn machine in a movie theater in 1939. During these travels, Lippert calculated he personally met close to 90% of all theatre owners and film distributors.

In 1942, he opened his first theater and introduced the first drive-in theater on the West Coast in 1945. His big break came in World War II, when he conceived the idea of all night movies for night shift workers at the local shipyards. With a new income stream, he began to expand his collection of theaters; he also started his own distribution company. In the next decade, his distribution company grew to 28 regional offices in the United States with additional offices in foreign countries. Lippert Pictures produced, financed and/or distributed close to 200 motion pictures.

With this network of contacts, a distribution network and over 150 theaters of his own, Lippert made the leap to producing his own films.

Lippert produced/released hundreds of movies in the 1940's and into the 1950's. He had brand recognition; fans knew when a film carried the Lippert banner that they were in for something different. His two most recognizable films were *Rocketship X-M* (1950) and *Little Big Horn* (1951). *Time* dubbed him the "Quickie King" in 1951, after he made *Superman and The Mole Men.*

In 1955, he went to work for 20th Century Fox, making hundreds of what were then called second features for them. He was an unabashed B-movie maker and was once quoted as saying he didn't worry about what the critics said: he made pictures people want to see.

He had several production companies under various names like Lippert Productions and Screen Guild Productions. The three Lippert companies associated with the Fox Fly films were Regal Pictures, Associated Pictures and Lippert Films Limited. *The Fly* was one of the few that got away from him, and that was only after Fox took over his options on the story. Lippert may barely have even noticed at the time — between 1956 and 1966, he produced 120 full-length features, in addition to running his theatre chain and promoting a new concept to moviegoers — the multiplex, which he introduced in 1965.

Robert L. Lippert, Sr. died November 16, 1976 and is interred in Woodland Memorial Park, Colma, California.

Return of the Fly (1959) — Phillipe and Francois observe the results of using the rebuilt transport devices.

CHAPTER 8

SEQUELS AND REMAKES

RETURN OF THE FLY (1959)

ASSOCIATED PICTURES, 20TH CENTURY FOX, CINEMASCOPE, B&W, 84 MINUTES

Producer....................Bernard Glasser
Director and Screenwriter....................Edward L. Bernds,
based on the short story by George Langelaan
Cinematographer....................Brydon Baker
Editor....................Richard C. Meyer
First Assistant Editor....................Orven Schanzer
Music....................Paul Sawtell and Bert Shefter
Art Directors....................John Mansbridge and Lyle R. Wheeler
Set Decorators....................Joseph Kish and Walter M. Scott
Assistant Director....................Byron Roberts
Makeup....................Hal Lierley
Sound....................Bernard Freericks

CAST

Vincent Price....................Francois Delambre
Brett Halsey....................Philippe Delambre
John Sutton....................Inspector Beacham
David Frankham....................Ronald Holmes alias Alan Hinds
Danielle De Metz....................Cecile Bonnard
Jack Daly....................Granville - Reporter
Janine Grandel....................Madame Bonnard
Michael Mark....................Gaston - Watchman
Richard Flato....................Sergeant Dubois
Gregg Martel....................Cop
Barry Bernard....................Lt. MacLish
Pat O'Hara....................Inspector Evans
Francisco Villalobos....................Priest
Joan Cotton....................Nurse
Florence Strom....................Nun
Ed Wolff....................Philippe as the Fly

Given the success of the first film, plans were immediately made for a sequel. It was announced that filming would start on February 2, 1959. A totally different Lippert crew was assembled to make this film on a shoestring. Vincent Price returned as the brother and uncle, Francois Delambre. With a now grown up Philippe Delambre, Francois and Philippe would be central to the story. It is now fifteen years later. They are the only main characters retained from the short story by Langelaan. This and a score by Paul Sawtell and Bert Shefter are first two elements theses films have in common. There is also a night watchman named Gaston, who is supposed to be the same character from the first film, but is played by a totally different actor, Mark Manson.

James Clavell apparently wanted to direct this sequel, but lost the job to Edward L. Bernds, who was also working for Lippert at this time. Bernds was told to write the screenplay. Edward Bernds was probably best known for directing *The Three Stooges* up to this point. Fox decided the sequel had to film on the Fox lot, so the film cost more than it would have if Lippert's crew had been able to do it some other place, but director Bernds was flexible and fast and got the film done despite the added studio overhead.

The sequel was filmed in black and white, to save money. However, it was still done in the Technicolor process, which gave it a much better look than most of the other cheap, quick, science fiction films that were being cranked out at this time. All the studios were quick to take advantage of the teen audience and their flocking to drive-in theatres in droves to see this kind of picture.

Vincent Price wanted to read the sequel script first and then signed on the basis of what he read. His signing merited a newspaper mention on March 4, 1959. The first draft contained a wonderful part for him. When a producer mandated revision cut most of the scenes Price had liked, Vincent lobbied the director to put them back in. The scenes in question were with Danielle De Metz, who was playing Cecile, the housekeeper's daughter, and were described as sweet and tender. Naturally, they were the first scenes to be cut.

Bernds did all he possibly could, short of filming the cut scenes and while the final script was a disappointment to Price, it did not keep Vincent from doing the film. He really wanted to work, after a period of being gray-listed. Price took most anything at this time in his movie career. The entire film was shot in ten days. Price would later joke that they should have called the sequel, *The Zipper*. Such was Vincent's sense of humor.

Price's contract with Fox was renewed for *Return of the Fly* and he later explained what happened to the script he had first been given. When Vincent read it, he was very excited about the possibilities, but the producers proceeded to put in a lot of gimmicks in the belief that the film needed the gimmicks to be popular. In the end, to his mind, these gimmicks lessened and nearly ruined the dramatic effect that could have made the sequel a superior picture.

Herbert Marshall was also sought to reprise his Inspector Charas role, but amid claims he was too ill, was the reality that the film's budget could not afford him. John Sutton, who had worked with Vincent Price before in films such as *Tower of London* and *The Private Lives of Elizabeth and Essex* in 1939 and *The*

Invisible Man Returns in 1940, was hired as Inspector Beacham. Sutton was also in the 1948 version of *The Three Musketeers*. In total Sutton made eight films with Vincent Price, their last collaboration coming on *The Bat* in 1959. Much is made of this relationship in *Return of the Fly*, that only Beacham knows what's going on and can be trusted, because he (supposedly) worked with Charas on the original case.

Brett Halsey, who played the grown up son of Andre, was still an unknown at this time and was paid a paltry $1000 (his pay at the time) for his five days of work. Halsey was told take it or leave it. Brett took the role in hopes it would be a more high profile part than the ten previous films he had made and get him noticed. That decision, at least, worked out for Halsey, as he signed a Fox Studio contract at a much higher rate of pay after doing this film.

David Hedison was on the lot during the making of *Return of the Fly*, filming the pilot of his first television series, *Five Fingers*. David and Brett have been friends since 1959 and have done joint personal appearances together at science fiction conventions. He shared the following story about Brett Halsey.

Lippert really wanted Brett for the part and made a big selling point that Halsey would not have to wear the fly head make-up, like Hedison had to. That made Brett happy, but he had one final request of Lippert before he would agree to take the role. Lippert was sure he was going to ask for the moon and the budget (as stated above) could not afford that. Halsey leaned forward and told Lippert he wanted a dressing room as big as Gardner McKay's.

Gardner McKay (in 1959) was the handsome star of the Fox TV Series *Adventures in Paradise*. He was getting the most fan mail at the time and had all female attention. The other young males on the Fox lot wanted their piece of that.

Lippert nearly fell out of his chair when he found out that was all Brett wanted, so Halsey got his dressing room, in fact, because it was a movie, he may have been given an even larger one than the one Gardner McKay had.

Halsey, like Hedison, took his role seriously. He wasn't interested in playing it campy, despite the elements of the over-large fly head and the man/hamster hybrid that is created and then destroyed during the film. Halsey was pleased with the opportunity the film gave him. Brett said it launched his career and led to a life with show business marriages and children he would not have had otherwise.

Halsey liked Bernds; he had worked for him in *High School Hellcats* (1958). The twist to that film was the girls were the juvenile delinquents, at least until they were reformed. Halsey said Bernds was very capable, but seemed to have gotten trapped in the niche of making quick, efficient B-movies. The director was calm and collected and very good at what he did. Bernds may have seemed an odd choice to helm the sequel to *The Fly*, but this assignment was not his first genre film. Besides *Space Master X-7*, Edward had also directed *World without End* (1956), *Queen of Outer Space* (1958) and then did *Valley of the Dragons* (1961).

Halsey had a rather interesting career before he did this film. Starting out as an uncredited extra in 1953, he had parts in *All I Desire* (1953), and was one of

Publicity shot for the *Five Fingers* episode "Thin Ice" with star David Hedison and guest star Brett Halsey.

PHOTO COURTESY OF THE PERSONAL COLLECTION OF DAVID HEDISON, 2008

the Kettle kids in *Ma and Pa Kettle at Home* and became a squire in *The Black Shield of Falworth* in 1954.

After a name change from Charles Hand to Brett Halsey, he was hired by Universal and cast as an extra in several films, beginning with *Return of the Creature* in 1955. Halsey was also in *To Hell and Back* (1955) and a Tab Hunter service picture called *The Girl He Left Behind* (1956) and *I Want to Live* (1958) with Susan Hayward.

Halsey did several other JD flicks (as they were called), including one with an as equally as unknown Jack Nicholson called *The Cry Baby Killer* (1958) as well as *Hot Rod Rumble, The Girl in Lovers Lane* and *Speed Crazy.*

Brett was also cast in television shows such as *Gunsmoke* (in 1956) and *Perry Mason* and *Highway Patrol*. He appeared in at least four Fox television series, including guest stints on David Hedison's *Five Fingers* and Gardner McKay's *Adventures in Paradise*. Let us hope there were no fights over dressing rooms!

Halsey has had a long career, managing to find work in many mediums. He was reunited in Rome with Vincent Price in *Twice Told Tales* in 1963 during his Italian period doing sword and sandal epics and has been in most everything from *Fantasy Island* to *Godfather III* to being on a soap opera. Halsey has lived all over the world and spent the last few years teaching acting in Costa Rica, before moving back to California.

Halsey's nemesis in *Return of the Fly* was David Frankham, who was making his American screen debut at the age of 33. Frankham had previously worked as a radio announcer in the service and after the war he worked on BBC radio. He gave up that career up and moved to America, to give acting a try. Armed with letters of introduction graciously written by Alec Guinness, he had the right look for *Return of the Fly* and carved out a career playing crazed killers in movies and television after this. He would co-star again with Vincent Price in *Master of The World* in 1961 and *Tales of Terror* in 1962 and had a good 20 year career in film and television after *Return of the Fly*.

Both actors became friends with Vincent Price, who was a kind and generous man, who would take them on trips with him and tell them what paintings to buy for investment. Frankham credits Price for getting him started out on the right foot and being a genial mentor through those three early movies.

The Fly sequel was made strictly as a moneymaker for Fox. Price knew this and sandwiched his part into a monstrously busy schedule of films, art lectures and promotion of his new art book. This second *Fly* film is hardly ever mentioned in essays on Price's career. Fox was disappointed in the box office receipts for this film, but considering the weak story and even more ludicrous "fly" makeup used in this film, it is remarkable to has survived and have loyal fans, even after all these years.

A reporter accosts Philippe at Helene's funeral which forces François to reveal the truth and show his nephew André's ruined lab. Philippe is determined to perfect his father's process. It supposedly being fifteen years later, Price had grey added to his hair to look older. Francois refuses to finance the project and Philippe says he will use his own money to do it.

Hired away by Philippe from his uncle to be his lab assistant, Dr. Alan Hinds (David Frankham) had his own agenda. He is actually Ronald Holmes, an escaped convict. He wants to sell the blueprints of the transmitter to local mortician and well known fence Max Berthold (Dan Seymour). Together Philippe and Alan rebuild the transporter chambers in the basement of Philippe's grandfather's house, until Francois finds out what they are doing. Philippe threatens to sell his half of Delambre Freres Electronics to continue to finance the rogue project, unless Francois funds him. Francois reluctantly agrees.

The three of them perfect the transportation process, correcting the problems of gigantism that occur with the first guinea pig sent through, but manage to finally send a rabbit through that comes back normal size.

When Detective Evans (Pat O'Hara) catches up with Hinds that evening to arrest him on his old murder warrant while he's taking pictures of the plans of the transporter device, Hinds knocks the policeman out. He then disintegrates the lawman to hide his body until he can dispose of it. When Hinds reintegrates Evans, he is horrifyingly recombined with a guinea pig that was disintegrated earlier in the day by Philippe and left to be brought back at a later time. Hinds crushes the rodent (which has human hands) first with his shoe and then a heavy piece of equipment when they both come back switched. He puts the dead rodent in a box. He sends the mutated Evans over a cliff in his own car trunk, along with the guinea pig to destroy any evidence of what Hinds has done in the resulting car fire.

Alan is confronted by Philippe when he returns to the lab. Philippe heard the machine and demands to know what going on. They fight and Hinds knocks him out as well. He then puts Philippe in the transporter and repeats the disintegration process, after throwing in a fly, since he now knows Philippe is deathly afraid of them.

The mutated Philippe runs away when he is reintegrated, leading the police to believe he is the one who shot Francois. Hinds makes his escape from the estate by stealing François' car. He shoots the older Delambre in the side during his getaway.

Philippe is saved by combined efforts of Cecile, her mother, Madame Bonnard, Francois, and Inspector Beacham. Madame Bonnard, the Housekeeper, is the first to suspect Hinds is up to no good and calls the police. Cecile may be Philippe's fiancée, but this is not made clear. They do, however, care for each other.

Francois is taken to the hospital to be treated and will only tell his story to Inspector Beacham, who knows the details of the first incident from working with Inspector Charas. They hatch a plan to capture both the fly with Philippe's head and his body with the fly head, claw hand and (apparently for good measure) claw foot. They manage to corral both, but not before the fly hybrid stalks and kills both Berthold and Hinds to keep them from selling the plans to the transporter.

The mutant man/fly returns to the house and is taken to the basement. Francois leaves his sickbed to operate the machine. They are put together in the transporter and untangled. Philippe falls into the arms of the woman he loves and the film ends. Without saying whether or not Philippe will be charged in the death of the two men the Fly killed. So we are left with a transporter that works, when used properly, and no continuation.

A stuntman, circus giant Ed Wolff, was hired to wear Hal Lierley's version of the makeup, which dramatically increased the size of the second fly head. Wolff had health problems and couldn't run with the giant head on, without fear of him having a heart attack, so a smaller, healthier stunt man (Joe Becker) did the now famous chase scene through the woods.

Return of the Fly was released on a co-bill with *The Alligator People,* but there was apparently one opportunity Fox publicity did not want to miss. They moved up the opening of *Return of the Fly* two weeks in New York City to pair the film (as a double feature) with the opening of *Son of Robin Hood,* starring Al Hedison, the original Fly, beginning August 12, 1959 and for the duration of the screening there.

***Return of the Fly* (1959) — Francois and Cecile attempt to separate Philippe from the Fly.**

The regular bill of *The Return of the Fly* with *The Alligator People,* which starred Beverly Garland as the hapless wife confronted with mutated alligator husband, Richard Carlson, opened in Los Angeles and most everywhere else on August 26, 1959. Vincent Price had four other films playing at this same time, including *House of Haunted Hill* and *The Tingler,* so *Return of the Fly* did not receive the press coverage that these two larger hits did.

Fox dutifully ran local announcements that the film was playing in Los Angeles and other theatres for three weeks and then let it play out. *Return of the Fly* lasted until at least December 1959 in most areas and was still playing in some drive-ins in 1960. Price for the most part, carried the film, and is credited for lifting the script out of the B-movie category. The Technicolor process helped the film look better, but it never should have been made in black and white.

The two movies were re-released together in England under a co-bill with Vincent Price as the star and everyone else listed under the respective film titles. They earned an X rating from the British review board.

The film was released on 16 mm as a rental and while not nearly as popular as the original movie still enjoyed a long and healthy rental life. The first single VHS release was as a high priced rental, as was the Betamax version. The first widely available VHS came out in 1992. The 1996 laserdisc release had this film second billed with *The Fly* and nearly all releases after that have the two films together. The VHS was re-released as a single for the last time on January 1, 1998. The last VHS release came on September 5, 2000 as a two tape set of both *The Fly* and *Return of the Fly*.

There were at least two European PAL VHS releases, one in English and one in German. Early VHS versions have a 78 minute version of the movie. Later American DVD releases extend the film to the original 84 minutes with restoration of whatever scenes that caused the film to be rated X when it was first released overseas in 1960, but some of the PAL DVD versions state it is a 74 minute version.

The first American DVD of *Return of the Fly* came out (as stated above) in 2000 as double set with the first film. The PAL version (Region 2) was released on October 22, 2001 as a two disc two DVD set. A German edition DVD *Die Rukkehr die Fliege* was released on April 7, 2005 under the Studio Classics Banner. The British version (also a single disc) followed on July 4, 2005. The Studio Classics 2005 DVD release is easily recognizable by the angled movie posters on the DVD covers.

Return was also part of the seven disc Mega set released (Region 2) in England on May 29, 2006 and the four disc Trilogy set (Region 1) released in North America September 11, 2007.

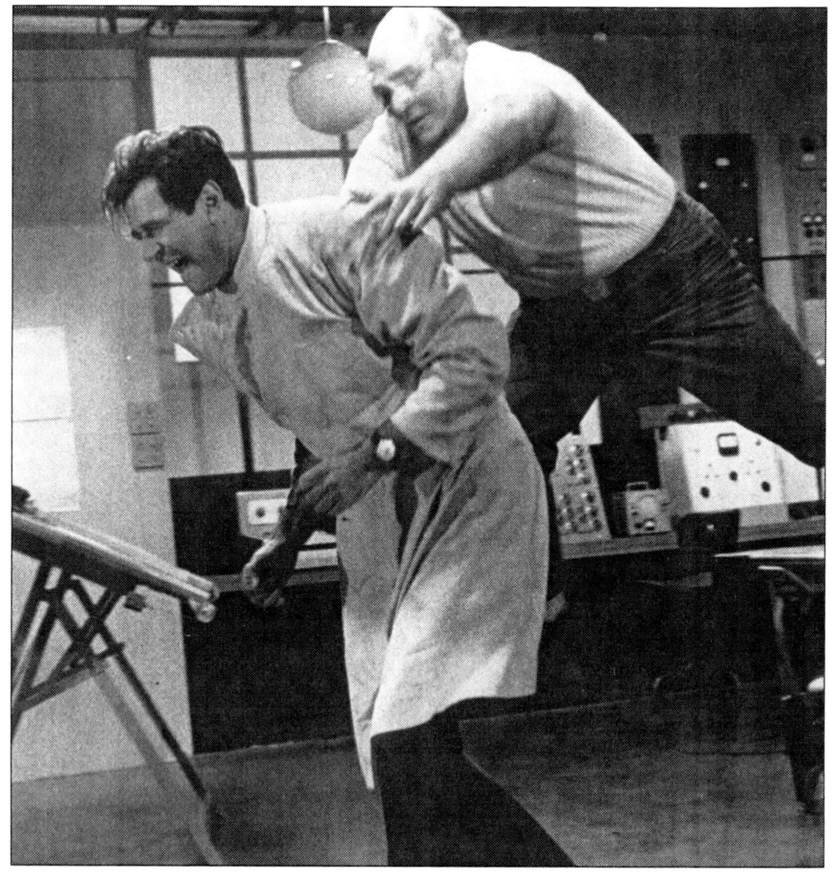

Curse of the Fly (1965) — Mutated lab assistant Samuels attacks Martin Delambre.

CURSE OF THE FLY (1965)

LIPPERT FILMS LIMITED, DISTRIBUTED BY 20TH CENTURY FOX, CINEMASCOPE, B&W, 86 MINUTES

Producers............................ Robert L. Lippert and Jack Parsons
Director .... Don Sharp
Screen Writer .... Henry Spaulding *(Langelaan is uncredited)*
Editor ....Robert Winter
Cinematographer...Basil Emmott
Music.............................. Bert Shefter and Johnny Pearson
Assistant Director.....................................Gordon Gilbert
Art Director .... Harry White
Makeup.. Don O'Gorman
Hairstyles... Barbara Bernard
Sound .... Jack May and Clive Smith
Special effects Makeup..................................Harold Fletcher
Title Design.. Francis Rodker

CAST

Brian Donlevy....................................... Henri Delambre
George Baker...Martin Delambre
Carol Gray .... Patricia Stanley
Yvette Rees.. Wan
Bert Kwouk ....Tai
Mary Manson ....Judith Delambre
Michael Graham......................................Albert Delambre
Rachel Kempson .... Madame Fournier
Jeremy Wilkins .... Inspector Ronet
Warren Stanhope .... Hotel Manager
Charles Carson.................................... Inspector Charas
Mia Anderson..Nurse
Arnold Bell..Hotel Porter
Stan Simmons........................Heavyset Creature — Samuels

Curse of the Fly was made in 1965, because Robert Lippert thought there might be some life left in the property. Although their relationship to André et al. varies depending on the review, the matter-transmitting Delambres make a final appearance. The family is now represented by Henri (Brian Donlevy) and his two sons, Martin (George Baker) and Albert (Michael Graham).

Harry Spalding's script has Martin, who suffers from periodic bouts of rapid aging caused by inherited fly genes that he controls with a serum, marrying an escaped mental patient, Patricia Stanley (Carole Gray). Martin found her running down the road in her underwear. This scene of her escape is considered by many to be the highlight of the film.

They spend a week together at a hotel in Montreal where Martin is picking up equipment for the transporter and fall in love, after deciding not to tell each other anything about either of their past lives.

Martin needs to install the new equipment to help get his father back to Montreal. The elder Delambre had transported himself to London and was badly burned by radiation when he did so. His injuries were severe enough to put his other son Albert off the whole transportation experiment, but he agrees to send his father back after he recovers enough, since Henri is having problems explaining why he's in London without his passport. The transport is made and Henri makes it back in one piece, thanks to Albert's wrap job to protect him from further burns.

Martin is assisted by Tai and Wan, the two Chinese house servants. Tai is dutiful, but Wan resents what happened to Judith. She doesn't like that Martin has shut her away in the stable, so he won't have to look at her disfigured face and body from a previous failed experiment. Wan lets Judith out from time to time. Wan is not happy Martin has brought home a new wife. She does several things to make Pat doubt her new found sanity, using the deformed Judith to terrorize her.

About this time the Mental Institution comes looking for Pat. The local Inspector investigator finds out she was last seen with Martin Delambre. Inspector Ronet takes the Institute Matron out to the Delambre estate to reclaim her patient. Pat immediately runs away from Madame Fourier out of the room and into the garden. Martin refuses to give Pat up. He produces a valid marriage license. The Matron is not happy, but they leave when asked to.

Pat runs to a part of the estate she has never been to before to escape being taken back. There discovers the locked barn stalls of the "failed" experiments, the two Lab assistants, Dill and Samuels and Judith. Pat is horrified by what she sees in the stables.

Ronet, his curiosity piqued by this odd family, makes an appointment to see Inspector Charas, now played by another actor (Charles Carson), but still the authority on the "Delambre case." Charas is now (understandably) in a nursing home and thus make a few mistakes in relating the sad story of the tragic family to this new investigator. He shows Ronet a photo of the mutated Philippe while describing what happened to Andre. He states, however, that Martin is Andre's grandson and how three generations have suffered from the tragedy. He then says the son (Henri?) fixed the problem, and never mentions Francois (the Uncle), nor does he explain why Philippe changed his name to Henri after he married Cecile and had children, if Donlevy's character is indeed supposed to be Philippe.

This may have been done unintentionally by the screenwriter, as Andre's son is called Henri in the short story, which Lippert had the option on. The name change to Philippe was made in the first films by the studio and Clavell, so this "flub" in the history may have made to avoid a rights issue. Or Lippert's decision to have the script written in Los Angeles and the movie filmed in the

England caused major communication errors. Screenwriter Spaulding was not happy he was not allowed any input while the film was being made.

Henri is convinced Ronet will find out about the failed experiments locked in the barn and since Albert is determined to defect from the project, Henri proposes they abandon Montreal and everyone must move to London to start over. That is, after they have disintegrated the three failed human experiments so there is no evidence of what they have done left at the estate.

Martin is opposed, but evidently realizes it's the only way to be free of Judith, so he can start over with Pat. Henri insists Martin send the first two mistakes — lab assistants Dill and Samuels - through the machine together to London, forcing Albert to kill the resulting fused blob that materializes at the other end. This will bind him to them, lest he be charged with murder and keep him from defecting.

Wan turns Judith loose in an attempt to kill Pat, but she attacks Tai instead. He kills Judith with a wrench. Tai and Wan then disintegrate Judith to hide what they have done. They tell Martin and Henri when they ask, that she ran away, so no one will try to reintegrate her.

Albert has had more than enough and tries to warn Martin not to send Henri through when he is called to do the next transfer. Martin sends Henri anyway, not knowing that the disillusioned Albert has already smashed the reintegrator machine at the other end and there was nothing left for Henri (or Judith) to reintegrate into, so they both remain disintegrated, until someone rebuilds the machines to reintegrate them. It is a quicker, more merciful "death" that the one from radiation that was slowly consuming both of them.

Martin stays integrated, ostensibly to take the blame, but his aging spasm hits almost immediately, he can't get to his serum and he ages to death, right in front of his hysterical second wife. Martin's last words are (of course) "Help me, Help me."

Pat shows Martin's dead body to Ronet, and is probably then returned to the mental institution, although this is not made clear. The film ends with her and the Inspector walking away into the house and the caption: Is this the end? It is, for the franchise, until it is revived in 1986, with the green lighting of a remake of the first film.

This third film, in which no one turns into a fly, but mutated and irradiated victims abound, is considered to be well directed by Don Sharp, whose best known film for Hammer up to this time was *Kiss of the Vampire* (1963).

Inventive as he was, Sharp was severely hobbled by a twenty eight day shooting schedule and the standard Lippert budget of less than $100,000. Lippert was well known for his "90 thousand" genre film budgets and considered it a point of pride he could make his films on that. Lippert hired Brian Donlevy because he was Brian Donlevy, with a career in film that stretches back to 1923. He is probably best remembered for his turns in *Command Decision* (1948) with Clark Gable and playing Quantrill in *Kansas Raiders* (1950). He was in *Brigham Young* (1940) with Vincent Price and in *Destry Rides Again* (1939) with James

Stewart as well as the 1946 version of *The Virginian* with Joel McCrea, playing Trampas, who was a villain in the film versions of this classic novel.

Donlevy played Quatermass in two British movies in the mid 1950's, thus he was familiar to British audiences. Donlevy claimed that the only film people remembered by the time he made *Curse of the Fly* was *The Great McGinty (1940)*. He does better in most reviews than the film.

Donlevy came to London to film at Shepperton Studios and found himself a target of the press. By Fox accounts, he was cordial to everyone on the street who recognized him and was even polite to reporters, telling them there had to be dozens more people around more newsworthy then him to ask questions of. He even thanked Tallulah Bankhead for filming a movie at the same time. She wasn't any easier to interview than he was, but the reporters spent more time chasing after her than chasing after him! If they did find him, Donlevy would remind them, he preferred to make films, rather than talk about them.

George Baker became much better known after this film, landing a small part in the James Bond movie, *On Her Majesty's Secret Service* (1969). He first worked with Roger Moore in *The Persuaders* television series in 1971 and then did a second Bond film with Moore; *The Spy Who Loved Me* in 1977.

Both Baker and fellow Fly and Bond alumnus David Hedison would work with Moore again in *North Sea Hijack*, which was released in the United States in 1980 as *ffolkes*. George Baker is probably best known today (at least in England) for playing Inspector Wexford in a series of British TV movies based on the detective books known collectively as The Ruth Rendell Mysteries.

South African Carole Gray made five films between 1964 and 1966, including *Curse*, and was promoted as a singer, ballerina, professional ball room dancer, and musical comedy star. She married well and left show business after her fifth film.

Curse of the Fly was released on a double bill with *Devils of Darkness*, which also starred Carole Gray. It came and went with lackluster box office and remained the hardest movie of the first trilogy to actually see, until its release on DVD in the UK on in May 26, 2006 and in North America on September 11, 2007 as part of multi-DVD sets.

According to most sources the film was never released on VHS or Betamax, but highlights of the film could be purchased on a Super 8 reel. The movie never made it onto a Laserdisc, but was sold to television. There are several mentions of bad pan-and-scan television screenings over the years. One such screening took place on a Saturday night in Milwaukee, Wisconsin when station WVTV showed the film on October 11, 1986. There was also a mention that the film had been sighted on cable and definitely most recently on The Fox Movie Channel since the DVD came out. It last aired on March 26, 2008 and will most likely air again this year.

This third film has had more releases on DVD in Europe and Australia as a Region 2 and/or a Region 4 than in North America. There are at least four different DVD covers on the various PAL versions of this film offered for sale around the world. The Region 1 (North America) DVD has entirely different cover art than any of these. *Curse of the Fly* was also released in Germany and Italy under the titles *Der Fluch der Fliege* and *La Maledizone della Mosca.*

Channel 4 (British Television) refers to the film as a daft British bookend to the series, that is still entertaining, albeit for unintentional reasons. The British seem fond of the film because of the casting of favorites George Baker and Carole Gray, even if there is isn't much in the way of plot to recommend it. Yvette Rees as a Chinese servant is considered the worst casting, particularly since they did cast Bert Kwouk as the male servant, but she is not the only one suffering under bad make-up in this film.

Some reviews laud the Lovecraftian elements of the film and others credit its moments of eerie moodiness, but mostly the film is dismissed as ludicrous with even more bad science than its predecessors. One reviewer gleefully points out that's the earth rotation would speed up Henri's reentry so much that he would splatter on the glass on the reintegration chamber upon reintegration, so once again the machine does not work the way it would in real life and thus conquer the fourth dimension as touted in the film publicity.

The screenwriter thought Brian Donlevy was miscast, others critics fault the pacing and the script, questioning why a third film was even made, since there is no fly transformation and the story is now stretched beyond anything logical, except as a "curse."

The lack of box office, plus the body count made it extremely unlikely a fourth film would be made and no attempt was made for another twenty years.

the Fly (1986) — David Cronenberg, Jeff Goldblum and Geena Davis.

THE FLY (1986)
20TH CENTURY FOX, 95 MINUTES

Producer...Stuart Cornfeld
Director ....David Cronenberg
Co-Producers .... Mark Boyman and Kip Ohman
Writers.......................Charles Edward Pogue and David Cronenberg, based on the short story by George Langelaan
Cinematographer...Mark Irwin
Editor ....Ronald Sanders
Music...Howard Shore
Production Design... Carol Spier
Art Director.. Rolf Harvey
Set Decorator ....Elinor Rose Galbraith
Costume Design..Denise Cronenberg
Makeup..Shonagh Jabour
Hairstyles .... Ivan Lynch
Wardrobe .... Trysha Bakker
Sound .... David Evans
Creature Effects .... Chris Walas
Special Effects...................................... Louis Craig and Ted Ross
Visual Effects.. Hoyt Yeatman

CAST

Jeff Goldblum .... Seth Brundle
Geena Davis .... Veronica Quaife
John Getz.. Stathis Borans
Joy Buechel .... Tawny
Leslie Carlson... Dr. Brent Cheevers
George Chuvalo .... Marky
Michael Copeman..2nd Man in Bar
David Cronenberg... Gynecologist
Carol Lazare ....Nurse
Shawn Hewitt .... Clerk

The Fly was remade in 1986. Screenwriter Charles Edward Pogue suggested the idea of remaking the 1958). Pogue's prior film had been *Psycho III*, considered the weakest of the sequels and one Anthony Perkins only agreed to participate in because he was allowed to direct. The original director was Robert Bierman, who had one full-length movie credit to his name at the time, a straight to cable thriller. This combination of writing and directing would have created an entirely different film, but Bierman left the project before production started when an accident in Africa killed his daughter.

David Cronenberg was brought in as a replacement, mostly at the insistence of Mel Brooks who was quietly underwriting the film. Cronenberg's contract allowed him to modify the script as he saw fit, and he made significant changes to the script; reworking key plot points, overhauling the dialogue and even changing the names of the characters. The concept of a fly-human hybrid was Pogue's idea, but not much else of his script remained unscathed.

The new film starred Jeff Goldblum as researcher Seth Brundle in a much more modern retelling of the same old problem; namely Man and fly DNA become deadly when combined. While experimenting with his transport pods, Seth accidentally splices his genes to those of the fly, and his lover, Ronnie Quaife (Geena Davis), is forced to witnesses his inevitably degeneration into what he calls Brundlefly. Throw in a love triangle and uncontrollable insect urges; the end result is Ronnie pregnant by Seth and her employer and former lover Borans menaced and then maimed — he had a hand and foot dissolved by fly vomit - by the hybrid man-fly.

In the end, Seth begs Ronnie to kill him as he cannot stand what his blended DNA has made him become. She doesn't think she can, but finally does end his life.

This version of *The Fly* won the 1986 Academy Award for Best Makeup and is not for the faint of stomach. Audience members who could take it loved the realistic and often times quite gross transformation of man into Brundlefly.

This remake was released on VHS and Betamax for rental in 1987, with VHS re-releases in 1992 and 1997. An EP laserdisc version was also released. The first DVD version of the 1986 remake came on September 5, 2000 when Fox re-released all the films, except *Curse of the Fly* on both VHS and DVD simultaneously.

The film was re-released on October 4, 2005 as a 2 Disc Special Edition DVD with bonus material, which then became part of the 7 Disc Mega DVD Set in Europe in 2006. This particular version was also released in Canada on October 4 in a bi-lingual version that gave the viewer 2 discs — one of *The Fly* (in English) and one of *La Mouche* (in French). A single disc was also released simultaneously. It had a different gold Award Series cover and played up the title that this was *David Cronenberg's The Fly* in large type. A second single disc came out on in March of 2006 with the familiar black and green cover and a newly repackaged double pack called *The Fly Collector Set*, consisting of single discs of *The Fly* and *Fly II* came out on August 8, 2007. A double pack of *The Fly* Two Disc Collector's Edition and the DVD of the 1968 *Planet of the Apes* was released in North America on July 25, 2006.

The European releases are many and all have different cover art. The first PAL DVD came out on October 22, 2001 and was a double disc release of *The Fly* and *Fly II*. The next release was as singles on August 15, 2005. 2006 brought the release of another double disc with both films as an alternate to the Megaset. Both versions were released on May 29. There is also a Cinema Resolve Edition that came out on July 3, 2006 which is the British Version of the NTSC 2 disc Special Edition with all the extras and another alternative to the Megaset. This DVD is also available in a French Version. There was also a DIVX version of this film for as long as that format lasted in 2006.

The 1986 version of *The Fly* is the first of the film series to be recorded on Blu-Ray Disc, which is the system that was chosen by Fox from the beginning, so there will be no HD DVD version of any of these films. The Fox Blu-Ray disc was released on October 9, 2007 in North American and can purchased through European retailers, provided one has the Blu-Ray player required to view it.

The 1986 version of *The Fly* was a huge hit, so naturally talk of a sequel started. Cronenberg was not interested in coming back or repeating himself, but Fox managed to have their sequel by recruiting Chris Walas, who won the Academy Award for the Brundlefly make-up, to direct.

Walas had always wanted to make a "Son of" horror movie and that's what he did. A good old monster runs amuck in the sterile halls of Bartok Industries. On February 10, 1989, Fox released *Fly II,* with the tag line: Like Father, Like Son. Not quite, but it made for good copy.

the Fly II (1989) — Lee Richardson, Eric Stoltz and Daphne Zuniga.

THE FLY II (1989)
20TH CENTURY FOX 105 MINUTES

Producer.....Steven-Charles Jaffe
Executive Producer.....Stuart Cornfeld
Director.....Chris Walas
Writers.....Story by Mick Garris, Screenplay by Jim Wheat, Ken Wheat, and Frank Darabont; based on characters created by George Langelaan
Cinematographer.....Robin Vidgeon
Editor.....Sean Barton
Music.....Christopher Young
Associate Producer.....Gillian Richardson
Production Design.....Michael S. Bolton
Art Director.....Sandy Coltrane
Set Decorator.....Rose Marie McSherry
Costume Design.....Christopher Ryan
Makeup.....Jayne Dancose and Sydney Silvert
Hairstyles.....Sherry Linder-Gygll and Brenda Gibson
Sound.....Leslie Schatz

Special Effects by Chris Walas, Inc.
Visual Effects by Available Light Limited and Video Image

CAST

Eric Stoltz.....Martin Brundle
Daphne Zuniga.....Beth Logan
Lee Richardson.....Anton Bartok
John Getz.....Stathis Borans
Frank C. Turner.....Shepard
Anne Marie Lee.....Dr. Jainway
Gary Chalk.....Scorby
Saffron Henderson.....Veronica "Ronnie" Quaife
Harley Cross.....10 year old Martin
Matthew Moore.....four year old Martin
Rob Roy.....Wiley
Andrew Rhodes.....Hargis
Pat Bermell.....Mackenzie
William S. Taylor.....Dr. Trimble
Jerry Wasserman.....Simms
Duncan Fraser.....Obstetrician
Janet Hodgkinson.....Nurse
Sean O'Byrne.....Perinatologist
Mike Winlaw.....Neonatologist
Allan Lysell.....Guard A
Suzanne Ristic.....Guard #1

Danny Virtue..Guard #2
Kimelly Anne Warren..Maria
Ken Camroux...Lindner
Bruce Harwood...Technician
Lorena Gale...Women
Bill Dow..Man
David Mylrea...Flywalker
Robert Metcalfe..Observer #1
Garwin Sanford...Observer #2
Tom Heaton...Manager
Cecilia Warren..Anchorwoman
Andrea Mann...Cute Girl
Sterling Cottingham...................................Newborn Baby Martin
Rodney Clough, Junior....................................1 1/2 year old Martin
Jeff Goldblum.................................Seth Brundle in archive footage

In the fifth film, Ronnie dies giving birth to Seth's son and Martin (Eric Stoltz) is raised by the evil industrialist who owned the telepods. Martin eventually mutates into the inevitable fly creature after five years of accelerated growth, thanks to his fly DNA. This is an event Anton Bartok has been anticipating, since all his experiments with the pod technology have ended in failure. Martin shows every sigh of being a genius when he is mature and will be able to fix the pods so they can finally be marketed.

Martin manages to escape his father's fate in a happy ending by figuring out a cure for himself once he gets the pods working. Martin does this by transferring all his mutant fly DNA to Bartok. Anton comes out of the pod an even more hideous beast than Martin's pet dog was turned into, after an earlier failed transporter experiment.

Thus Martin Brundle managed to survive his transformation in very much the same way Philippe is saved in *The Return of the Fly* and gets the girl (Daphne Zuniga). The films have come full circle.

Walas set out to make an old-fashioned monster movie and on this level the film succeeds. Eric Stoltz gives Martin a wide-eyed innocence that works very well and this is considered one of his better roles. Stoltz is probably best known for being in the film *Mask*. This sequel was about as well received as *Curse of the Fly* and only made 20 million dollars, so there was zero interest in making a *Fly III*.

Fly II was released on VHS and Betamax for rental in 1989, with VHS re-releases in 1992 and 1997. A laserdisc version was also released in 1989. The first DVD version of the sequel came on September 5, 2000 when Fox re-released all these films, except *Curse of the Fly* on both VHS and DVD simultaneously. This would be the last VHS release.

The film was re-released on October 5, 2005 as a 2 Disc Special Edition DVD with bonus material, which then became part of the 7 Disc Mega DVD Set in Europe on May 29, 2006 as well as being part of all the double feature releases mentioned above. This Special Edition *Fly II* DVD released in 2005 contains the AMC documentary *The Fly Papers* that aired on AMC in 2000 as part of its special features. This AMC documentary that covers all five films made and is quite good.

The film has mostly been released on double DVD discs (as stated above) and the film can be readily bought as a single DVD or in tandem with the 1986 version of *The Fly* in both North America and Europe. The film was even released in Turkey under the title *Sinek II*. Another poster touts it as *Muva II*.

Both the 1986 Fly and the 1989 sequel have extensive bonus materials of documentaries and commentaries that go more deeply into the making of both of these films than I ever could. Renting either 2 disc Special Edition DVDs is recommended. These materials, in particular, the three hour documentary, *Fear of the Flesh*, will tell you more than you ever wanted to know about either film.

THE FLY (2006) FOX SEARCHLIGHT FILMS

Directed by Todd Lincoln
Written by Todd Lincoln and Martin Scheck. (Never made)

Fox Searchlight optioned a treatment by Todd Lincoln and his writing partner Martin Scheck and the film was announced in *Fangoria* Magazine in early 2006. Todd's ideas for his version; he was also set to direct the film, ended up being too outside the box for Fox. Someone still became a Fly, but who, how and why was a completely brand new scenario.

The Studio was looking for a more straightforward remake of one of the earlier versions and eventually passed on this, releasing Lincoln to work on other projects such as *Hack/Slash*. One of Lincoln's best ideas was to definitely write a role in his film for David Hedison, the original 1958 leading man, so it is disappointing that this 2006 version was never green lighted by the studio so that event could happen for the fiftieth anniversary.

Fox Searchlight remains attached to the project as a distributor, but there has been no new activity since November of 2007. There was forum talk in February 2008 if there was any interest in reviving the movie remake, but so far it is only talk. The time to film anything for the anniversary has passed, but the idea persists that another film could and should be made in the near future.

HOWARD SHORE'S *THE FLY* OPERA (2008)

David Cronenberg has been planning a third installment of his Brundle saga for some time — he is doing it as an opera. Brundlefly is set to sing on September 7, 2008 in Los Angeles. This U.S. premiere with a libretto by David Henry Hwang, has been scheduled to run September 7-27, 2008.

David Cronenberg will direct. The opera will be based on his celebrated 1986 horror film and on the original 1957 short story by George Langelaan. Both

Cronenberg and Shore believe the material is made to be an opera. Howard Shore, in particular, believes that Langelaan's story of love and death, and true love surviving in the face of physical decay and ultimate sacrifice are elements that can be adapted beautifully to this genre.

The opera reunites three of the principals involved in the 1986 movie, the director/screenwriter, soundtrack composer and costume designer. Plácido Domingo will conduct, and bass-baritone Daniel Okulitch has been cast in the title role. Mezzo-sopranos Ruxandra Dunose and Beth Clayton and tenors Kurt Streit and Jay Hunter Morris are the other principals.

The sets are being designed by Dante Ferretti and the costumes are by Denise Cronenberg, the director's sister. *The Fly* is a co-production with Théâtre du Châtelet in Paris where the World Premiere will be held on July 2, 2008.

It was not known at the time this book was printed if this opera version will be released on DVD. So keep watching for announcements, between the push to remake the film and The Opera, the Fly saga may continue to evolve into 2009.

Sculpt and build-up by S.M. Clark. Kit available from CultTVman hobby shop (www.culttvman.biz).

PHOTO COURTESY OF S.M. CLARK, 2008

CHAPTER 9

THE FLY IN POPULAR CULTURE

The Ninth Season Halloween episode of the animated series *The Simpsons* is probably the Fly parody that has been seen by most everyone, as it has been shown annually in syndication ever since it's first airing. Homer buys two transport pods from Springfield's resident mad scientist Professor Frink at his garage sale. After telling Bart not to touch the machines, Bart experiments with them anyway and promptly mixes up the family dog and cat into two creatures: one with two heads and one with two butts. The second creature he promptly gives to his sister Lisa. Bart then goes through the machine to become a SuperFly but it doesn't quite work out the way he wanted it to, as he becomes a tiny head on a fly that can talk and his body ends up with a large yellow eyed fly head that can't talk. Marge promptly adopts the creature and happily keeps feeding it. Lisa is responsible for getting her brother back in one piece, at least until Homer finds out and picks up an axe to destroy the machine, but ends up chasing Bart with it, instead. The show won a Golden Reel Award for sound editing and the dramatic underscore was nominated for an Emmy.

This is not the only television show to reference the first film, but it is one of the most faithful. The "Fly vs. Fly" segment of "Treehouse of Horror VIII" (Season 9, episode 4) would be the last Simpsons episode that Brad Bird worked on but his affection for classic movies would continue in his future projects such as *The Iron Giant* and *The Incredibles.*

Gary Larson took his *Far Side* cartoon to television for a Halloween a special in 1994. *Tales from the Far Side* included a great send-up of the original film, making *The Fly* the in-flight movie on a planeload of (what else) flies! Helene whips off the cloth revealing Andre and everyone cheers! Until the little plane is hit by lightning and everyone starts screaming in time with the movie. Then the plane crashes — into a human car's windshield.

The short lived Marvel cartoon series *Spider-Woman* (1979) had an episode called "Spider Woman Vs. The Fly," where the (obligatory) mad scientist is transformed into the fiendish "Fly" after experimenting (of course) with animal splicing. The television show list goes on with *Jimmy Neutron* "My Son, the Hamster"; *Dexter's Laboratory* "Sole Brother"; *Spongebob Squarepants* "SquidBob TentaclePants"; *The Grim Adventures of Billy and Mandy* "Zip Your Fly"; *Johnny Bravo* "I, Fly"; *Family Guy* "8 Simple Rules for Buying My Teenage Daughter" and *Eerie, Indiana* "Heart on a Chain."

The cartoon television show that borrowed the heaviest from the original film was *Teenage Mutant Ninja Turtles.* Their sub par villain Baxter Stockman was a man-fly with a lab coat, wings and major attitude.

Stockman appears as a recurring villain in almost all of the various incarnations of the Turtles franchise, but it only in the 1987-1996 animated television series that Baxter turns into a Fly. Baxter episodes include: "Enter: The Fly," "Return of the Fly," "Bye, Bye, Fly," "Son of Return of the Fly II," "Landlord of the Flies" and "Revenge of the Fly." Even the episode titles are spoofs. The Fly Baxter Stockman also appeared in five TMNT video games based on this cartoon series, was a character was in the 1990 Video TMNT: Coming Out of their Shell Tour (1990) and in four episodes of the 2003-2005 cartoon series. An action figure of Baxter was produced for the 2007 movie line of toys, but he is not listed as being a character in the actual film. Maybe that's why Baxter looks more like a Doctor Octopus ripoff than a fly in his latest appearance.

The Fly is also referenced in such diverse movies as *Howling III* (1987); *The Exorcist III* (1990); *Awakenings* (1990); *Beetlejuice* (1990); *City Slickers* (1991); *Terminator 2: Judgment Day* (1991); *Addams Family Values* (1993); *Wolf* (1994); *Multiplicity* (1996); *The First Wives Club* (1996); *Doctor Dolittle* (1998); *Galaxy Quest* (1999); *Nutty Professor II: The Klumps* (2000); *Little Nicky* (2000); *Emperor's New Groove* (2000); *Charlie and the Chocolate Factory* (2005); *Wallace and Gromit in the Curse of the Wererabbit* (2005) and the forgettable *Mansquito* (2005). Quality issues aside, *The Fly* remains a classic of the genre, and always ripe for further parody.

In 2005, The American Film Institute held a contest to determine the most influential movie lines ever uttered. 400 nominations from 100 years of film were accepted. "Help me! Help me! was nominated from *The Fly* and ended up listed as #123. "Be Afraid. Be Very Afraid" from *The Fly* (1986) was also nominated.

The Fly was a Fox property and as such never enjoyed the opportunities for licensed merchandising that the Universal Monsters enjoyed, so there are far fewer collectibles associated with this film series, but several licensed items do exist. There has been one Fly action figure based on the original movie and that was not licensed as such. In 1977, in the wake of the success of monster figure from AHI (under license from Universal) and Mego (characters in the public domain), Tomland released "Famous Monsters of the Movies," four monsters not released by the competition — Yeti, Cyclops, Morlock and The Fly. However, Tomland neglected to secure the rights to the characters and had to change the names of the series to "Famous Monsters of Legend."

There were three versions of the Tomland Fly figure. All versions are 8 inches tall with 14 points of articulation. All wear a lab coat over a shirt, tie and pants. The difference is color — one wears matching tan lab coat and pants, the second sported a white outfit and the third was a glow-in-the-dark variation that had the tan lab coat with white pockets. The shirt is blue and the tie is red in all versions, but there's some variation in the shades during the run. The carded figure was in distribution for about a year. The figure was sold in Europe under the Combex brand while American dolls were sold as Tomland or Kresge (K-Mart).

All variants include the trademark bunny logo stamped on the lower back and are considered highly collectible, especially the glow-in-the-dark version.

A modified version of the figure was also released as an alien named "Oov" on a blister card in a "Star Raiders" series, to cash in on some of the Star Wars figure mania. This version commonly has the tan lab coat but with white pockets. The series was also released in a glow-in-the-dark series with Oov's hands and head replace with glowing parts. The head was subsequently reused for another alien "Dado" in 1978 in the glow-in-the-dark Space Raiders line. The figure was updated with new limbs and re-released in both the 1979 Space Fighter line and the 1982 Space People line.

The easiest collectible for anyone to purchase was the above mentioned Baxter Stockman from the *Teenage Ninja Mutant Turtles* cartoon television series. This mass produced five inch action figure was first released in 1987 by Playmates Toys and reissued in 1989. The fly swatter accessory is a different color in the re-issue. One only has to read the character card to see where creator Kevin Eastman got his inspiration for this character. Baxter is a mutant with the mind of a scientist and the body of a common housefly. Stockman's favorite catchphrase is "Help me!" and is never seen without his lab coat. A series of trading cards also produced from the first cartoon show feature Baxter as a fly. The Baxter cards appear in Card Series Two and were numbered in the 120's and 140's.

Another common collectible is a Bart Simpson action figure with the head of a fly, made in 2000, also by Playmates Toys. Bart is one of four "Treehouse of Horror" Figures made for this ToysRUs exclusive "Springfield Cemetery" Playset. The other figures were Homer as King Kong, Ned Flanders as the Devil and Mr. Burns as a white haired Dracula. A "Treehouse of Horror" themed Monopoly game was produced by Parker Brothers. A 112 card "Treehouse of Horrors" UNO game by Sabada was also made.

A Gee key chain figure of Superfly Bart with multifaceted fly eyes was produced by Toys2R in Hong Kong as part of a Bart 3 inch Gee collection. The figure is number 8 in a first set release of 12 in 2007. The collection was to include 24 different figures. There was also a bendable figure of Bart with the Fly head that was part of a Best of Bart set of five. These were made by bendie figure company NJ Croce in California as part of their Simpsons license from Fox.

In 1994, Fox commissioned a series of collectibles based on paper publicity items from the first film. The original "screaming" poster was reissued and sold for $8.00. A smaller post card version of the same poster was encased in Lucite and became a paperweight. All the collectibles in this line were touted as "a limited edition of 1,958." Two t-shirts — a white Tee with the poster art stenciled on it and a black Tee with a red target and a B&W picture of *The Fly* monster and the tag line: She would scream for the rest of her life were also produced. The final item was a framed blueprint of the plans of the disintegrator/reintegrator booths with 4 stills from the movies.

PMC Publishing, an Italian company, released a series of movie poster trading cards in 1995, including card #76, the 1958 film poster in full-color. The

1993 Joe Dante film *Matinee* stars John Goodman as a thinly disguised William Castle premiering a new film in Key West on the eve of the Cuban Missile Crisis. The film being premiered is of a very familiar theme — *Mant!* "Half Man, Half Ant, All Terror."

In 2007, Breygent Marketing Inc. of Canada reproduced the original poster from the first film for their *Classic Science Fiction and Horror Posters Collection Trading Cards* 49 card set. *The Fly* poster is card #33. These card boxes also included hand sketched poster art (randomly inserted) of some of the classic posters, including seven different treatments of *The Fly* poster.

With the success of the Universal Monsters as Aurora model kits in the 1960s, it might be assumed that Fox creations would follow suit. Fox simply never exploited their films as effectively. They had a number of films that would lend themselves to the series: The robot Gort from *The Day the Earth Stood Still* (1951) and any of the assorted giant creatures from *Journey to the Center of the Earth* (1959) or *The Lost World* (1960) would lend themselves to a plastic kit. *The Fly* would be a natural and although Aurora didn't create a Fly model kit, there were a number of later releases. Among the notable kits were two from Geometric Designs, a ¼ scale bust with circular base and a 1/25 scale full figure in their Micro-Mania line.

The most recent kit was a limited edition re-release of a kit from Creature Arts, underwritten by CultTVman's Fantastic Modeling. Sculpted by S.M. Clark and designed as an action shot of Andre smashing his equipment, the kit was sized and stylistically posed to evoke the Aurora model kits. The re-release was a very limited edition, produced in honor of David Hedison's appearance at the 2005 Wonderfest in Louisville, Kentucky. The boxed kit contained 10 parts including a base and nameplate. The model included waterslide decals for the equipment panels and a special certificate of authenticity signed by David Hedison.

A Japanese garage kit company, Monster Shop USA produced a vinyl figure and lab diorama in 1993. It was marketed as being the original Fly, but with an oversized head, it was strictly from *Return of the Fly*, one of the few merchandising pieces for the sequel. A trading card (#19) produced in 1961 by NuCards as part of their Horror Monster series. A second card (#103) was released two years later in the "Terror Monster Series" from Rosan Printing Company. A 12-inch *Return of the Fly* doll was made in 2003 by Majestic Studios, a Hong Kong based company who specialized in licensed action figures, particularly those from films that have slipped through the cracks and never had any figures made. "Philippe" was the first in their line of *Film Freaks* and debuted at the 2003 New York Toy Fair. It was released in the United States in 2004 and was sold at various science fiction conventions that year.

There were two resin figures that came out in the late 1980's, probably in response to the 1986 sequel movie starring Jeff Goldblum. The first one was made in Germany, and was about 3 inches tall. The figure was half business suited man (in brown resin) on one side and half black resin insect on the other side, making him look more like the Batman villain Two Face than our movie monster. The second figure was made in Japan by Bandai as one of their classic deformed monsters about 1 centimeter tall. This was cast in either green or white plastic. The claw and head is the closest match to the 1958 movie monster ever made.

MacFarlane Toys made a six inch action figure of Brundlefly from the 1986 movie in their Series III collection of Movie Maniacs. He came with a

Sculpt and build-up by S.M. Clark. Kit available from CultTVman hobby shop (www.culttvman.biz).

PHOTO COURTESY OF S.M. CLARK, 2008

poster from the 1986 film and was released to toy stores in September of 2000. Sideshow Collectibles then released 20th anniversary 1:6 scale maquettes of Brundlefly and Martinfly in 2006 in limited editions of 250 each.

Now that we have seen some of the impact *The Fly* has had on pop culture, let us now turn to a critical analysis of these films. As a classic film, *The Fly* has been reviewed and deconstructed many times over the past fifty years and for the most part the reviews have been favorable. There is something about this movie that strikes home with all who have seen it; despite the fact what happens in the film hasn't happened yet, given the current state of our technology.

The low budget, low risk "weirdie" (as this kind of film has now been classified by film scholars) with its combination of science fiction, horror, and fantasy all blended together in exploitable fashion — became it's own genre. These films supposedly promised the moviegoer of the late 1950's terror or wonder, but mostly delivered mediocre acting performances and unintentional comedy.

A staple during the late 1950's and early 1960's, these films were one of the few genres the studios made any money on in theatres at that time, despite their cheap special effects, bad monster makeup and labored shocks. It was a rare film that lived up to the high concept title it had been given. You were more likely to suffer through the angst and bad slang of *Teenagers from Outer Space* (1959) than see a movie that had any dramatic quality.

Andre successfully transports a guinea pig.

The Fly became a model for this genre, because it eschewed the sensationalism that was rampant in these films. The movie was filmed with restraint and implied so much by simple suggestion. The monster of the title remained hidden under a dark cloth for most of the film, so we could only guess at what hideous thing he had become.

When Andre is finally revealed, the extremely effective photography leaves us with an image we will never forget. This remains the central scene of the film. This movie has two lasting images that grab the audience and never let go.

Major suspension of disbelief is critical when watching this story as filmed. It is the skillfully crafted story that carries the viewer through, slowly revealing more and more until the puzzle is solved. This slow reveal was the way films were made in the 1950's and it serves admirably here to give this particular movie its unnerving eeriness.

The disembodied yowl of the disintegrated cat is one scene that is always mentioned in this regard; as well as the scene where Francois sits in the garden and the audience can hear the tiny voice yelling for help and he can not. There is the frantic chase by Helene, Philippe and Emma to catch the white headed fly, only to have it fly out the window. There is the hollow knocking we hear from Andre on the other side of his locked lab door. It is the unbearable tension of this film that slowly, inexorably, builds into the sad inevitability that Andre will not be saved from what he has done to himself.

The film succeeds because of the serious way this story is presented. The viewer is asked to believe in something ludicrous and they actually do. We root

Helene tries to understand how important Andre's work is to him.

for the doomed character because he was a good person trying so hard to do the right thing, only to have everything go horribly wrong.

There is stateliness to the film. Clavell hints something awful has happened, but withholds the shock of what until the very end. Everyone is so terribly decent and soft-spoken about the murder. Francois never once reproaches Helene for having killed his brother. We believe that he feels helping her and ultimately taking care of her is the nobler thing he has to do — under the circumstances.

The moral of *The Fly* is an old one. Just as Daedalus and Icarus learned, when the search for knowledge goes too far, it is considered blasphemous and thus, one will be punished with an unnatural death. The film implies it is okay to kill "a thing," since it is no longer human. In fact, our beliefs demand that we must kill it. Andre has crossed over this unwritten, unspoken and unfortunate cultural line that mandates that the unexplainable and unclassifiable must be destroyed.

It is precisely this belief that carries the movie and made it the classic it is today. Trying to make sense of the fantasy science involved and the physical reality of what would really happen in the transporter mutation will only give one a headache. The elements used were chosen because they create dramatic tension. The science to explain their use is riddled with 1950's inaccuracies and implausibilities. Since we still don't have a working transporter fifty years after this film was made to tell us what would really happen, the story must remain what it is: science fiction; with the emphasis on the fiction.

Why has *The Fly* lasted as a film we will watch over and over again? It has become in its own way modern myth. Over the span of fifty years, this film has developed its own niche mythology about how and why transporter accidents occur.

This ever developing mythos roughly parallels the development of the Grandfather Paradox so prevalent in backwards time travel stories and movies. Both are staples in the cautionary 'don't do this unless you want to come to bad end' style of modern filmmaking. One must use teleportation wisely or end up as a mutated accident and then have to do away with oneself.

The fly mythos depends on our inherent mistrust of technology. As we became increasingly dependent on electronic devices after 1958; were we not caught in an ever-increasing (spider) web of ever more advanced technologies? So much so, that this simple fantasy story of careless technological experimentation which ends in spectacular disaster has become more relevant today than it was to audiences in 1958? We have yet to build a computer that can take over the world, but that hasn't kept our paranoia from making that myth the plot of several other movies.

Langelaan put his World War II experiences with technology's escalating destructive power into the original 1957 short story as François Delambre's dislike of private home telephones. Are the recent spate of movies that feature terrorization by cell phone only the latest manifestation of our deeply imbedded cultural distrust of all new technology? Has anything really changed in fifty years? Are we as afraid and paranoid now as we were in 1958, when this film resonated with that fear and took off at the box office?

All the filmed sequels only reinforce this developed mythos that messing with technology one does not understand leads to disaster. You end up mutated or worse: totally disintegrated and/or the victim of a mercy killing.

The other reason the fly films remain popular to this day is that they have more substance than the average "atomic monster run amuck" films of their eras. The original film unfolds more as a mystery, with Francois having to figure out the various clues to solve how his brother was murdered. Then he discovers Andre committed suicide, rather than lose his soul to the monster he had become.

The second film is more about love and revenge, as the son does not repeat his father's mistake, but is inadvertently transformed into a fly hybrid by his assistant, who then tries to murder him by disintegration, so he can steal the transportation process and sell it to the highest bidder.

There is a certain justice inherent in both of these films and the inadvertent nature of both transformations leaves no one to blame for the ensuing deaths, but both strongly reinforce the idea and developing mythos that this science should not and cannot be used. All the principals involved have no idea how to use it wisely or they become corrupted by the promise of what it can achieve. The third film is the first to abuse of the science of transportation. This abuse is the main reason the principals die in the third installment.

These ideas and mythos carry over to the 1986 sequel, where Seth is also undone by love and greed and becomes something he does not want to be and asks to be destroyed. His son Martin exacts revenge over the greed and

The camera prepares to roll and shoot a close-up of Andre's blackboard message to Helene.

mismanagement of transporter technology by Bartok. Martin managed emancipation from his pre-determined ill fate. His transmutation is not done by his own hand and thus is reversible because of his innocence.

Martin Brundle and Philip Delambre were able to overcome their dual existence paradox and live because someone loved them enough to help them make it right. Henri and Martin Delambre could not find that kind of love and died.

Andre Delambre and Seth Brundle were both killed by the woman who loved them enough to release them from the torment of what they had done to themselves. Not your average love stories by any means, but interesting enough in each version to compel viewers to watch the films over and over again.

So what is the pop culture legacy of *The Fly*? What makes the first film such a classic that it is still watched? It is a combination of many factors, the story, the cast and the fantastic elements, but ultimately, it is the universality of Andre's struggle with what he had hoped to do with the technology and what actually happened to him. That struggle touches everyone who has ever watched this film.

Al Hedison in full makeup as Andre the Fly.
PHOTO COURTESY OF THE PERSONAL COLLECTION OF DAVID HEDISON, 2008

CHAPTER 10

A LITTLE SOMETHING I WROTE ON *THE FLY*

OR, *THE SQUEAK HEARD 'ROUND THE WORLD*
BY MARTY BAUMANN

I met David Hedison at a 1998 party that was being thrown in the midst of a horror, sci-fi and memorabilia convention called Chiller in Arlington, Virginia. Dozens of fans were crowded into a hotel suite along with a handful of celebrity guests, all of them veterans of vintage fantasy films and television programs. Hedison was charming and distinguished, with a neatly trimmed gray beard and snowy hair. "Yes, it's true," he told those cloistered in his corner of the room. "I can't walk down the street without someone yelling, 'Help me! Help me!' "

He'd first shrieked that desperate plea some 40 years earlier as *The Fly* ("The monster created by atoms gone wild," as one arresting tagline urgently screamed). Hedison (known at the time as Al Hedison) portrayed Andre Delambre in the 1958 shocker about a scientist testing his theories of matter transportation and managing to scramble his molecules with those of a housefly in the process. The climactic scene — and surely this is no spoiler considering the film's vaunted reputation — finds Hedison's tiny, withered head atop the body of a fly, ensnared in a spider's web, wailing in a squeak of a voice as eight-legged Death stalks nearer.

That squeaky "Help me" is one of the most memorable and oft-referenced bits of dialogue in screen history. It evokes titters from contemporary audiences who simultaneously find the scene repulsive. I think it elicited the same reaction 50 years ago; bemusement mingled with revulsion, smiles of astonishment curdling into horrified disgust. If you're reading this, you've surely seen the film. Admit it; initially you likely wanted to laugh at the sheer banality of the tiny peeping man stuck in the web. But, outlandish though it may be, the scene touches the queasy core of your gut. The initial amusement is fleeting. You empathize with the prostrate fly's helplessness and cringe at the idea of his being devoured by an arachnid.

Horror films are popular because we like to be scared, as long as we don't relinquish our control over the situation. Watching in the safety of a movie theater or the comfort of our home we realize this control. The fright is very real, but a giggle diffuses it, alleviates tension and returns us to reality. If it is the job of the horror filmmaker to try to make the outlandish seem real, then certainly *The Fly* is among the boldest attempts. C'mon! An itsy, bitsy fly with a man's head? On its surface, the notion is amusing, but deep down; you feel the fly-man's vulnerability. Of course, there are the jaded few who aren't about to admit to being frightened outright by something so patently preposterous as the predicament of a tiny, screeching man-fly, so they mask embarrassing squeamishness with a laugh.

The provocation of these intertwined natural reactions — amusement co-mingling with horror, being simultaneously entertained and repulsed by Hedison's helplessness — were key to *The Fly's* success. That's the power of the squeaking fly. Like Frankenstein's monster, it is repugnant and sympathetic. It repels as it attracts and entertains. That's the key to a good horror yarn. Importantly, let's not confuse horror with the dehumanizing, sadistic, misogynist torture pornography that passes for horror these days; films that feature no element of the supernatural or scientific, that seem to exist solely to degrade humanity in general, and women in particular.

Public response at the time of *The Fly's* release was astounding. It was one of only a handful of 1950s sci-fi films that accrued legendary status in its own time. Upon its release, the buzz (if you'll pardon the irresistible pun) was incredible, generating long lines at box offices the world over. "Help me" became a catchphrase, a punch line, the film's signature. There were songs written in homage including a bit of exotica by jazz drummer Bobby Christian interrupted at intervals by a helium-voiced vocalist piping, "Help me! Help me!" Very few genre films are so completely assimilated into the greater web (again, do pardon me) of popular culture. It warranted two sequels, the so-so *Return of the Fly* and the forgettable *Curse of the Fly*. Grossmeister David Cronenberg remade it in 1986, and the successful remake merited a sequel, *The Fly 2*. (As this is written, rumors of yet another film remake continue to circulate.)

Interestingly, Hedison was disappointed with several aspects of the finished original film, in particular the way his voice was sped up on the soundtrack for the classic "Help me" finale. Hedison maintains that it would have been far more frightening had they retained his natural voice. ("I was screaming my lungs out on the set!") I wonder if it would have been half as memorable. There's something altogether unsettling in that pitiable little peep. We pity Andre Delambre, and sympathy, as novelist Joseph Conrad pointed out, is a form of fear.

It's a misconception that, in the 1950s and '60s, all serious, aspiring actors were ashamed to appear in horror films. Not in Hedison's case, at least. He embraced the source material — a short story by George Langelaan that appeared in Playboy, adapted for the screen by James Clavell — with gusto. He may have studied serious drama with legendary acting coach Uta Hagen, but Hedison saw the potential — both dramatic and financial — in the story of the half-man, half-fly. When both Michael Rennie (*The Day the Earth Stood Still*) and Rick Jason (TV's *Combat!*) passed on the project and the script landed on Hedison's doorstep, he jumped at the opportunity. Whereas Jason objected to the prospect of having his face obscured for much of the film, Hedison raced to production chief Buddy Adler brimming with suggestions as to how the makeup might be rendered. Inspired by what had been accomplished in the

1931 version of *Dr. Jekyll and Mr. Hyde,* he suggested that a gradual transformation realized through a succession of increasingly grotesque make-ups, would be more disturbing. (Cronenberg's *Fly,* starring Jeff Goldblum as the transformed scientist, employed this to genuine effect.) Unfortunately, Hedison's suggestions were dropped in favor of outfitting him with a rubber mask.

The mask is one of the film's few weak links. It is an otherwise well-cast, well-written, snappily directed story, with much to set it apart from your average B-movie shocker. In large measure, it is about family. Hedison's love for his wife and son is the story's hub. On subordinate levels, it explores the responsibilities that come with rapid advances in science, man's meddling in the natural order of things, and, most audaciously, it addresses euthanasia. This is an ambitious agenda for a monster movie.

The cast is superb. Hedison, who might otherwise appear too youthful without that dash of grey in his hair, is arresting in the lead role of Andre. Vincent Price as Andre's concerned, compassionate brother, Francois, turns in a typically solid performance, and Herbert Marshall, nearing the twilight of a long, lustrous career, is happily cast as the local police inspector. (The story of how Price and Marshall ruined take after take by giggling uncontrollably at the very idea of encountering a tiny peeping fly-man has become B-movie legend.) Patricia Owens as Andre's devastated bride is the focus of one of horrordom's most iconic scenes, the "fly's-eye view" through a honeycombed lens, displaying multiple images of her screaming in terror.

Director Kurt Neumann was no stranger to fantastic cinema. His credits included the pioneering sci-fi adventure *Rocketship X-M,* the underrated *She Devil* and the low-budget but nonetheless effective *Kronos.* Sadly, the director did not live to enjoy the enormous worldwide success of *The Fly*. Neumann's wife passed away shortly after the film premiered. *The Hollywood Reporter* ran her obituary notice on the same page with a rave review of *The Fly*. Soon after, Neumann also died unexpectedly.

Hedison had been in England filming *The Son of Robin Hood* when *The Fly* was released. He returned to the States to find that it was a smash, eventually becoming one of 20th Century-Fox's biggest grossers of the year. He saw it alone in a neighborhood theater, seated in the last row. He thought the color production was effective, well made, with a fine score. But he was ultimately disappointed that his make-up suggestions weren't employed, and he was genuinely taken aback at the sound of his shrieking, peeping, "Help me!" He still insists that his original, unenhanced screams would have proven more genuinely terrifying.

And he may be right. But it's the squeaking fly that made film history. It is the singular sequence that lingers in memory long after viewing the film. After five decades, mention of *The Fly* invariably provokes a high-pitched response of, "Help me! Help me!" from even nascent genre-film buffs. History can't be unmade. Fifty years later, Hedison's plea remains one of the most identifiable sounds in all of pop culture, and the film enjoys a reputation that few horror movies of its vintage can rival.

CHAPTER 11

GEORGE LANGELAAN

George Langelaan was born in Paris on January 19, 1908. He spent his youth in France, becoming equally proficient in English and French and learning the newspaper trade first hand. His father George, Sr. was an English journalist of Dutch descent and his mother was a Parisian. His father worked from Paris as a field reporter for a number of European and American newspapers until 1905, when he became the personal secretary to Norman Angell, newly appointed head of the Paris office of the British newspaper *The Daily Mail.* Angell resigned the *Daily Mail* in 1912 to devote himself to writing and lecturing on a book that had brought him great notoriety (and eventually a Nobel Peace Price). In 1910, Angell published *Europe's Optical Illusion,* an anti-war stance that the economies of Europe had grown and integrated across borders to the point that war was obsolete for strictly economic reasons. World War I would render the argument moot.

Instead of following Angell, George Langelaan, Sr. stayed with the *Mail.* When he was offered the position of personal secretary of Lord Northcliffe, the publisher of *The Daily Mail,* the senior Langelaan moved to London while the family moved into the French Countryside with relatives. George Senior remained in London until Northcliffe's death in 1922. He returned to France, collected his family from his in-laws, returned to Paris and continued in the journalism field for various news services.

The son was the beneficiary of his father's contacts. After attending Journalism school in the United States, Langelaan returned home and immediately found work. By 1928, Langelaan was a Paris-based staff writer for the Associated Press.

When the Spanish Civil War erupted in 1936, Langelaan was a correspondent for the *New York Times,* crossing over the French border into Spain and reporting on the status of the war. His reports were usually interesting, enough to warrant placement on page two. His June 1936 interview with the rebels predicting that Madrid would fall within a week made front page of the *New York Times* (the claim was optimistic — a siege of Madrid starting in November of 1936 would drag on for three years). Langelaan was doing more than making headlines — he was also keeping British Army Intelligence apprised of the rebel forces and their aid from Fascist Italy and Nazi Germany.

Langelaan, with barely two weeks of formal military training, found himself working with British Army Intelligence in Belgium when the Germans invaded in 1940. As the British tried to conducted reconnaissance, they found themselves trying to help with the stream of refugees. The German war machine continued into France and Langellan and the British found themselves trapped behind enemy lines. They escaped Belgium as part of the Dunkirk evacuation and returned to England. His bilingual skills were immediately brought back into use for the British crown — George Langelaan became an operative of SOE, the Special Operations Executive, formed as an independent British secret service. He joined Section F; a team of highly trained operatives and parachuted into France in September 1941 to help organize the resistance and dabble in sabotage when opportunity arose.

To prevent being recognized in France by his friends and associates, Langelaan insisted on plastic surgery; he had his ears tacked and his chin modified. With a new moustache and a new face, George Langelaan became George Langdon and was dropped into France to make contact with the Resistance. His missions continued until his capture by the Vichy government. A subsequent escape from a POW camp and his trek over the Pyrenees on foot to freedom brought him back to England just in time to be parachuted back into the espionage game, first in Algiers and then the fabled Casablanca in Morocco. Langelaan landed at Omaha Beach on D Day and was part of one the first advance political warfare teams that entered the liberated Paris as symbol of hope to the French. After the war, Langelaan returned to his beloved Paris. He and his father both wrote for the newspapers; the father used the byline "G. Langelaan" and the son used "George Langelaan." His father retired and wrote a travel book *Paris in a Week, and a Day at Versailles (1949)*, aimed at the English tourists. It would be updated annually through 1968 with George Jr. updating the text starting in 1959 under the alias G. Langham.

George Jr. continued to work for the Paris bureau of various news services but also began to write stories based on his experiences in the war. Recollections of the war had become popular in France; his first book *Un Nommé Langdon: Mémoires d'un Agent Secret (1950)* was successful enough to warrant translation into Spanish *Yo Fui Agente Secreto en Francia (1952)*, but never found a market in the English or American markets.

Carl Laemmle, Jr., son of the founder of Universal Pictures and a successful producer in his own right, had gotten wind of the interest in a James Bond film that was building through 1955 and 1958. In the wake of the success of the film version of *The Fly*, Laemmle learned that Langelaan was an English spy with a biography already in print. In 1958, Laemmle announced his return from retirement. His last film had been *Showboat* in 1936, after which he and his father had been forced out of the studio, and his return to the business would be "a mystery story called *The Cloakless Agent* based on an original story by United Press writer George Langelaan of Paris."

The project never developed, but it did create enough interest for the English language version of Langelaan's memoirs to finally be published. 1959 saw the release in England of *Knights of the Floating Silk* and in the United States as *The Masks of War*.

Langelaan would continue to exploit his background in espionage, running a column called "The Notebooks of Secret Agent 751 PP" (his actual designation in the SOE) for the weekly children's periodical *Pilote* that talked about the training, skills and processes of espionage. Espionage would continue to be a reliable source of income for Langelaan for the rest of his life — he was one of a number of authors who churned out the French language "Secret Agent" series of men's adventure novels. Langelaan headlined the series, writing 8 of the 40 titles in the series from 1964 to 1966 (All eight of his titles in the series were reissued in 1992). In 1970, he became a columnist for a short lived magazine devoted to spies and spying. *Revue Espionnage* only lasted a year, but it proved Langelaan still kept abreast of the field. But even as Langelaan wrote of spies, he was dabbling in other genres.

The publication of "The Fly" in *Playboy*, June 1957 was the first in a series of stories in English, as opposed to all the previous espionage tales, which had been written exclusively for the French language markets. Only one of his English stories was derived from his days as a spy; "I Rescued a Harem Wife" ran in *Suspense* August 1960. The rest of his stories, like "The Fly," skirted the line between science fiction and horror, such as four of his stories that ran in *Argosy*, a British short story magazine (not to be confused the American pulp magazine of the same name). Langelaan was in good company; other authors in the magazine included names such as Roald Dahl, Ray Bradbury and Arthur C. Clarke.

The last story he wrote for the England language markets was "The Other Hand," published in *Fantasy and Science Fiction*, October 1961. The story of a man who seeks to have his arm surgically removed when he finds it is possessed by an evil spirit; the story was later made into an episode of *Night Gallery* as "The Hand of Borgus Weems." Premiering September 15, 1971 (Season 2, Episode 3), it was directed by John Meredyth Lucas and starred George Maharis and Ray Milland.

1962 was looking very promising for Langelaan. *Nouvelles De L'anti-Monde*, a collection of his stories (including "The Fly") was due out. One of his *Argosy* stories, "Strange Miracle" from the August 1958 issue was being made into an episode of *Alfred Hitchcock Presents*, broadcast February 13, 1962. Suddenly, George Langelaan's father died unexpectedly.

A month after his father's death, Langelaan was walking in the Paris neighborhood of Montmartre along a street he had frequently walked with his father. Suddenly he got the impression his father was there with him and trying to give him a message.

The death and visitation from his father affected Langelaan's perspective and interest. He essentially stopped writing in English. A co-author was brought in to pick up the slack on the updates for *Paris in a Week, and a Day at Versailles* and Langelaan abandoned his science fiction and horror writings. He stopped enforcing his copyrights on stories — when Peter Haining was compiling stories for his horror anthology *The Ghouls* in 1971, there was no copyright notice concerning the use of "The Fly" and no subsequent reprint has shown one.

Now convinced there were realms of reality unexplored, his interests led him to a new movement gaining momentum in France, a literary style and philosophy the French referred to as *Réalisme fantastique*.

Réalisme fantastique, literally "Fantastic Realism," looked at occult, paranormal, futuristic technologies, UFOs and Fortean phenomena as factual events that were on the extreme edges of human perception, relying on intuition and empirical data, not scientific reasoning to explain.

Langelaan joined the staff of the fledgling bi-monthly magazine *Planète,* founded by Louis Pauwels and Jacques Bergier in the wake of the success of their book *Le Matin des Magiciens.* The book was an introduction the occult and Fortean phenomena. Both Bergier and Pauwels were journalists, and their populist approach, stripped of mystery and esoteric trappings, made the book stand apart from the usual fare on the topic. It was subsequently translated into English in 1963 as *The Morning of the Magicians* and became a bestseller.

Under the banner of réalisme fantastique, Langelaan published two books. *Le dictionnaire des faits maudits (The Dictionary of Accursed Facts)* was actually a 1967 compilation of Langelaan's contributions to the *Planète* with such topics as UFOs, ESP and the rise of Satanism in Great Britain. The book was named as homage to Charles Fort, a kindred investigator who had published The *Book of the Damned* in 1919 England.

The second of Langelaan's contribution to *réalisme fantastique* was *Treize Fantômes* (Thirteen Ghosts). Published in 1971, *Treize Fantômes* was a collection of haunted houses in the UK and Europe that Langelaan had investigated. Langelaan never wrote or talked about his childhood with one notable exception in *Treize Fantômes* where he recounts an incident when he was a child, which increased the impact of his father's visitation. When he was 8, he and his mother were staying with his maternal grandfather. His mother was frightened by a man suddenly appearing before her. His grandfather merely shrugged it off as a ghost, nothing important.

Langelaan's only other book was Les Nouveaux Parasites (1969), co written with Jean Barral. The book is a discussion of industrial espionage — how to recognize it and how to prevent it. Langelaan's high profile from the "Secret Agent" pulp novels and his *Planète* work had undermined his credibility as a mainstream expert and the book did not sell well.

One of Langelaan's acquaintances from his work at the *Planète* was Marcel Belline, a noted clairvoyant whose specialty was predicting deaths. Langelaan had visited Belline in January of 1972 and learned what he already suspected — his time was coming. Belline offered advice on how to prepare for the transition and a greatly relieved Langelaan prepared his estate and put his affairs in order. He died in Paris February 9, 1972 at the age of 68.

The Planète ended publication that year, but published one last book, *L'Histoire Invisible,* an anniversary book celebrating a decade of research. The 400 page book came out within weeks of Langelaan's death and included an early article by Langelaan, "On Sait Qui a Tué Kennedy," his take on the conspiracies surrounding the assassination of Kennedy.

George Langelaan did not believe in religion but, keeping with his *réalisme fantastique* roots, he did believe in reincarnation. His name, transliterated from the Dutch, was Long Path, or Long Journey, appropriate for the endless travel of the immortal soul from one incarnation to the next. Whether he was correct or not, he has achieved immortality through the suffering of Andre Delambre and the cautionary tale of "The Fly."

Andre explains his transport process.

CHAPTER 12

THE FLY

BY GEORGE LANGELAAN

Telephones and telephone bells have always made me uneasy. Years ago, when they were mostly wall fixtures, I disliked them, and nowadays, when they are planted in every nook and corner, they are a downright intrusion. We have a saying in France than a coalman is a master in his own house; with the telephone that is no longer true, and I suspect that even the Englishman is no longer king in his own castle.

At the office, the sudden ringing of the telephone annoys me. It seems that, no matter what I am doing, in spite of the switchboard operator, in spite of my secretary, in spite of the doors and walls, some unknown person is coming into the room and onto my desk to talk into my very ear, confidentially — whether I like it or not. At home, the feeling is still more disagreeable, but the worst is when the telephone rings in the dead of night. If anyone could see me turn on the light and get up blinking to answer it, I suppose I would look like any other sleepy man annoyed at being disturbed. The truth in such a case, however, is that I am struggling against panic, fighting down a feeling that a stranger has broken into the house and is in my bedroom. By the time I manage to grab the receiver and say: "*Ici Monsieur Delambre. Je vous ecounte,*" I am outwardly calm, but I only get back to a more normal state when I recognize the voice at the other end and when I know what is wanted of me.

This effort at dominating a purely animal reaction and fear had become so effective that when my sister-in-law called me at two in the morning, asking me to come over, but first to warn the police that she had just killed my brother, I quietly asked her how and why she had killed André.

"But, François! ... I can't explain all that over the telephone. Please call the police and come quickly."

"Maybe I had better see you first, Hélène?"

"No, you better call the police first; otherwise they will start asking you all sorts of awkward questions. They'll have enough trouble as it is to believe I did alone ... And, by the way, I suppose you ought to tell them that André ... André's body, is down at the factory. They may want to go there first."

"Did you say that André is at the factory?"

"Yes ... under the steam-hammer."

"Under the what!"

"The steam-hammer! But don't ask so many questions. Please come quickly, François! Please understand that I'm afraid ... that my nerves won't stand it much longer!"

Have you ever tried to explain to a sleepy police officer that your sister-in-law has just phoned to say that she had killed your brother with the steam-hammer? I repeated my explanation, but he would not let me.

"*Oui, Monsieur, oui,* I hear ... but who are you? What is your name? Where do you live? I said, where do you live?"

It was then that Commissiare Charas took over the line and the whole business. He at least seemed understand everything. Would I wait for him? Yes, he would pick me up and take me over to my brother's house. When? In five or ten minutes.

I just managed to pull on my trousers, wriggle into a sweater and grab a hat and coat, when a black Citroen, headlights blazing, pulled up at the door.

"I assume you have a night watchman at your factory, Monsieur Delambre. Has he called you? asked Commissiare Charas, letting in the clutch as I sat down beside him and slammed the door of the car.

"No, he hasn't. Though of course my brother could have entered the factory through his laboratory where he often works late at night ... all night sometimes."

"Is Professor Delambre's work connected with your business?"

"No, my brother is, or was, doing research for the Ministere de l'Air. As he wanted to be away from Paris and yet within reach of where skilled workmen could fix up or make gadgets big and small for his experiments, I offered him one of the old workshops of the factory and he came to live in the first house built by our grandfather on top of the hill at the back of the factory."

"Yes, I see. Did he talk about his work? What sort of research work?"

"He rarely talked about it, you know; I suppose the Air Ministry could tell you. I only know that he was about to carry out a number of experiments he had been preparing for some months, something to do with the disintegration of matter, he told me."

Barely slowing down, the Commissaire swung the car off the road, slid it through the open factory gate and pulled up sharp by a policeman apparently expecting him.

I did not need to hear the policeman's confirmation. I knew now that my brother was dead, it seemed that I had been told years ago. Shaking like a leaf, I scrambled out after the Commissaire.

Another policeman stepped out of a doorway and led us toward one of the shops where all the lights had been turned on. More policemen were standing by the hammer, watching two men setting up a camera. It was tilted downwards, and I made an effort to look.

It was far less horrid than I had expected. Though I'd never seen my brother drunk, he looked just as if he were sleeping off a terrific binge, flat on his stomach across the narrow line on which the white-hot slabs of metal were rolled up to the hammer. I saw at a glance that his head and arm could only be a flattened mess, but that seemed quite impossible; it looked as he had somehow pushed his head and arms right into the metallic mass of the hammer.

Having talked to his colleagues, the Commissiare turned toward me:

"How can we raise the hammer, Monsieur Delambre?"

"I'll raise it for you."

"Would you like us to get one of your men over?"

"No, I'll be all right. Look, here is the switchboard. It was originally a steam-hammer, but everything is worked electrically here now. Look, Commissiare, the hammer is been set at fifty tons and its impact at zero."

"At zero ...?"

"Yes, level with the ground if you prefer. It is also set for single strokes, which means it has to be raised after each blow. I don't know what Hélène, my sister-in-law, will have to say about all this, but one thing I'm sure of: she certainly did not how to set and operate the hammer."

"Perhaps it was set that way last night when work stopped?"

"Certainly not. The drop is never set at zero, Monsieur le Commissaire."

"I see. Can it be raised gently?"

"No. The speed of the upstroke cannot be regulated. But in any case it is not very fast when the hammer is set for single strokes."

"Right. Will you show me what to do? It won't be very nice to watch, you know."

"No, no, Monsieur le Commissiare. I'll be all right."

"All set?" asked the Commissaire of the others. "All right then, Monsieur Delambre. Whenever you like."

Watching my brother's back, I slowly but firmly pushed the upstroke button.

The unusual silence of the factory was broken by the sigh of compressed air rushing into the cylinders, a sigh that always makes me think of a giant taking a deep breath before solemnly socking another giant, and the steel mass of the hammer shuddered and then rose swiftly. I also heard the sucking sound as it left the metal base and thought I was going to panic when I saw André's body heave forward as a sickly gush of blood poured all over the ghastly mess bared by the hammer.

"No danger of it coming down again, Monsieur Delambre?"

"No, none whatever," I mumbled as I threw the safety switch and, turning around, I was violently sick in front of a young green-faced policeman.

For weeks after, Commissiare Charas worked on the case, listening, questioning, running all over the place, making out reports, telegraphing and telephoning right and left. Later, we became quite friendly and he owned that he had for a long time considered me as suspect number one, but had finally given up that idea because, not only was there no clue of any sort, but not even a motive.

Hélène, my sister-in-law, was so calm throughout the whole business that the doctors finally confirmed what I have long considered the only possible solution: that she was mad. That being the case, there was of course no trial.

My brother's wife never tried to defend herself in any way and even got quite annoyed when she realized the people thought her mad, and this of course was considered proof she was indeed mad. She owned up to the murder of her husband and proved easily that she knew how to handle the hammer; but she would never say why, exactly how, or under what circumstances she had killed my brother. The great mystery was how and why my brother had so blithely stuck his head under the hammer, the only possible explanation for his part in the drama.

The night watchman had heard the hammer all right; he had even heard it twice, he claimed. This was very strange, and the counter-stroke which was always set back to nought after a job, seem to prove him right, since it marked the figure two. Also, the foreman in charge of the hammer confirmed that after cleaning up the day before the murder, he had as usual turned the stroke-counter back to nought. In spite of this, Hélène maintained that she had only used the hammer once, and this seemed just another proof of her insanity.

Commissaire Charas, who had been put in charge of the case, at first wondered if the victim was really my brother. But of that there was no possible doubt, if only because of the great scar running from his knee to his thigh, the result of a shell that had landed within a few feet of him during the retreat in 1940; and there were also the fingerprints of his left hand which corresponded to those found all over his laboratory and his personal belongings up at the house.

A guard had been put on his laboratory and the next day half-a-dozen officials came down from the Air Ministry. They went through all his papers and took away some of his instruments, but before leaving, they told the Commissiare that the most interesting documents and instruments had been destroyed.

The Lyons police laboratory, one of the most famous in the world, reported that André's head had been wrapped up in a piece of velvet when it was crushed by the hammer, and one day Commissaire Charas showed me a tattered drapery which I immediately recognized as the brown velvet cloth I had seen on a table in my brother's laboratory, the one on which his meals were served when he could not leave his work.

After only a very few days in prison, Hélène had been transferred to a nearby asylum, one of the three in France where insane criminals are taken care of. My nephew, Henri, a boy of six, the very image of his father, was entrusted to me, and eventually all legal arrangements were made for me to become his guardian and tutor.

Hélène, one of the quietest patients of the asylum, was allowed visitors and I went to see her on Sundays. Once or twice the Commissaire had accompanied me and, later, I learned that he had also visited Hélène alone. But we were never able to obtain any information from my sister-in-law, who seemed to have become utterly indifferent. She rarely answered my questions and hardly ever those of the Commissaire. She spent a lot of her time sewing, but her favorite pastime seemed to be catching flies, which she invariably released unharmed after having examined them carefully.

Hélène only had one fit of raving — more like a nervous breakdown than a fit, said the doctor who had administered morphia to quieten her — the day she saw a nurse swatting flies.

The day after Hélène's one and only fit, Commissiare Charas came to see me.

"I have a strange feeling that there lies the key to the whole business, Monsieur Delambre," he said.

I did not ask him how it was that he already knew all about Hélène's fit.

"I do not follow you, Commissaire. Poor Madame Delambre could have showed an exceptional interest for anything else, really. Don't you think that flies just happen to be the border-subject of her tendency to raving?"

"Do you believe she is really mad?" he asked.

"My dear Commissaire, I don't see how there can be any doubt. Do you doubt it?"

"I don't know. In spite of all the doctors say, I have the impression that Madame Delambre has a very clear brain ... even when catching flies."

"Supposing you were right, how would you explain her attitude with regard to her little boy? She never seems to consider him as her own child."

"You know, Monsieur Delambre, I have thought about that also. She may be trying to protect him. Perhaps she fears the boy or, for all we know, hates him?"

"I'm afraid I don't understand, my dear Commissiare."

"Have you noticed, for instance, that she never catches flies when the boy is there?"

"No. But come to think of it, you are quite right. Yes, that is strange ... Still, I fail to understand."

"So do I, Monsieur Delambre. And I'm very much afraid that we shall never understand, unless perhaps your sister-in-law should get *better*."

"The doctors seem to think that there is no hope of any sort you know."

"Yes. Do you know if your brother ever experimented with flies?"

"I really don't know, but I shouldn't think so. Have you asked the Air Ministry people? They know all about the work."

"Yes, and they laughed at me."

"I can understand that."

"You are very fortunate to understand anything, Monsieur Delambre. I do not ... but I hope to someday."

"Tell me, Uncle, do flies live a long time?"

We were just finishing our lunch and, following and establishing an established tradition between us, I was just pouring some wine into Henri's glass for him to dip a biscuit in.

Had Henri not been staring at his glass gradually being filled to the brim, something in my look might have frightened him.

This was the first time he had ever mentioned flies, and I shuddered at the thought that Commissaire Charas might quite easily have been present. I could imagine the glint in his eye as he would have answered my nephew's question with another question. I could almost hear him saying:

"I don't know, Henri. Why do you ask?"

"Because I have again seen the fly *Maman* was looking for."

And it was only after drinking off Henri's glass of wine that I realized he had answered my spoken thought.

"I did not know that your mother was looking for a fly."

"Yes, she was. It has grown quite a lot, but I recognized it all right."

"Where did you see this fly, Henri, and ... how did you recognize it?"

"This morning on your desk, Uncle François. Its head is white instead of black and it has a funny sort of leg."

Feeling more and more like Commissaire Charas, but trying to look unconcerned, I went on:

"And when did you see this fly for the first time?"

"The day that Papa went away. I had caught it, but *Maman* made me let it go. And then after, she wanted me to find it again. She'd changed her mind," and shrugging his shoulders just as my brother used to, he added, "You know what women are."

"I think that fly must have died long ago, and you must be mistaken, Henri," I said, getting up and walking to the door.

But as soon as I was out of dining room, I ran up the stairs into my study. There was no fly anywhere to be seen.

I was bothered, far more than I cared to even think about. Henri had just proved that Charas was really closer to a clue than had seemed when he told me about his thoughts concerning Hélène's pastime.

For the first time I wondered if Charas did not really know much more than he let on. For the first time also, I wondered about Hélène. Was she really insane? A strange, horrid feeling was growing on me, and the more I thought about it, the more I felt that somehow, Charas was right: Hélène was *getting away with it!*

What could possibly have been the reason for such a monstrous crime? What led up to it? Just what had happened?

I thought of all the hundreds of questions that Charas had put to Hélène, sometimes gently like a nurse trying to soothe, sometimes stern and cold, sometimes barking them furiously. Hélène had answered very few, always in a calm quiet voice and never seeming to pay any attention to the way the question had been put. Though dazed, she had seemed perfectly sane then.

Refined, well-bred and well-read, Charas was more than just an intelligent police official. He was a keen psychologist and had an amazing way of smelling out a fib or an erroneous statement even before it was uttered. I knew that he had accepted as true the few answers she'd given him. But then there had been all those questions which she never really answered: the most direct and important ones. From the very beginning, Hélène had adopted a very simple system. "I cannot answer that question," she would say in her low quiet voice. And that was that! The repetition of the same question never seemed to annoy her. In all the hours of questioning that she underwent, Hélène did not once point out to the Commissiare that he had already asked her this or that. She would simply say, "I cannot answer that question," as though it was the very first time that particular question had been asked and the very first time she had made that answer.

This cliché had become the formidable barrier beyond which Commissioner Charas could not even get a glimpse, an idea of what Hélène might be thinking. She had very willingly answered questions about her life with my brother — which seemed a very happy and uneventful one — up to the time of his end. About his death, however, all she would say that she had killed him with the steam-hammer, but she refused to say why, what had led up to the drama, and how she got my brother put his head under it. She never actually refused outright; she would just go blank and, with no apparent emotion, would switch over to, "I cannot answer that question for you."

Hélène, as I have said, had shown the Commissiare that she knew how to set and operate the steam-hammer.

Charas could only find one single fact which did not coincide with Hélène's declarations, the fact that the hammer been used twice. Charas was no longer willing to attribute this to insanity. That evident flaw in Hélène's stonewall defense seemed a crack which the Commissaire might possibly enlarge. But my sister-in-law finally cemented it by acknowledging:

"All right, I lied to you. I did use the hammer twice. But do not ask me why, because I cannot tell you."

"Is that your only ... misstatement, Madame Delambre?" had asked the Commissaire, trying to follow up what looked at last like an advantage.

"It is ... and you know it, Monsieur le Commissaire."

And, annoyed, Charas had seen that Hélène could read him like an open book.

I had thought of calling on the Commissaire, but the knowledge that he would inevitably start questioning Henri made me hesitate. Another reason also made me hesitate, a vague sort of fear that he would look for and find the fly Henri had talked of. And that annoyed me a good deal because I could find no satisfactory explanation for that particular fear.

André was definitely not the absent-minded sort of professor who walks around in the pouring rain with a rolled umbrella under his arm. He was human, had a keen sense of humor, loved children and animals and could not bear to see anyone suffer. I had often seen him drop his work to watch a parade of the local fire brigade, watch the Tour de France cyclists go by, or even follow a circus parade all around the village. He liked games of logic and precision, such as billiards and tennis, bridge and chess.

How was it then possible to explain his death? What could have made him put his head under that hammer? It could hardly have been the result of some stupid bet or a test of his courage. He hated betting and had no patience with those who indulged in it. Whenever he heard a bet proposed, he would invariably remind all present that, after all, a bet was but a contract between a fool and a swindler, even if it turned out to be a toss-up as to which was which.

It seemed there were only two possible explanations to André's death. Either he had gone mad, or else he had a reason for letting his wife kill him in such a strange and terrible way. And just what could have been his wife's role in all this? They surely could not have been both insane?

Having finally decided not to tell Charas about my nephew's innocent revelations, I thought I myself would try to question Hélène.

She seemed to have been expecting my visit for she came into the parlor almost as soon as I made myself known to the matron and been allowed inside.

"I wanted to show you my garden," explained Hélène as I looked at the coat slung over her shoulders.

As one of the "reasonable" inmates, she was allowed to go into the garden during certain hours of the day. She had asked for and obtained the right to a little patch of ground where she could grow flowers, and I had sent her seeds and some rosebushes out of my garden.

She took me straight to a rustic wooden bench which had been in the men's workshop and only just set up under a tree close to her little patch of ground.

Searching for the right way to broach the subject of André's death, I sat for a while tracing vague designs on the ground with the end of my umbrella.

"François, I want to ask you something," said Hélène after awhile.

"Anything I can do for you, Hélène?"

"Now, just something I want to know. Do flies live very long?"

Staring at her, I was about to say that her boy had asked the very same question a few hours earlier when I suddenly realized that here was the opening I had been searching for and perhaps even the possibility of striking a great blow, a blow perhaps powerful enough to shatter her stonewall defense, be it sane or insane.

Watching her carefully I replied:

"I don't really know, Hélène; but the fly you were looking for was in my study this morning."

No doubt about it I had struck a shattering blow. She swung her head around with such force that I heard the bones crack in her neck. She opened her mouth, but said not a word, only her eyes seemed to be screaming with fear.

Yes, it was evident that I had crashed through something, but what? Undoubtedly, the Commissaire would have known what to do with such an advantage; I did not. All I knew was that he would never given her time to think, to recuperate, but all I could do, and even that was a strain, was to maintain my best poker-face, hoping against hope that Hélène's defenses would go on crumbling.

She must have been quite a while without breathing, because she suddenly gasped and put both her hands over her still open mouth.

"François ... did you kill it?" she whispered, her eyes no longer fixed, but searching every inch of my face.

"No."

"You have it then ... You have it on you! Give it to me!" she almost shouted, touching me with both her hands, and I knew that had she felt strong enough she would have tried to search me.

"No, Hélène, I haven't got it."

"But you know now ... you have guessed, haven't you?"

"No, Hélène. I only know one thing, and that is that you are not insane. But I mean to know it all, Hélène, and, somehow, I am going to find out. You can choose: either you tell me everything and I'll see what is to be done well or ..."

"Or what? Say it!"

"I was going to say it, Hélène ... or I assure you that your friend the Commissaire will have that fly first thing tomorrow morning."

She remained quite still, looking down at the palms of her hands on her lap and, although was getting chilly, her forehead and hands were moist.

Without even brushing aside a wisp of brown hair blown across her mouth by the breeze she murmured: "If I tell you ...will you promise to destroy that fly before doing anything else."

"No, Hélène. I can make no such promise before knowing."

"But, François, you must understand. I promised André that fly would be destroyed. That promise must be kept and I can say nothing until it is."

I could sense the deadlock ahead. I was not yet losing ground, but I was losing the initiative. I tried a shot in the dark:

"Hélène, of course you understand that as soon as the police examine that fly, they will know that you are not insane, and then ..."

"François, no! For Henri's sake! Don't you see? I was expecting that fly; I was hoping it would find me here but it couldn't know what had become of me. What else could it do but go to others it loves, to Henri, to you ... you who might know and understand what was to be done!"

Was she really mad, or was she simulating again? But mad or not, she was cornered. Wondering how to follow up and how to land the knockout blow without running the risk of seeing her slip away out of reach, I said very quietly:

"Tell me all, Hélène. I can then protect your boy."

"Protect my boy from what? Don't you understand that if I am here, it is merely so Henri won't be the son of a woman who was guillotined for having murdered his father? Don't you understand I would far prefer the guillotine to the living death of this lunatic asylum?"

"I understand, Hélène, and I'll do my best for the boy whether you tell me or not. If you refuse to tell me, I'll still do the best I can to protect Henri, but you must understand that the game will be out of my hands, because Commissaire Charas will have the fly."

"But why must you know?" said, rather than asked, my sister-in-law, struggling to control her temper.

"Because I must and will know how and why my brother died, Hélène."

"All right. Take me back to the ... house. I'll give you what your Commissaire would call my 'Confession.'"

"You mean to say that you have written it!"

"Yes. It not really meant for you, but more likely for *your friend*, the Commissaire. I had foreseen that, sooner or later, he would get too close to the truth."

"You then have no objection to his reading it?"

"You will act as you think fit, François. Wait for me a minute."

Leaving me at the door the parlor, Hélène ran upstairs to her room. In less than a minute she was back with a large brown envelope.

"Listen, François; you are not nearly as bright as was your poor brother, but you are not unintelligent. All I ask is that you read this alone. After that, you may do as you wish."

"That I promise you, Hélène," I said, taking the precious envelope. "I'll read it tonight and although tomorrow is not a visiting day, I'll come down to see you."

"Just as you like," said my sister-in-law without even saying good-bye as she went back upstairs.

It was only on reaching home, as I walked from the garage to the house, that I read the inscription on the envelope:

TO WHOM IT MAY CONCERN

(Probably Commissaire Charas)

Having told the servants I would have only a light supper to be served immediately in my study and that I was not to be disturbed after, I ran upstairs, threw Hélène's envelope on my desk and made another careful search of the room before closing the shutters and drawing the curtains. All I could find was a long since dead mosquito stuck to the wall near the ceiling.

Having motioned to the servant to put her tray down on the table by the fireplace, I poured myself a glass of wine and locked the door behind her. I then disconnected telephone — I always did this now at night — and turned out all the lights but the lamp on my desk.

Slitting open Hélène's fat envelope, I extracted a thick wad of closely written pages. I read the following lines neatly centered in the middle of the top page:

This is not a confession because, although I killed my husband, I am not a murderess. I simply and very faithfully carried out his last wish by crushing his head and right arm under the steam-hammer of his brother's factory.

Without even touching the glass of wine by my elbow, I turned the page and started reading.

For very nearly a year before his death (*the manuscript began*), my husband had told me of some of his experiments. He knew full well that his colleagues of the Air Ministry would have forbidden some of them as too dangerous, but he was keen on obtaining positive results before reporting his discovery.

Whereas only sound and pictures had been, so far, transmitted through space by radio and television, André claimed to have discovered a way of transmitting matter. Matter, any solid subject, placed in his "transmitter" was instantly disintegrated and reintegrated in a special receiving set.

André considered his discovery as perhaps the most important since that of the wheel sawn off the end of a tree trunk. He reckoned that the transmission of matter by instantaneous "disintegration-reintegration" would completely change life as we had known it so far. It would mean the end of all means of transport, not only of goods including food, but also of human beings. André, the practical scientist who never allowed theories or daydreams to get the better of him, already foresaw the time when there would no longer be any airplanes, ships, trains or cars and, therefore, no longer any roads or railway lines, ports, airports or stations. All that would be replaced by matter-transmitting and receiving stations throughout the world. Travelers and goods would be placed

Helene shields her face from the light of transportation.

in special cabins and, at a given signal, would simply disappear and reappear almost immediately at the chosen receiving station.

André's receiving set was only a few feet away from his transmitter, in an adjoining room of his laboratory, and he at first ran into all sorts of snags. His first successful experiment was carried out with an ash tray taken from his desk, a souvenir we had brought back from a trip to London.

That was the first time he told me about his experiments and I had no idea what he was talking about the day he came dashing into the house and threw the ash tray into my lap.

"Hélène, look! For a fraction of a second, a bare ten-millionth of a second, that ash tray had been completely disintegrated. For one little moment it no longer existed! Gone! Nothing left, absolutely nothing! Only atoms traveling through space at the speed of light! And the moment after, the atoms were once more gathered together in the shape of an ash tray!"

"André, please ... please! What on earth are you raving about?"

He started sketching all over a letter I had been writing. He laughed at my wry face, swept all my letters off the table and said:

"You don't understand? Right. Let's start all over again. Hélène, do you remember I once read to you an article about the mysterious flying stones that seem to come from nowhere in particular, and which are said to occasionally fall in certain houses in India? They come flying in as though thrown from outside and that, in spite of closed doors and windows."

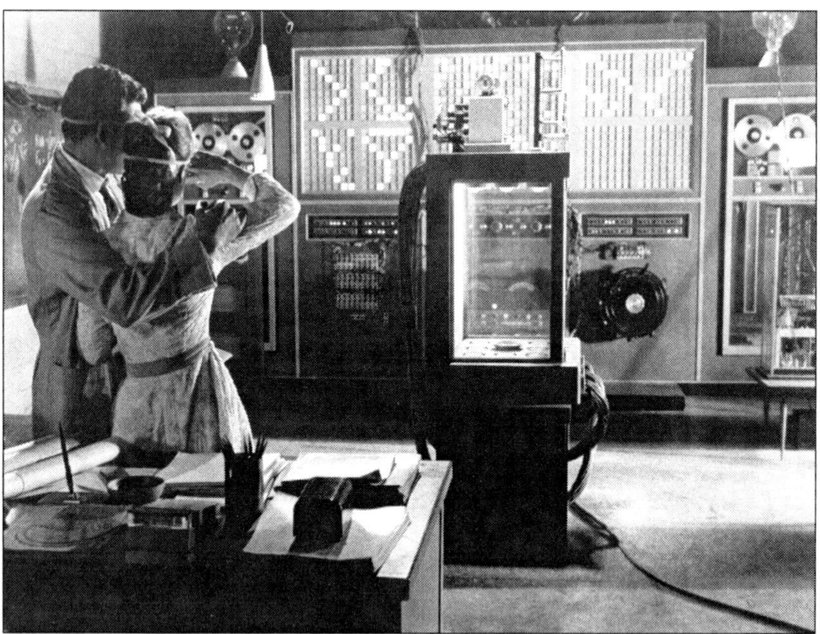

Andre transports a dish for Helene.

"Yes, I remember. I also remember that Professor Augier, your friend of the College de France, who had come down for a few days, remarked that if there was no trickery about it, the only possible explanation that the stones had been disintegrated after having been thrown from the outside, come through the walls, and then been reintegrated before hitting the floor or the opposite walls."

"That's right. And I added that there was, of course, one other possibility, namely the momentary and partial disintegration of the walls as the stone or stones came through."

"Yes, André. I remember all that, and I suppose you also remember that I failed to understand, and that you got quite annoyed. Well, I still don't understand why and how, even disintegrated, stones should be able to come through a wall or a closed door."

"But it is possible, Hélène, because of the atoms that go to make up matter are not close together like a bricks in a wall. They are separated by relative immensities of space."

"Do you mean to say you have disintegrated that ash tray, and then put it back together again after pushing it through something?"

"Precisely, Hélène. I projected it through the wall that separates my transmitter from my receiving set."

"And would it be foolish to ask how humanity is to benefit from ash trays that can go through walls?"

André seemed quite offended, but he soon saw that I was only teasing, and again waxing enthusiastic, he told me of some of the possibilities of his discovery.

"Isn't it wonderful, Hélène?" He finally gasped, out of breath.

"Yes, André. But I hope you won't ever transmit me; I'd be too much afraid of coming at the other end like your ash tray."

"What do you mean?"

"Do you remember what was written under that ash tray?"

"Yes, of course: MADE IN JAPAN. That was the great joke of our typically British souvenir."

"The words are still there, André; but ... look!"

He took the ash tray out of my hands, frowned, and walked over to the window. Then he went quite pale, and I knew that he had seen what had proved to me that he had indeed carried out a strange experiment.

The three words were still there, but reversed and reading:

NAPAJ NI EDAM

Without a word, having completely forgotten me, André rushed off to his laboratory. I only saw him the next morning, tired and unshaven after a whole night's work.

A few days later, André had a new reverse which put him out of sorts and made him fussy and grumpy for several weeks. I stood it patiently enough for awhile, but being myself bad tempered one evening, we had a silly row over some futile thing, and I reproached him for his moroseness.

"I'm sorry, *cherie*. I've been working my way through a maze of problems and have given you all a very rough time. You see, my very first experiment with a live animal proved a complete fiasco."

"André! You tried that experiment with Dandelo, didn't you?"

"Yes. How did you know?" he answered sheepishly. "He disintegrated perfectly, but he never reappeared in the receiving set."

"Oh, André! What became of him then?"

"Nothing ... there was just no more Dandelo; only the dispersed atoms of a cat wandering, God knows where, in the universe."

Dandelo was a small white cat the cook had found one morning in the garden and which we had promptly adopted. Now I knew how it had disappeared and was quite angry about the whole thing, but my husband was so miserable over it all that I said nothing.

I saw little of my husband during a next few weeks. He had most of his meals sent down to his laboratory. I would often wake up in the morning and find his bed unslept in. Sometimes, if he'd come in very late, I would find that storm-swept appearance which only a man can give a bedroom by getting up very early and fumbling around in the dark.

Andre is determined to solve the problem of the backward dish.

One evening he came to dinner all smiles, and I knew that his troubles were over. His face dropped, however, when he saw I was dressed for going out.

"Oh. Were you going out, Hélène?"

"Yes, the Drillons invited me for game of bridge, but I can easily phone them and put it off."

"No, it's all right."

"It isn't all right. Out with it, dear!"

"Well, I've at last got everything perfect and I wanted you to be the first to see the miracle."

"*Magnifique,* André! Of course I'll be delighted."

Having telephoned our neighbors to say how sorry I was and so forth, I ran down to the kitchen and told the cook that she had exactly 10 minutes in which to prepare a "celebration dinner."

"An excellent idea, Hélène," said my husband when the maid appeared with the champagne after our candlelight dinner. "We'll celebrate with reintegrated champagne!" and taking the tray from the maid's hands, he led the way down to laboratory.

"Do you think it will be as good as before its disintegration?" I asked, holding the tray while he opened the door and switched on the lights.

"Have no fear. You'll see! Just bring it here, will you," he said, opening the door of a telephone call-box he had bought and which had been transformed into what he called a transmitter. "Put it down on that now," he added, putting a stool inside the box.

Having carefully closed the door, he took me to the other end of the room and handed me a pair of very dark sun glasses. He put on another pair and walked back to a switchboard by the transmitter.

"Ready, Hélène?" said my husband, turning out all the lights. "Don't remove your glasses until I give the word."

"I won't budge, André, go on," I told him, my eyes fixed on the tray which I could just see in a greenish shimmering light through the glass-paneled door of the telephone booth.

"Right," said André, throwing a switch.

The whole room was brilliantly illuminated by an orange flash. Inside the cabin I had seen a crackling ball of fire and felt its heat on my face, neck and hands. The whole thing lasted but a fraction of a second, and I found myself blinking at green-edged black holes like those one sees after having stared at the sun.

"*Et Voila*! You can take off your glasses, Hélène."

A little theatrically perhaps, my husband opened the door of the cabin. Although André had told me what to expect, I was astonished to find that the champagne, glasses, tray and stool were no longer there.

André ceremoniously led me by the hand into the next room, in the corner of which stood a second telephone booth. Opening the door wide, he triumphantly lifted the champagne tray off the stool. Feeling somewhat like a good-natured kind-member-of- the-audience that has been dragged onto the music hall stage by the magician, I repressed from saying, "All done with mirrors," which I knew would have annoyed my husband.

"Sure it is not dangerous to drink?" I asked as the cork popped.

"Absolutely sure, Hélène," he said handing me a glass. "But that is nothing. Drink this off and I'll show you something much more astounding."

We went back into the other room.

"Oh, André! Remember poor Dandelo!"

"This is only a guinea pig, Hélène. But I'm positive it will go through all right."

He set the furry little beast down on the green enameled floor of the booth and quickly closed the door. I again put on my dark glasses and saw and felt the vivid crackling flash.

Without waiting for André to open the door, I rushed into the next room where the lights were still on and looked into the receiving booth.

"Oh, André! *Cheri!* He's there are right!" I shouted excitedly, watching the little animal trotting round and round. «It's wonderful, André. It works! You succeeded!"

"I hope so, but I must be patient. I'll know for sure in a few weeks' time."

"What do you mean? Look! He's as full of life as when you put him in the other cabin."

"Yes, so he seems. But we'll have to see if all his organs are intact, and that will take some time. If that little beast is still full of life in a month's time, we can then consider the experiment a success."

I begged André to let me take care of the guinea pig.

"All right, but don't kill it by overfeeding," he agreed with a grin for my enthusiasm.

Although not allowed to take Hop-la — the name I had given the guinea pig — out of its box in the laboratory, I had tied a pink ribbon around its neck and was allowed to feed it twice a day.

Hop-la soon got used to its pink ribbon and became quite a tame little pet, but that month of waiting seemed a year.

And then one day, André put Miquette, our cocker spaniel, into his "transmitter." He had not told me beforehand, knowing full well that I would never agree to such experiment with our dog. But when he did tell me, Miquette had been successfully transmitted half a dozen times and seemed to be enjoying the operation thoroughly; no sooner was she let out of the "reintegrator" then she dashed madly into the next room, scratching at the "transmitter" door to have "another go," as André called it.

I now expected that my husband would invite some of his colleagues and the Air Ministry specialists to come down. He usually did this when he had finished a research job and, before handing them long detailed reports which he always typed himself, he would carry out an experiment or two before them. But this time, he just went on working. One morning I asked him when he intended throwing his usual "surprise party," as we called it.

"No, Hélène; not for a long while yet. This discovery is much too important. I have an awful lot of work to do on it still. Do you realize that there are some parts of the transmission proper which I do not yet myself fully understand? It works all right, but you see, I can't just say to all these eminent professors that I do this and that and, poof, it works! I must be able to explain how and why it works. And what is even more important, I must be ready and able to refute every destructive argument they will not fail to trot out, as they usually do when faced with anything really good."

I was occasionally invited down to the laboratory to witness some new experiment, but I never went unless André invited me, and only talked about his work if he broached the subject first. Of course it never occurred to me that he would, at that stage at least, have tried an experiment with a human being; though, had I thought about it — knowing André — it would have obvious that he would have never allowed anyone into the "transmitter" before he had been through to test it first. It was only after the accident that I discovered he had duplicated all his switches inside the disintegration booth, so he could try it out by himself.

The morning André tried this terrible experiment, he did not show up for lunch. I sent the maid down with a tray, but she brought it back with a note she had found pinned outside the laboratory door: "Do not disturb me, I am working."

He did occasionally pin such notes on his door and, though I noticed it, I paid no particular attention to the unusually large handwriting of his note.

It was just after that, as I was drinking my coffee, that Henri came bouncing into the room to say he caught a funny fly, and would I like to see it. Refusing to even look at his closed fist, I ordered him to release it immediately.

"But *Maman*, it has such a funny white head!"

Marching the boy over to the open window, I told him to release the fly immediately, which he did. I know that Henri had caught the fly merely because he thought it looked curious or different from other flies, but I also knew his father would never stand for any form of cruelty to animals, and that there would be a fuss should he discover that our son had put a fly in a box or bottle.

At dinner time that evening, André had still not show up and, a little worried I ran down to the laboratory and knocked at the door.

He did not answer my knock, but when I heard him moving around and a moment later he slipped a note under the door. It was typewritten:

HÉLÈNE, I AM HAVING TROUBLE. PUT THE BOY TO BED AND COME BACK IN AN HOUR'S TIME. A.

Frightened, I knocked and called, but André did not seem to pay any attention and, vaguely reassured by the familiar noise of his typewriter, I went back to the house.

Having put Henri to bed, I returned to the laboratory, where I found another note slipped under the door. My hand shook as I picked it up because I knew by then that something must be radically wrong. I read:

HÉLÈNE, FIRST OF ALL I COUNT ON YOU NOT TO LOSE YOUR HEAD OR DO ANYTHING RASH BECAUSE YOU ALONE CAN HELP ME. I HAVE HAD A SERIOUS ACCIDENT. I AM NOT IN ANY PARTICULAR DANGER FOR THE TIME BEING THOUGH IT IS A MATTER OF LIFE AND DEATH. IT IS USELESS CALLING TO ME OR SAYING ANYTHING. I CANNOT ANSWER, I CANNOT SPEAK. I WANT YOU TO DO EXACTLY AND VERY CAREFULLY ALL THAT I ASK. AFTER HAVING KNOCKED THREE TIMES TO SHOW THAT YOU UNDERSTAND AND AGREE, FETCH ME A BOWL OF MILK LACED WITH RUM. I HAVE HAD NOTHING ALL DAY AND CAN DO WITH IT.

Shaking with fear, not knowing what to think and repressing a furious desire to call André and bang away until he opened, I knocked three times as requested and ran all the way home to fetch what he wanted.

In less than five minutes I was back. Another note had been slipped under the door:

HÉLÈNE, FOLLOW THESE INSTRUCTIONS CAREFULLY. WHEN YOU KNOCK I'LL OPEN THE DOOR. YOU ARE TO WALK OVER TO MY DESK AND PUT DOWN THE BOWL OF MILK. YOU WILL THEN GO INTO THE OTHER ROOM WHERE THE RECEIVER IS. LOOK CAREFULLY AND TRY TO FIND A FLY WHICH OUGHT TO BE THERE BUT WHICH I AM UNABLE TO FIND. UNFORTUNATELY I CANNOT SEE SMALL THINGS VERY EASILY.

BEFORE YOU COME IN YOU MUST PROMISE TO OBEY ME IMPLICITLY. DO NOT LOOK AT ME AND REMEMBER THAT TALKING IS QUITE USELESS. I CANNOT ANSWER. KNOCK AGAIN THREE TIMES AND THAT WILL MEAN I HAVE YOUR PROMISE. MY LIFE DEPENDS ENTIRELY ON THE HELP YOU CAN GIVE ME.

I had to wait a while to pull myself together, and then I knocked slowly three times.

I heard André shuffling behind the door, then his hand fumbling with the lock, and the door opened.

Out of the corner of my eye, I saw that he was standing behind the door, but without looking around, I carry the bowl of milk to his desk. He was evidently watching me and I must all costs appear calm and collected.

"*Cheri*, you can count on me," I said gently, and putting the bowl down under his desk lamp, the only one alight, I walked into the next room where all lights were blazing.

My first impression was that some sort of hurricane must have blown out of the receiving booth. Papers were scattered in every direction, a whole row of test tubes lay smashed in a corner, chairs and stools were upset and one of the window curtains hung half torn from its bent rod. In a large enamel basin on the floor a heap of burned documents was still smoldering.

I knew that I would not find the fly André wanted me to look for. Women know things that men only suppose by reasoning and deduction; it is a form of knowledge very rarely accessible to them and which they disparagingly call intuition. I already knew that the fly André wanted was the one that Henri had caught and which I had made him release.

I heard André shuffling around in the next room, and then a strange gurgling and sucking as though he had trouble in drinking his milk.

"André, there is no fly here. Can you give me any sort of indication that might help? If you can't speak, rap or something ... you know: once for yes, twice for no."

I had tried to control my voice and speak as though perfectly calm, but I had to choke down a sob of desperation when he rapped twice for "no."

"May I come to you, André? I don't know what can have happened, but whatever it is, I'll be courageous, dear."

After a moment of silent hesitation, he tapped once on his desk.

At the door I stopped aghast at the sight of André standing with his head and shoulders covered by a brown velvet cloth he taken from a table by his desk, the table on which he usually ate when he did not want to leave his work. Suppressing a laugh that might have easily turned to sobbing, I said:

"André, we'll search thoroughly tomorrow, by daylight. Why don't you go to bed? I'll lead you to the guest room if you like, and won't let anyone else see you."

His left hand tapped the desk twice.

"Do you need a doctor, André?"

"No," he rapped.

"Would you like me to call Professor Augier? He might be of more help..."

Twice he rapped "no" sharply. I did not know what to do or say. And then I told him:

"Henri caught a fly this morning when he wanted to show me, but I made him release it. Could it have been the one you are looking for? I didn't see it, but the boy said its head was white."

André emitted a strange metallic sigh and I just had time to bite my figures fiercely in order not to scream. He had let his right arm drop, and instead of his long fingered muscular hand, a gray stick with little buds on it like a branch of a tree hung out in his sleeve almost down to his knee.

"André, *mon cheri*, tell me what happened. I might be of more help to you if I knew. André ... oh it's terrible!" I sobbed, unable to control myself.

Having rapped once for yes, he pointed to the door with his left hand.

I stepped out and sank down crying as he locked the door behind me. He was typing again and I waited. At last he shuffled to the door and slid a sheet of paper under it.

HÉLÈNE, COME BACK IN THE MORNING. I MUST THINK AND WILL HAVE TYPED OUT AN EXPLANATION FOR YOU. TAKE ONE OF MY SLEEPING TABLETS AND GO STRAIGHT TO BED. I NEED YOU FRESH AND STRONG TOMORROW, MA PAUVRE CHERIE. A.

"Do you want anything for the night, André?" I shouted through the door.

He knocked twice for no, and a little later I heard the typewriter again.

The sun full on my face woke me up with a start. I had set the alarm-clock for five but had not heard it, probably because of the sleeping tablets. I had indeed slept like a log without a dream. Now I was back in my living nightmare and crying like a child I sprang out of bed. It was just on seven!

Running into the kitchen, without a word for the startled servants, I rapidly prepared a trayload of coffee, bread and butter with which I ran down to laboratory.

André opened the door as soon as I knocked and closed it again as I carried the tray to his desk. His head was still covered, but I saw from his crumpled suit and his open camp bed that he must have at least tried to rest.

On his desk lay a typewritten sheet for me which I picked up. André opened the other door, and taking this to mean that he wanted to be left alone, I walked into the next room. He pushed the door to and I heard him pouring out the coffee as I read:

DO YOU REMEMBER THE ASH TRAY EXPERIMENT? I HAVE HAD A SIMILAR ACCIDENT. I TRANSMITTED MYSELF SUCCESSFULLY THE NIGHT BEFORE LAST. DURING THE SECOND EXPERIMENT YESTERDAY A FLY WHICH I DID NOT SEE MUST HAVE GOT INTO THE "DISINTEGRATOR." MY ONLY HOPE IS TO FIND THAT FLY AND GO THROUGH AGAIN WITH IT. PLEASE SEARCH FOR IT CAREFULLY SINCE, IF IT IS NOT FOUND, I SHALL HAVE TO FIND A WAY OF PUTTING AN END TO ALL THIS.

If only André had been more explicit! I shuddered at the thought that he must be terribly disfigured and then cried softly as I imagined his face inside-out, or perhaps his eyes in place of his ears, or his mouth at the back of his neck, or worse!

André must be saved! For that, the fly must be found!

Pulling myself together, I said:

"André, may I come in?"

He opened the door.

"André, don't despair; I'm going to find that fly. It is no longer in the laboratory, but it cannot be very far. I suppose you're disfigured, perhaps terribly so, but there can be no question to putting an end to all this, as you say your note; that I will never stand for. If necessary, if you do not wish to be seen, I'll make you a mask or cowl so that you can go on with your work until you get well again. If you cannot work, I'll call Professor Augier, and he and all your other friends will save you, André."

Again I heard that curious metallic sigh as he rapped violently on his desk.

"André, don't be annoyed; please be calm. I won't do anything without first consulting you, but you must rely on me, have faith in me and let me help you as best I can. Are you terribly disfigured, dear? Can't you let me see your face? I won't be afraid ... I am your wife, you know."

But my husband again rapped a decisive "no" and pointed to the door.

"All right. I am going to search for the fly now, but promise me that you won't do anything foolish; promise you won't do anything rash or dangerous without first letting me know all about it!"

He extended his left hand, and I knew I had his promise.

I will never forget that ceaseless day-long hunt for a fly. Back home, I turned the house inside-out and made all the servants join in the search. I told them that a fly had escaped from the Professor's laboratory and that it must be captured alive, but it was evident that they already thought me crazy. They said so to the police later, and that day's hunt for a fly most probably saved me from the guillotine later.

I questioned Henri and as he failed to understand right away what I was talking about, I shook him and slapped him, and made him cry in front of the round-eyed maids. Realizing that I must not let myself go, I kissed and petted the poor boy and at last made him understand what I wanted of him. Yes, he remembered, he had found the fly just by the kitchen window; yes, he had released it immediately as told to.

Even in the summer time we had very few flies because our house is on the top of the hill and the slightest breeze coming across the valley blows around it. In spite of that, I managed to catch dozens of flies that day. On all the window sills and all over the garden I had put saucers of milk, sugar, jam, meat — all things likely to attract flies. Of all those we caught, and many others which we failed to catch but which I saw, none resembled the one Henri had caught the day before. One by one, with a magnifying glass, I examined every unusual fly, but none had any thing like a white head.

At lunchtime, I ran down to André with some milk and mashed potatoes. I also took some of the flies we had caught, but he gave me to understand they could be of no possible use to him.

"If that fly has not been found tonight, André, we'll have to see what has to be done. And this is what I propose: I'll sit in the next room. When you can't answer by the yes - no method of rapping, you'll type out whatever you want to say and then slip it under the door. Agreed?"

"Yes," rapped André.

By nightfall we had still not found the fly. At dinner time, as I prepared André's tray, I broke down and sobbed in the kitchen in front of the silent servants. My maid thought that I had had a row with my husband, probably about the mislaid fly, but I learned later that the cook was already quite sure that I was out of my mind.

Without a word, I picked up the tray and put it down again as I stopped by the telephone.

That this is really a matter of life and death for André, I had no doubt. Neither did I doubt that he fully intended committing suicide, unless I could make him change his mind, or at least put off such a drastic decision. Would I be strong enough? He would never forgive me for not keeping a promise, but under the circumstances, did that really matter? To the devil with promises and honor! At all costs André must be saved! And having thus made up my mind, I looked up and dialed Professor Augier's number.

"The Professor is away and will not be back before the end of the week," said a polite neutral voice together at the other end of the line.

That was that! I would have to fight alone and fight I would. I would save André, come what may.

All my nervousness had disappeared as André let me in and, after placing the tray of food down on his desk, I went into the other room, as agreed.

"The first thing I want to know," I said as he closed the door behind me, "is what happened exactly. Can you please tell me, André?"

I waited patiently while he typed an answer which he pushed under the door a little later.

HÉLÈNE, I WOULD RATHER NOT TELL YOU, SINCE GO I MUST, I WOULD RATHER YOU REMEMBER ME AS I WAS BEFORE. I MUST DESTROY MYSELF IN SUCH WAY THAT NONE CAN POSSIBLY KNOW WHAT HAPPENED TO ME. I HAVE OF COURSE THOUGHT OF SIMPLY DISINTEGRATING MYSELF IN MY TRANSMITTER, BUT I HAD BETTER NOT BECAUSE, SOONER OR LATER, I MIGHT FIND MYSELF REINTEGRATED SOMEDAY, SOMEWHERE, SOME SCIENTIST IS SURE TO MAKE THE SAME DISCOVERY. I HAVE THEREFORE THOUGHT OF A WAY WHICH IS NEITHER SIMPLE NOR EASY, BUT YOU CAN AND WILL HELP ME.

For several minutes I wondered if André had not simply gone stark raving mad.

"André," I said at last, "whatever you may have chosen or thought of, I cannot and will never accept such a cowardly solution. No matter how awful the result of your experiment or accident, you are alive, you are a man, a brain ... and you have a soul. You have no right to destroy yourself! You know that!"

The answer was soon typed and pushed under the door.

I AM ALIVE ALL RIGHT, BUT I AM ALREADY NO LONGER A MAN. AS TO MY BRAIN OR INTELLIGENCE, IT MAY DISAPPEAR AT ANY MOMENT. AS IT IS, IT IS NO LONGER INTACT. AND THERE CAN BE NO SOUL WITHOUT INTELLIGENCE ... AND YOU KNOW THAT!

"Then you must tell the other scientists about your discovery. They will help you and save you, André!"

I staggered back frightened as he angrily thumped the door twice.

"André ... why? Why do you refuse the aid you know they would give you with all their hearts?"

A dozen furious knocks shook the door and made me understand that my husband would never accept such a solution. I had to find other arguments.

For hours, it seemed, I talked to him about our boy, about me, about his family, about his duty to us and the rest of humanity. He made no reply of any sort. At last I cried:

"André ... do you hear me?"

"Yes," he knocked very gently.

"Well, listen then. I have another idea. You remember your first experiment with the ash tray? ... Well, do you think that if you put it through again a second time, it might possibly have come out with the letters turned back the right way?"

Before I had finished speaking, André was busily typing and a moment later I read his answer:

I HAVE ALREADY THOUGHT OF THAT AND THAT WAS WHY I NEEDED THE FLY. IT HAS GOT TO GO THROUGH WITH ME. THERE IS NO HOPE OTHERWISE.

"Try all the same, André, you never know!"

I HAVE TRIED SEVEN TIMES ALREADY.

Was the typewritten reply I got to that.

"André! Try again, please!"

The answer this time gave me a flutter of hope, because no woman has ever understood, or will ever understand, how a man about to die can possibly consider anything funny.

I DEEPLY ADMIRE YOUR DELICIOUS FEMININE LOGIC. WE COULD GO ON DOING THIS EXPERIMENT UNTIL DOOMSDAY. HOWEVER, JUST TO GIVE YOU THAT PLEASURE, PROBABLY THE LAST I SHALL EVER BE ABLE TO GIVE YOU, I WILL TRY ONCE MORE. IF YOU CANNOT FIND THE DARK GLASSES, TURN YOUR BACK TO THE MACHINE AND PRESS YOUR HANDS OVER YOUR EYES. LET ME KNOW WHEN YOU ARE READY.

"Ready, André!" I shouted without even looking for the glasses and following his instructions.

I heard him moving around and then open and close the door of his "disintegrator." After what seemed very long wait, but probably not more than a minute or so, I heard a violent crackling noise and perceived a bright flash through my eyelids and fingers.

I turned around as the cabin door opened.

His head and shoulders still covered by the brown velvet carpet, André was gingerly stepping out of it.

"How do you feel, André? Any difference?" I asked touching his arm.

He tried to step away from me and caught his foot in one of the stools that I had not troubled to pick up. He made a violent effort to regain his balance, and the velvet carpet slowly slid off his shoulders and head as he fell heavily backwards.

The horror was too much for me, too unexpected. As a matter of fact, I am sure that, even had I known, the horror-impact could hardly have been less powerful. Trying to push both hands into my mouth to stifle my screams and although my fingers were bleeding, I screamed again and again. I could not take my eyes off him, I could not even close them, and yet I know that if

I looked at the horror much longer, I would go on screaming for the rest of my life.

Slowly, the monster, the thing that had been my husband, covered its head, got up and groped its way to the door and passed it. Though still screaming, I was able to close my eyes.

I who have ever been a true Catholic, who believed in God and another, better life hereafter, have only today but one hope: that when I die, I really die, and that there may be no afterlife of any sort because, if there is, then I shall never forget! Day and night, awake or asleep, I see it, and I know that I am condemned to see it forever, even perhaps into oblivion!

Until I am totally extinct, nothing can, nothing will ever make me forget that dreadful white hairy head with its low flat skull and its two pointed ears. Pink and moist, the nose was also that of a cat, a huge cat. But the eyes! Or rather, where the eyes should have been were two brown bumps the size of saucers. Instead of a mouth, animal or human, was a long hairy vertical slit from which hung a black quivering trunk that widened at the end trumpet-like, and from which saliva kept dripping.

I must have fainted, because I found myself flat on my stomach on the cold cement floor of the laboratory, staring at the closed door behind which I could hear the noise of André's typewriter.

Numb, numb and empty, I must have looked as people do immediately after a terrible accident, before they fully understand what has happened. I could only think of a man I once seen on the platform of a railway station, quite conscious, and looking stupidly at his leg still on the line where the train had just passed.

My throat was aching terribly, and that made me wonder if my vocal chords had not perhaps been torn, and whether I would ever be able to speak again.

The noise of the typewriter suddenly stopped and I felt I was going to scream again as something touched the door and a sheet of paper slid from under it.

Shivering with fear and disgust, I crawled over to where I could read it without touching it:

NOW YOU UNDERSTAND. THAT LAST EXPERIMENT WAS A NEW DISASTER, MY POOR HÉLÈNE. I SUPPOSE YOU RECOGNIZED PART OF DANDELO'S HEAD. WHEN I WENT INTO THE DISINTEGRATOR JUST NOW, MY HEAD WAS ONLY THAT OF A FLY. I NOW ONLY HAVE ITS EYES AND MOUTH LEFT. THE REST HAS BEEN REPLACED BY PART OF THE CAT'S HEAD. POOR DANDELO WHOSE ATOMS HAD NEVER COME TOGETHER. YOU SEE NOW THAT THERE CAN ONLY BE ONE POSSSIBLE SOLUTION, DON'T YOU? I MUST DISAPPEAR. KNOCK ON THE DOOR WHEN YOU ARE READY AND I SHALL EXPLAIN WHAT YOU HAVE TO DO. A.

Of course he was right, and it had been wrong and cruel of me to insist on a new experiment. And I knew that there was now no possible hope, that any further experiments could only bring about worst results.

Getting up dazed, I went to the door and tried to speak, but no sound came from my throat ... so I knocked once!

You can of course guess the rest. He explained his plan in short typewritten notes and I agreed, I agreed to everything!

My head on fire, but shivering with cold, like an automaton, I followed him to the silent factory. In my hand was a full page of explanations: what I had to know about the steam-hammer.

Without stopping or looking back, he pointed to the switchboard which controlled the steam-hammer as he passed it. I went no further and watched him come to a halt before the terrible instrument.

He knelt down, carefully wrapped the carpet around his head, and then stretched out flat on the ground.

It was not difficult. I was not killing my husband. André, poor André, had gone long ago, years ago it seemed. I was merely carrying out his last wish ... and mine.

Without hesitating, my eyes on the long still body, I firmly pushed the "stroke" button right in. The great metallic mass seemed to drop slowly. It was not so much the resounding clang of the hammer that made me jump as the sharp crackling which I had distinctly heard at the same time. My hus ... the thing's body shook a second and then lay still.

It was then I noticed he had forgotten to put his right arm, his fly leg, under the hammer. The police would never understand but the scientists would, and they must not! This had been André's last wish also!

I had to do it and quickly, too; the night watchman must have heard the hammer and would be around any moment. I pushed the other button up and hammer slowly rose. Seeing but trying not to look, I ran up, leaned down, lifted and moved forward the right arm that seemed terribly light. Back at the switchboard, again I pushed the red button, and down came the hammer second time. Then I ran all the way home.

You know the rest and can now do whatever you think right.

So ended Hélène's manuscript.

The following day I telephoned Commissaire Charas to invite him to dinner.

"With pleasure, Monsieur Delambre. Allow me, however, to ask: is it the Commissiare you are inviting or just Monsieur Charas?"

"Have you any preference?"

"No, not at the present moment."

"Well then, make it whichever you like. Will eight o'clock suit you?"

Although it was raining, the Commissaire arrived on foot that evening.

"Since you did not come tearing up to the door in your black Citroen, I take it you have opted for Monsieur Charas, off-duty?"

"I left the car up a side-street," mumbled the Commissaire with a grin as a maid staggered under the weight of his raincoat.

"*Merci*," he said a minute later when I handed him a glass of Pernod into which he tipped a few drops of water, watching it turn the golden amber liquid to pale blue milk.

"You heard about my poor sister-in-law?"

"Yes, shortly after you telephoned me this morning. I am very sorry, but perhaps it was all for the best. Being already in charge of your brother-in-law's case the inquiry naturally comes to me."

"I suppose it was suicide."

"Without a doubt. Cyanide, the doctors say quite rightly; I found a second tablet in the unstitched hem of her dress."

"*Monsieur est servi*," announced the maid.

"I would like to show you a very curious document afterwards, Charas."

"Ah, yes. I had heard that Madame Delambre had been writing a lot, but we could find nothing beyond the short note informing us she was committing suicide."

During our tête-à-tête dinner, we talk politics, books and films, and the local football club of which the Commissaire was a keen supporter.

After dinner, I took him up to my study, where a bright fire — a habit I picked up in England during the war — was burning. Without even asking him, I handed him his brandy and mixed myself what he called "crushed-bug juice in soda water" — his appreciation of whiskey.

"I would like you to read this, Charas; first, because it was partially intended for you and, secondly, because it will interest you. If you think Commissaire Charas has no objection, I would like to burn it after."

Without a word, he took the wad of sheets Hélène had given me the day before and settled down to read them.

"What you think of it all?" I asked some twenty minutes later as he carefully folded Hélène's manuscript, slipped it into the brown envelope, and put it into the fire.

Charas watched the flames licking the envelope, from which wisps of gray smoke were escaping, and it was only that when it burst into flames that he said, slowly raising his eyes to mine:

"I think it proves very definitely that Madame Delambre was quite insane."

For a long while we watched the fire eating up Hélène's "confession."

"A funny thing happened to me this morning, Charas. I went to the cemetery, where my brother was buried. It was quite empty and I was alone."

"Not quite, Monsieur Delambre. I was there, but I didn't want to disturb you."

"Then you saw me..."

"Yes. I saw you bury a matchbox."

"Do you know what was in it?"

"A fly, I suppose."

"Yes. I found it early this morning, caught in a spider's web in the garden."

"Was it dead?"

"No, not quite. I ... crushed it ... between two stones. Its head was ... white ... all white."

The End

SHORT STORY VERSUS FILM ADAPTATION

The Movie has always been considered a faithful adaptation of the short story, but there are several changes that did occur in the transition to the screen. Whether or not they really matter is up to the reader and the movie viewer.

In the film, André is a researcher at his family's electronics firm. He is trying to create an invention to patent to boost the fortunes of Delambre Frères, which is based in Montreal, Canada and he is in partnership with his brother and they jointly own the firm. He is never called Professor. In the short story, he is Professor Delambre, previously of the College de France and has left Paris — the short story takes place in France — to do (implied) top-secret research at his brother's manufacturing plant in the country. André appears to be in the employ of the French Government, with a contract from their Air Force or Department of Defense for any results of his research into disintegrating matter. François seems to have no interest in what André is working on, other than giving him a place to work at his factory. The short story never clarifies what François' factory makes, beyond having a metal press.

Another change from book to screen is the changing the name of André's son from Henri to Philippe. The short story has Helene naming the Guinea Pig Hop-la and the Delambres have a third pet in the house, a cocker spaniel named Miquette. This dog survives several trips in the transporter without harm in the story, but never appears in the film, unlike the poor disintegrated cat, Dandelo, who remains a victim in both versions. In the short story, Dandelo is a foundling, that perhaps being an easier way to accept his demise, as the two "house pets" survive, but in the film he is named as Philippe's pet. The whole cat disintegration with the disembodied yowling does lighten the mood of the film when it occurs and that may have been a deliberate choice by the either the screenwriter or the director, as does the bowl that reintegrates with Made in Japan turned backwards. They also serve as reminders that this is not a process to be messing with.

The short story has quite a different ending; Hélène commits suicide after giving François her written confession. François is alone when he finds and crushes the white-headed fly in the spider web with a stone. He is seen burying a matchbox at his brother's grave by Inspector (in the story he is called Commissaire) Charas, who guesses the contents of the matchbox, after he reads Hélène's confession. These two men decide to let the world continue to believe Hélène was mad and let the dead rest in peace. They burn her written explanation/confession of what really happened to André in François' fireplace.

The "accident" is much the same in both versions, except for the part where Hélène pleads with André to go through one more time (without the fly) to see if he will change back. It doesn't work in either case, but in the short story, André has already tried seven times and the eighth time he comes through reintegrated with a half cat/half fly head and this ends any hope of him being unscrambled. In addition, it is clearly noted that this final tragedy is Hélène's fault for insisting he go through one more time for her and that André should not have granted her request.

There also a debate in the short story as to whether or not André can commit suicide, being Catholic, but states he is transforming and will soon have no soul. No explanation is given of Hélène's reason for suicide, she is not mad or impaired, but she, depending on the interpretation, either committed murder or at least assisted a suicide. At the time the story was written in 1957 there was no doubt (in the story at least) that she will be executed by guillotine per French law if she is declared sane by Charas.

Nothing is mentioned in the short story about François having unrequited love for Hélène, in fact, he is more concerned about finding out how his brother died than he is in protecting Hélène and he is remarkably blasé about her death. This is a subplot added to the film, to support the happy (?) ending, in that Charas is as guilty of murder by smashing the tiny fly in the spider web as Hélène was in smashing the transformed André in the press. Therefore, Hélène must go free — to walk off into the sunset with François and Henri, er, Philippe.

François is named Henri's guardian in the story, despite the fact he is single and shown to be a bit too fond of wine and other spirits. The story documents he has developed a habit of giving wine to his 6-year-old ward to dip his biscuit in shortly after being given custody of him. This may also be a reflection of French culture in 1957.

In reading the story, there are many lines of it that transfer directly to the screen as dialogue, particularly with Vincent Price. Hélène screams hysterically and faints when André's fly head is revealed, but there is no place in the short story where a blackboard is used to convey the final message, nor is there any mention of a tiny fly/man found in a spider web, screaming, "Help me."

As Hollywood adaptations go, this one is closer than most, but still takes some license, for mostly dramatic purposes. The above scenes turned out to be good additions, as they have become the most quoted and remembered images whenever and wherever this film is discussed.

Charles Herbert poses with the Fly figure and a Vincent Price bust, Summer 2006.

PHOTO COURTESY OF CORTLANDT HULL, THE WITCH'S DUNGEON, 2008

AFTERWORD

FINAL THOUGHTS ON *THE FLY* BY CHARLES HERBERT

1958 was a very good year for me. I worked steadily all year, beginning with the *Jack Benny Show* and ending it with what I still consider the highlight of my career, *Houseboat* starring Cary Grant and Sophia Loren. That year I also appeared on *The Donna Reed Show* and *The Gail Storm Show*. I did *Colossus of New York* that year with Ross Martin as my father and of course, 1958 was the year of *The Fly*.

I was a ten year-old working with some of the biggest stars of the day and it was, for the most part, a lot of fun. Big star or not, a lot of adult actors weren't nice to child actors on the set. They didn't want to talk to you and they didn't want you stealing their close-ups. And some directors were better to work with than others. Michael Curtiz and Kurt Neumann, as examples, were serious, European-trained directors with no sense of humor who simply did not know how to work with children.

However, some actors were secure enough in their careers to treat child actors like real people. Cary Grant was wonderful to work with and Sophia Loren kept in contact for years afterwards through Christmas cards. And then of course, there was my "Uncle François," Vincent Price. Vincent Price was marvelous; he respected me as a person and a working actor and had no problem talking to me. Not Vincent! He had a tremendous sense of humor and he made the set a more relaxed environment. It was an honor to work with him.

The Fly was the biggest movie of that year. I was not a big horror fan (I still don't care for them) and that movie scared me. I was scared the first time I saw Al Hedison in the full makeup and it was even scarier when I sat through it in the movie theater. I still don't like insects! And why on earth did Al Hedison bother changing his name? Everyone else was changing their name to Biff, Rock, Rip, Tab – but David? I still wonder about that one.

1958 was also the year I met my friend Paul Petersen. Paul played my brother on *Houseboat*. That was another fun set, but meeting Paul was more important. You see, child actors have a tough enough time trying to figure out who they are. You have no identity when you are an actor. One week, you're David on *The Donna Reed Show* and the next week you're Roberto on *Houseboat*. Your childhood and teen years are when you're supposed to develop a sense of self. And unfortunately, a lot of former child actors discover that they are suddenly adults without a sense of who they are as a person off-screen. And that is where the problems start. I'm an example. I left show business with no education, no money and no one to turn to for support. It took me 30 years find myself but I survived. Others didn't and I am proud to work with Paul Petersen and "A Minor Consideration," his non-profit, foundation that offers guidance and support to young performers of yesterday, today and tomorrow.

Earlier this 50th anniversary year, I attended a convention in Pittsburgh that was a tribute to Vincent Price. Vincent is still a figurehead for horror movies. Karloff and Lugosi were great, but Vincent Price was the best. He was a great actor who could play anything because he was good person. You always liked him; no matter what how bad the villain he was playing, his terrific sense of humor and kind spirit also showed through. Vincent was practically a regular on *The Red Skeleton Show*. Vincent was a great clown and could laugh at himself, even when Red made him look an idiot. Price didn't care. He was having fun and Vincent Price liked to have fun. And the audience knew it. Comedians can do drama but dramatic actors rarely can do comedy — Vincent Price could do either. As long as you enjoyed yourself, that was all he wanted. Artist, chef and actor: Vincent's greatest talent was that he was a nice person. Period.

And for a 10 year-old, that made filming *The Fly* all the more memorable.

Charles Herbert
August 16, 2008

CONTRIBUTORS

David Hedison starred in The Fly as doomed scientist Andre Delambre, his first starring role in a film and he's never looked back. Best known as Captain Lee Crane on *Voyage to the Bottom of the Sea* and for appearing as Felix Leiter in two James Bond films, *Live and Let Die* and *Licence to Kill,* David remains active by working at the Actor's Studio, appearing in regional theater and making an occasional personal appearance. Visit him on the web at *www.davidhedison.com*

Charles Herbert was a familiar face to movie goers and television viewers throughout the 1950s and 1960s, appearing in twenty films in six years, along with countless television guest appearances. His career as a successful child actor came to an abrupt end when he grew. Today, he is actively involved in "A Minor Consideration," a non-profit foundation that offers guidance and support to young performers, past, present and future.

Marty Baumann is a writer, an illustrator and the creator of The Astounding B Monster, an award-winning website. He has written a book by the same name, devoted to B-movie history. Visit his web at *www.bmonster.com.*

Cortlandt Hull is the owner of Witch's Dungeon Classic Movie Museum in Bristol, Connecticut. A tribute to the monsters of the great movies of yesteryear, the museum doors have creaked open each Halloween since 1966. The displays feature realistic, life-size replicas of the classic creatures in tableaus from their films, with a number of figures created using the original molds and life masks. Hull, the great nephew of Henry Hull of *Werewolf of London* (1935) fame, was a friend of Vincent Price for over twenty years. Visit the Witch's Dungeon online at *www.preservehollywood.org.*

Diane C. Kachmar is a University Librarian at Florida Atlantic University. She maintains *www.davidhedison.com* and is the author of *Roy Scheider: A Film Biography* (2002).

David Goudsward is the author of a variety of books, ranging from archaeology in *Ancient Stone Sites of New England* (2006) to horror movie settings in *Shadows over New England* (2008).

Printed in the United States
205902BV00004B/31/P

9 781593 933159